Power Maths

Year 5
Textbook 5C

GW01396026

Sparks

Sparks is helpful.

He likes to help if you get stuck.

flexible

Flo

brave

Astrid

curious

Ash

determined

Dexter

Series editor: Tony Staneff
Lead author: Josh Lury

Consultants (first edition): Professor Liu Jian and Professor Zhang Dan
Author team (first edition): Liu Jian, Josh Lury, Catherine Casey, Belle Cottingham, Wei Huinv, Huang Lihua and Paul Wrangles

Pearson

Contents

Your teacher will tell you which page you need.

Unit 12 – Geometry – properties of shapes   6

Understand and use degrees   8
Measure acute angles   12
Measure angles up to 180°   16
Draw lines and angles accurately   20
Calculate angles around a point   24
Calculate angles on a straight line   28
Lengths and angles in shapes   32
Regular and irregular polygons   36
Parallel lines   40
Perpendicular lines   44
Investigate lines   48
3D shapes   52
End of unit check   56

Unit 13 – Geometry – position and direction   58

Read and plot coordinates   60
Problem solving with coordinates   64
Translate shapes   68
Translate points   72
Reflection   76
Reflection in horizontal and vertical lines   80
End of unit check   84

Unit 14 – Decimals   86

Add and subtract decimals within 1 (1)   88
Add and subtract decimals within 1 (2)   92
Complements to 1   96
Add and subtract decimals across 1   100
Add decimals with the same number of decimal places   104
Subtract decimals with the same number of decimal places   108
Add decimals with a different number of decimal places   112

Subtract decimals with a different number of decimal places   116

Problem solving with decimals (1)   120

Problem solving with decimals (2)   124

Decimal sequences   128

Multiply by 10   132

Multiply by 10, 100 and 1,000   136

Divide by 10   140

Divide by 10, 100 and 1,000   144

End of unit check   148

Unit 15 – Negative numbers   150

Understand negative numbers   152

Count through zero   156

Compare and order negative numbers   160

Find the difference   164

End of unit check   168

Unit 16 – Measure – converting units   170

Kilograms and kilometres   172

Millimetres and millilitres   176

Convert units of length   180

Imperial units of length   184

Imperial units of mass   188

Imperial units of capacity   192

Convert units of time   196

Timetables – calculating   200

Problem solving – units of measure (1)   204

Problem solving – units of measure (2)   208

End of unit check   212

Unit 17 – Measure – volume   214

Cubic centimetres   216

Compare volumes   220

Estimate volume   224

End of unit check   228

What have we learnt?   231

Let's get started!

How to use this book

These pages make sure we're ready for the unit ahead. Find out what we'll be learning and brush up on your skills!

Discover

Lessons start with **Discover**.

Here, we explore new maths problems.

Can you work out how to find the answer?

Don't be afraid to make mistakes. Learn from them and try again!

Share

Next, we share our ideas with the class.

Did we all solve the problems the same way? What ideas can you try?

Think together

Then we have a go at some more problems together. Use what you have just learnt to help you.

We'll try a challenge too!

This tells you which page to go to in your **Practice Book**.

At the end of each unit there's an **End of unit check**. This is our chance to show how much we have learnt.

Unit 12
Geometry – properties of shapes

In this unit we will …

⚡ Measure angles in degrees

⚡ Learn to measure angles with a protractor

⚡ Draw lines and angles accurately

⚡ Calculate missing angles

⚡ Learn about angles in shapes

⚡ Recognise, draw and label parallel and perpendicular lines

⚡ Accurately identify regular and irregular polygons

⚡ Recognise different 3D shapes from different views

Do you remember how to measure angles as turns? How do you describe the direction of the turn?

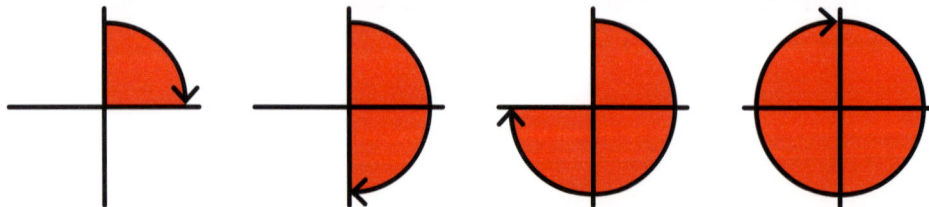

We will need some maths words. Which one can mean an angle that is a quarter turn?

angle   whole turn   right angle

acute angle   obtuse angle   degrees (°)

interior angle   clockwise   anticlockwise

parallel   perpendicular   regular

irregular   top view   plan view   side view

We will need this too! Can you see where the mark for 55 mm is?

0 1 2 3 4 5 6 7 8 9 10

cm

Understand and use degrees

Discover

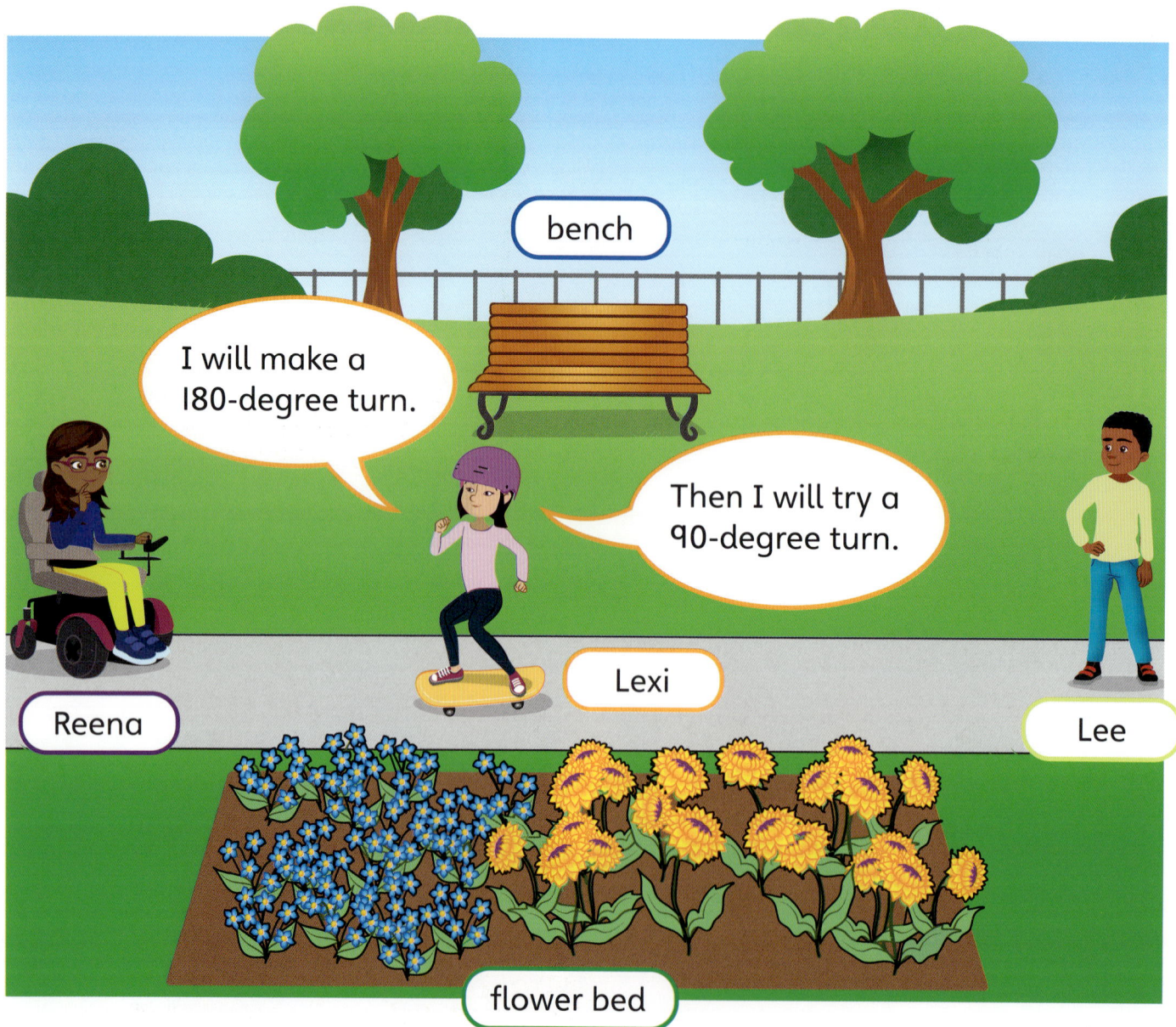

1 a) Who will Lexi be facing after a 180-degree turn?

b) Lexi then tries a 90-degree turn. What could she be facing now?

Share

a) A 360-degree turn is a whole turn.

A 180-degree turn is a half turn.

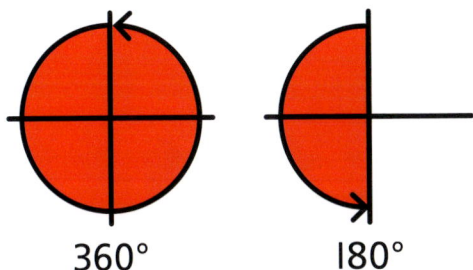

360°   180°

We measure turns in degrees. The ° symbol means degrees.

Lexi starts facing Reena.

After a 180-degree turn Lexi will be facing Lee.

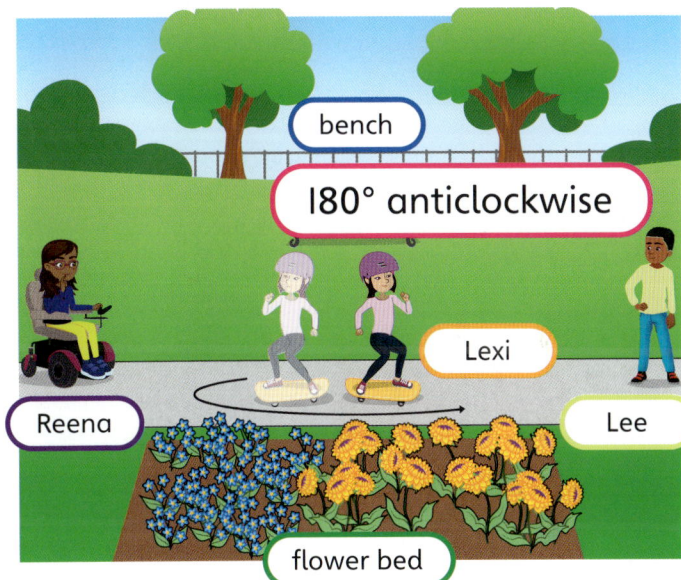

180° anticlockwise

bench

Lexi

Lee

Reena

flower bed

b) A 90-degree turn is a quarter turn.

anticlockwise

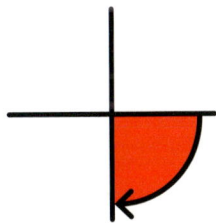

clockwise

This is also called a right angle.

Lexi starts facing Lee.

Lexi could turn 90° clockwise or 90° anticlockwise.
She could be facing the flowers or the bench now.

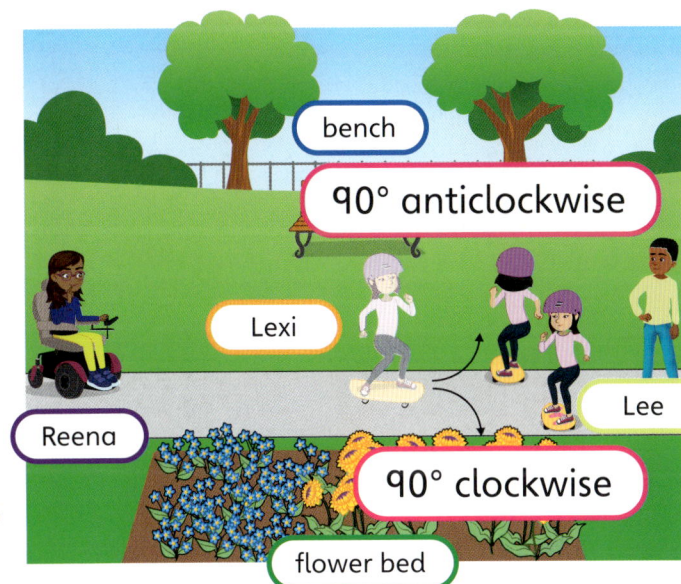

bench

90° anticlockwise

Lexi

Lee

Reena

90° clockwise

flower bed

Think together

1 Lexi starts facing Lee. She makes four 90-degree turns clockwise. How many degrees has she turned? What or who is she facing now?

Reena

Lee

2 Amelia is setting up the gym. She starts facing the bibs. She makes an anticlockwise turn and is now facing the gym mats.

How many degrees has she turned?

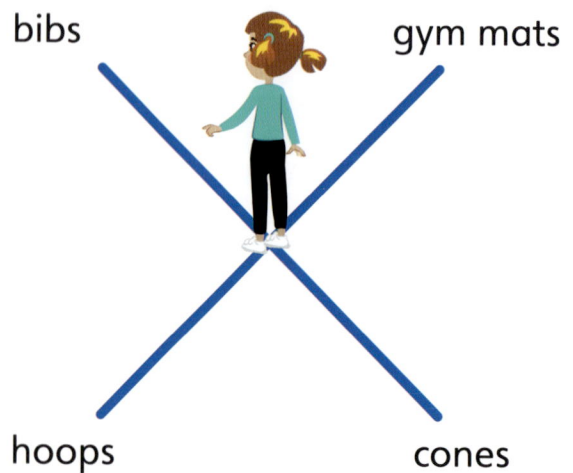

bibs   gym mats

hoops   cones

10

3 **a)** Mo is standing in the centre of points A to H.

Complete the table to describe which points he faces as he turns.

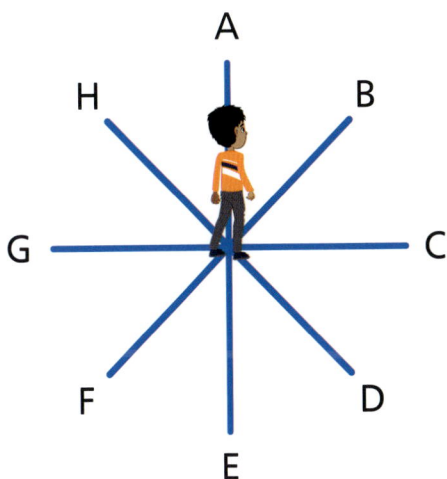

CHALLENGE

Start	Turn	Finish
facing B	180°	facing ☐
facing A	90° anticlockwise	facing ☐
facing E	☐° _____	facing C
facing G	☐° _____	facing A
facing G	☐° _____	facing H
facing ☐	45° clockwise	facing B

b) Mo faces G. Then he turns to face B.

Describe two different turns he could have made.

An angle less than 90° is acute. An angle greater than 180° is **reflex**. An angle between 90° and 180° is obtuse.

I think he could turn clockwise or anticlockwise.

→ **Practice book 5C p6**

Measure acute angles

Discover

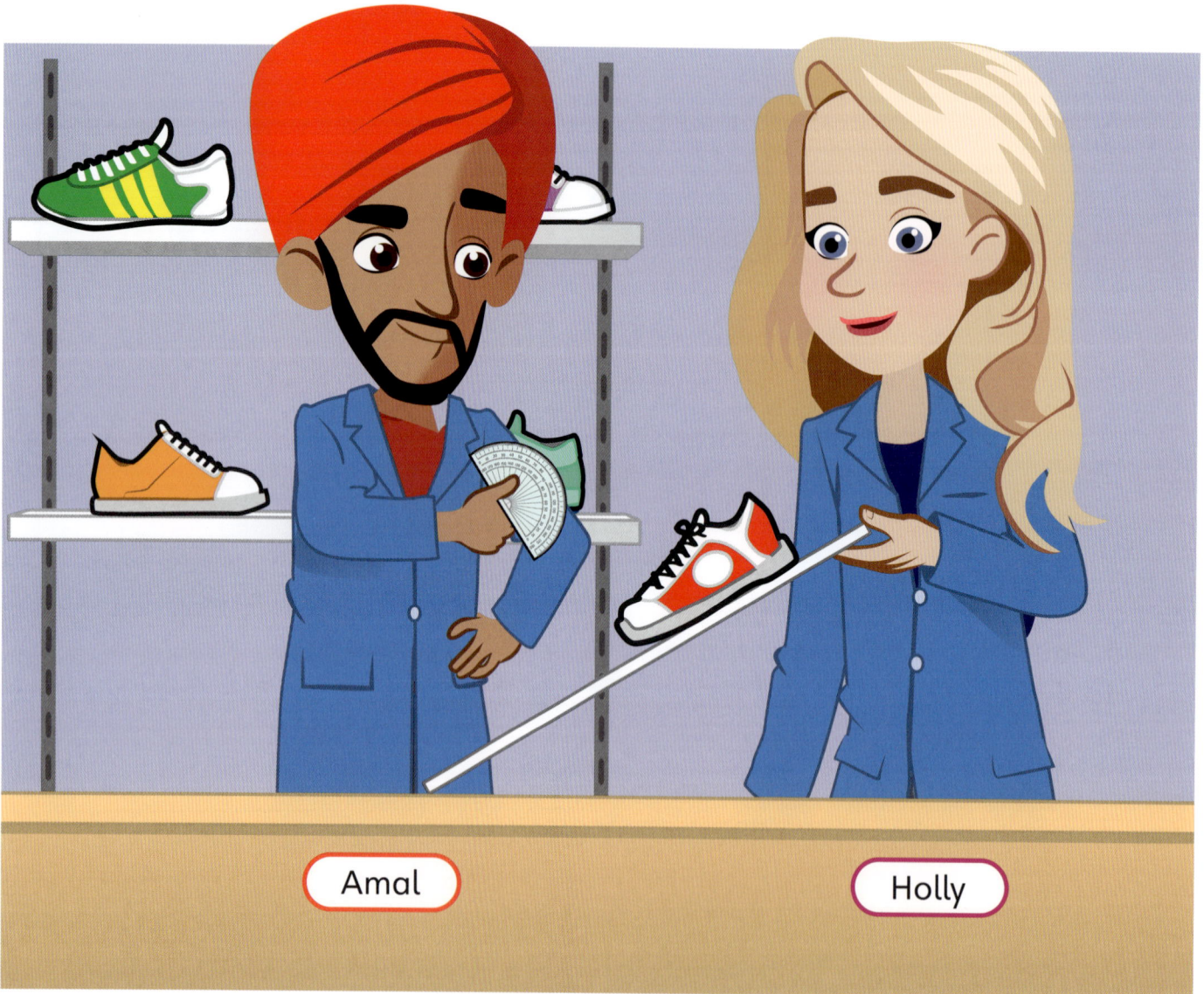

Amal

Holly

1 **a)** Amal and Holly are using a ramp to test the grip of some new trainers. What angle is the ramp at now?

b) Amal records the angle as 150°. Explain his mistake.

Share

a) You can use a protractor to measure the size of an angle.

Step 1

Make sure the zero line of the protractor matches the start of the angle turn.

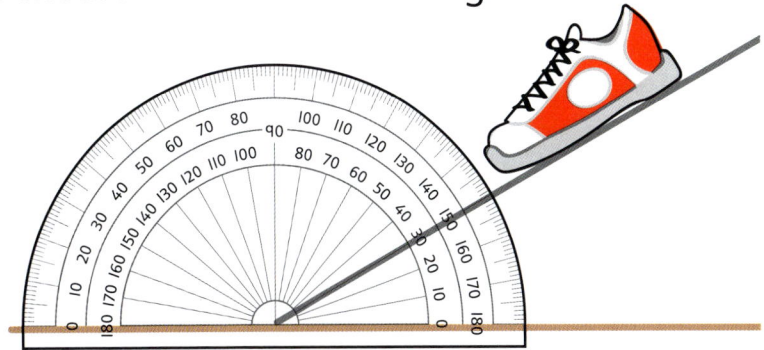

Step 2

Line up the centre mark with the exact point of the angle.

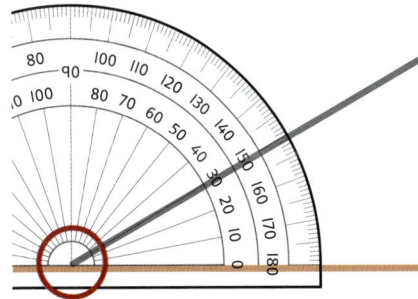

Step 3

Follow the scale from the zero mark to the completed turn. Read the angle from the scale.

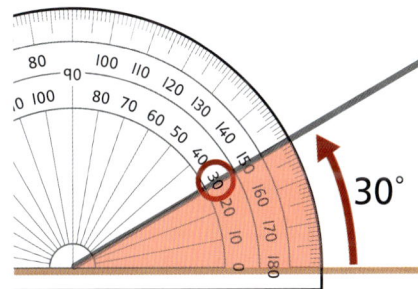

30°

The ramp is now at an angle of 30°.

b) Protractors often have two scales, so you can start measuring from the left or from the right. Amal's mistake is reading the wrong scale.

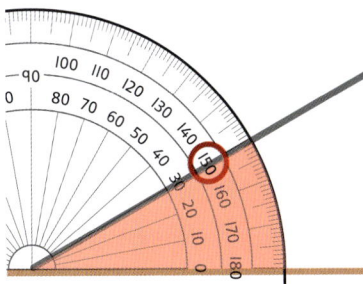

I saw that the angle is acute, because it is less than 90°. So I knew which scale to read.

Think together

1 Between which angles could the trainer have slipped down the ramp?

2 Measure these angles using a protractor.

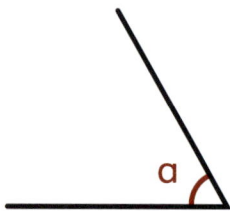

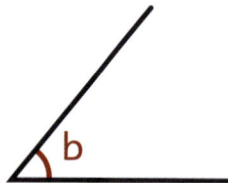

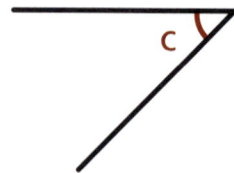

a

b

c

I wonder if it helps to turn the page around.

CHALLENGE

3 Estimate each of the angles in these triangles, then measure them accurately. How close were your estimates?

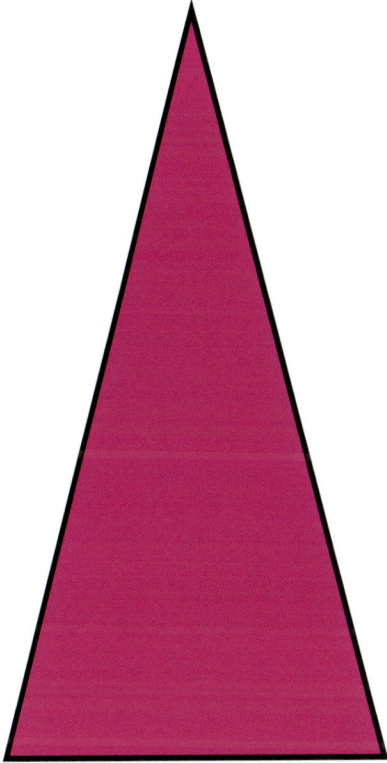

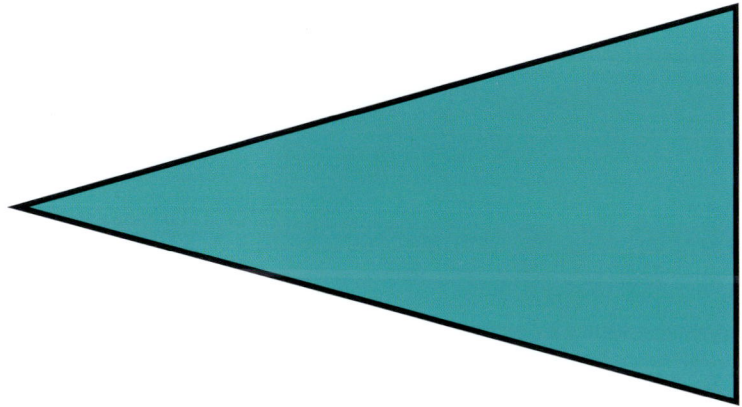

They look roughly the same size, but the angles look different.

I think all these angles are acute.

15

→ Practice book 5C p9

Measure angles up to 180°

Discover

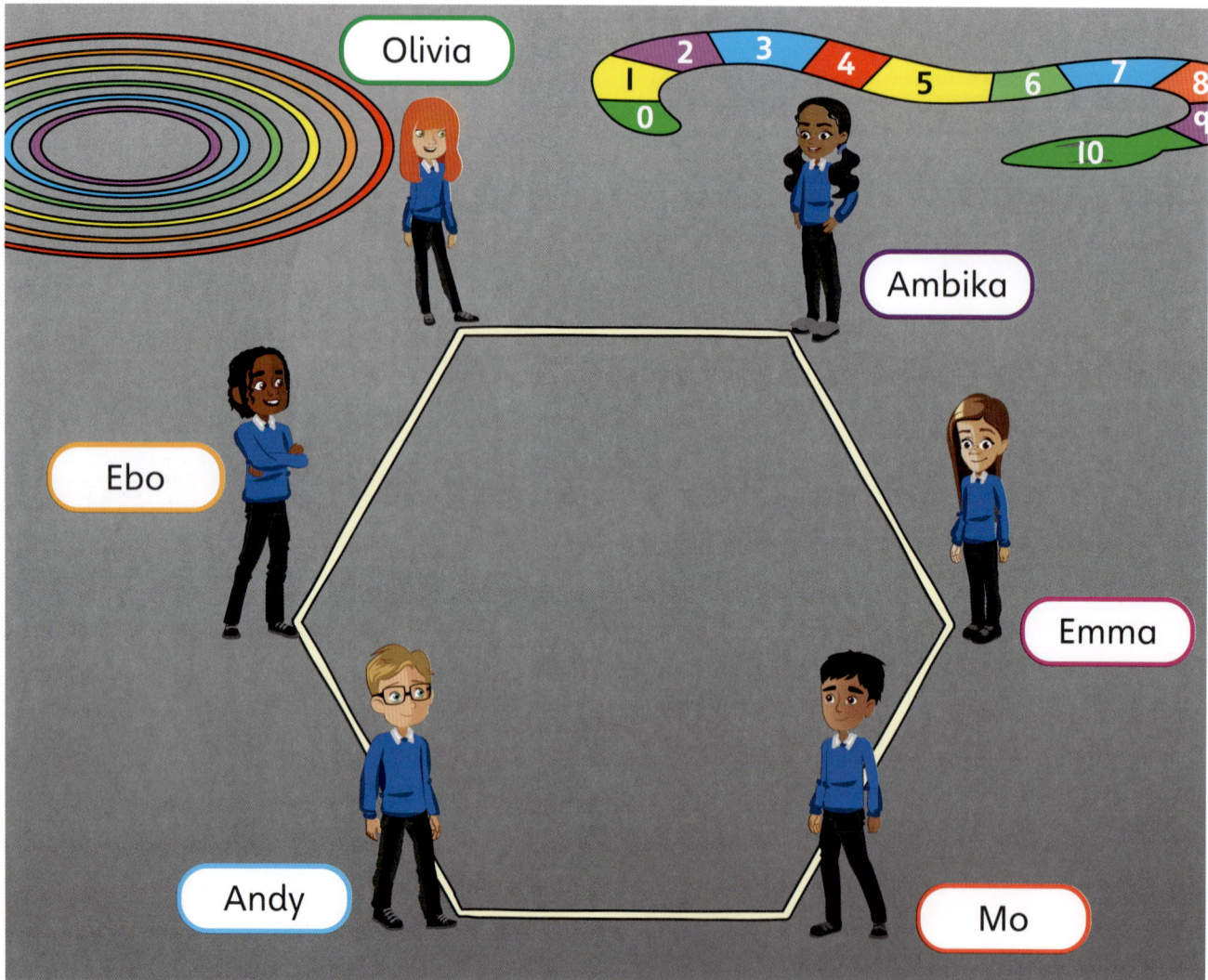

1 **a)** Mo turns from facing Andy to face Emma. What angle does he turn?

b) Emma turns from facing Mo to face Ambika. What angle does she turn?

Share

a) This turn makes an obtuse angle. It is greater than 90°.

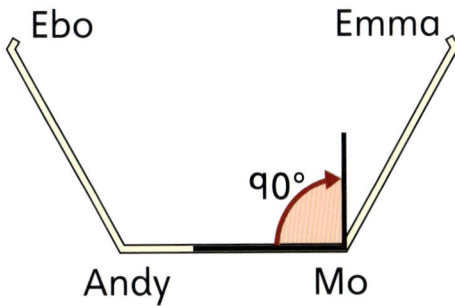

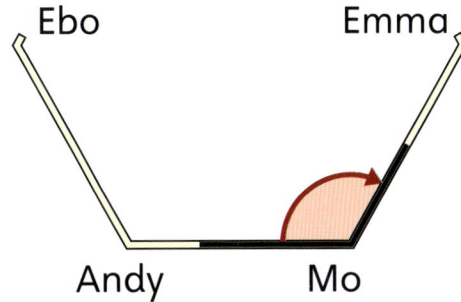

Ebo   Emma

90°

Andy   Mo

Ebo   Emma

Andy   Mo

> I knew which scale to use on the protractor because the angle is greater than 90°. It is obtuse.

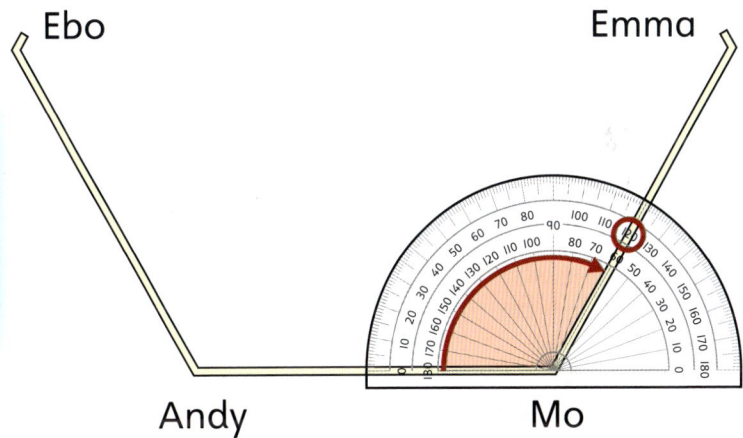

Ebo   Emma

Andy   Mo

Mo turns an angle of 120°.

b) Emma turns an angle of 120°.

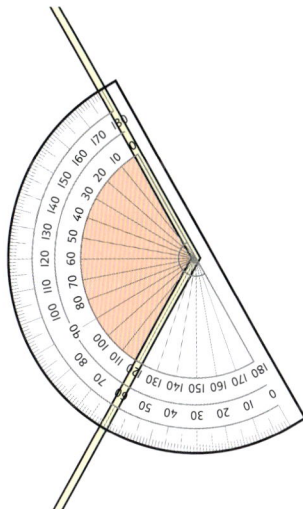

> I noticed that each angle inside the hexagon is 120°.

17

Think together

1 Measure the angles shown with a protractor.

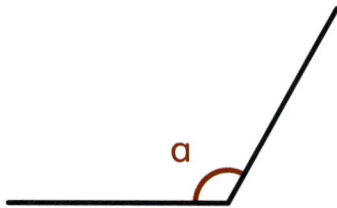

a

b

2 Put these angles in order, from smallest to greatest.

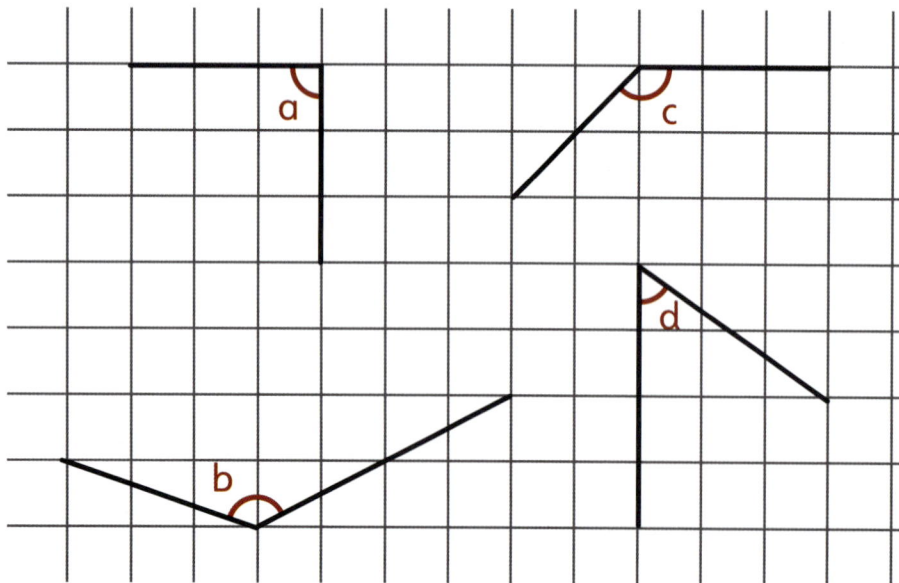

a

c

d

b

I can work out which is the smallest angle without measuring.

CHALLENGE

3 **a)** Amelia stands in the centre facing A. She turns to face C.

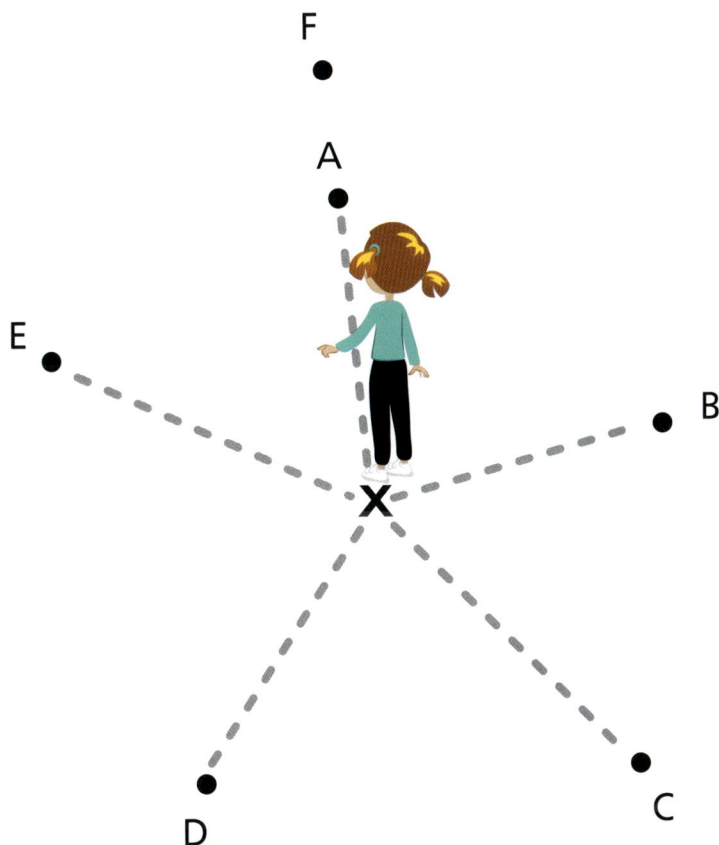

F

A

E

B

X

D

C

What angle does she turn?

I wonder if I could give two answers.

b) Then Amelia turns from facing C to face F.

What angle does she turn? What do you notice?

→ **Practice book 5C p12**

Draw lines and angles accurately

Discover

Let's draw some angles.

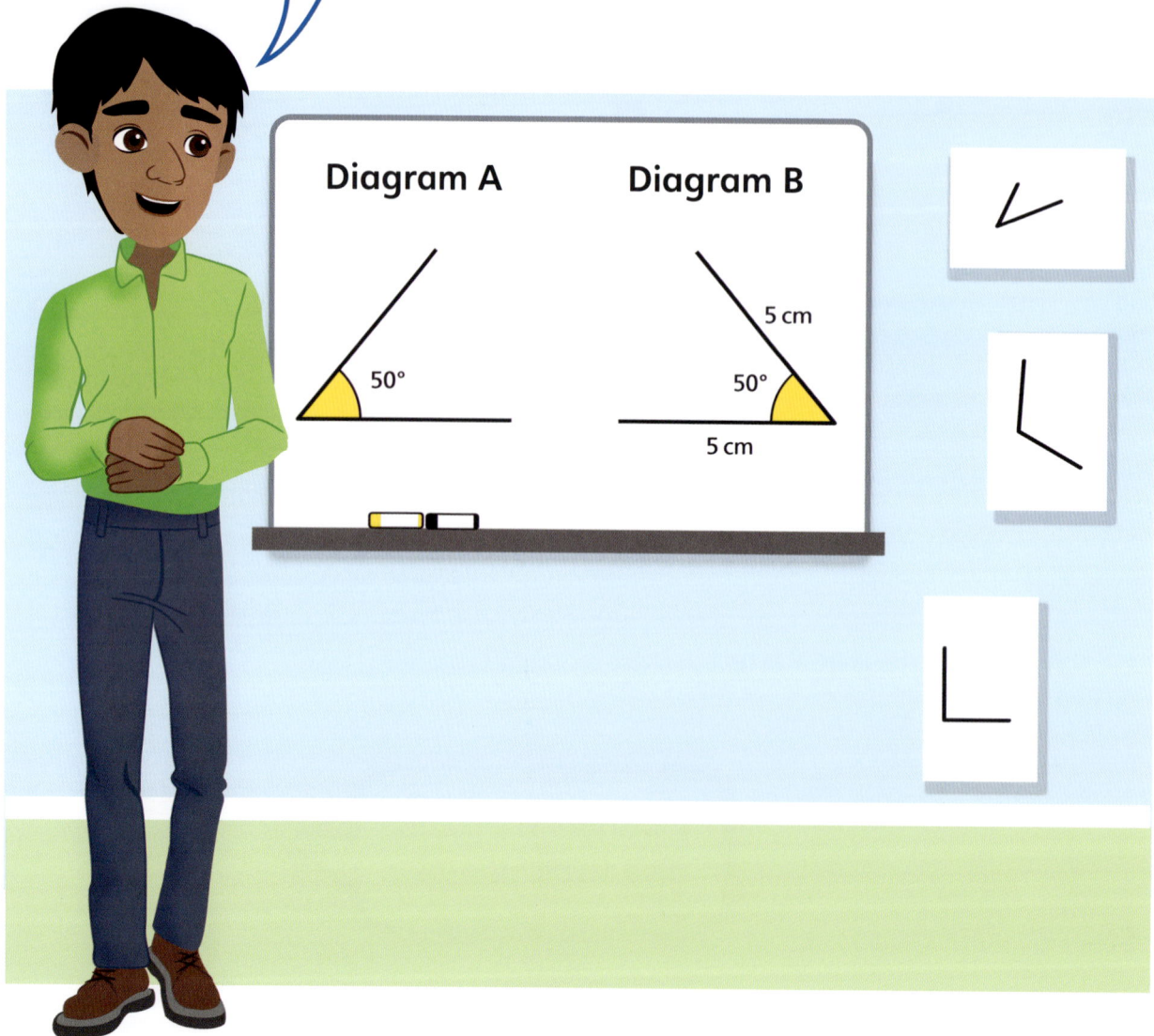

Diagram A

Diagram B

50°

5 cm

50°

5 cm

1 **a)** Draw a 50° angle.

b) Copy the angle in diagram B.

Share

a) You need a protractor, ruler and pencil to draw the angle accurately.

Step 1
Draw a straight line with a dot for measuring the angle.

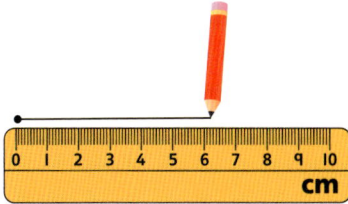

Step 3
Mark 50°

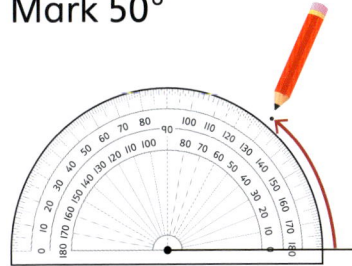

Step 2
Line up the protractor with the centre mark exactly on the dot.

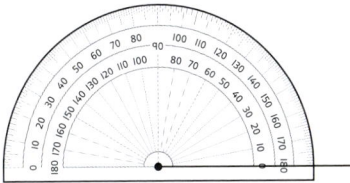

Step 4
Draw a straight line between the dots.

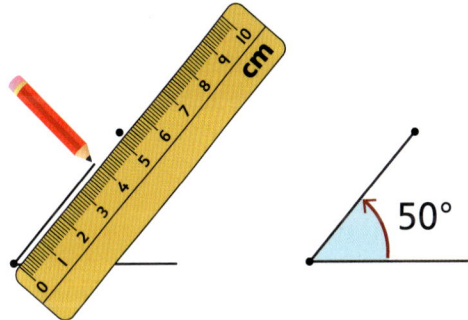

b) Step 1

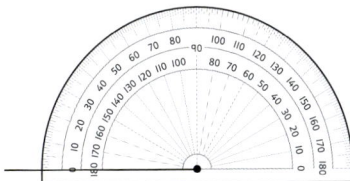

Step 2

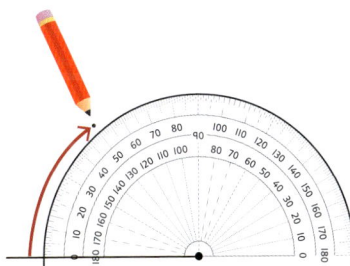

Step 3

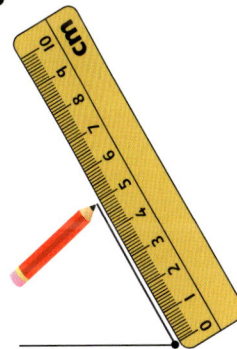

Think together

1 Copy each angle.

a)

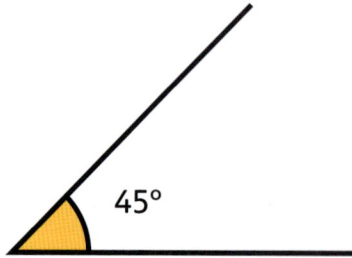

45°

b)

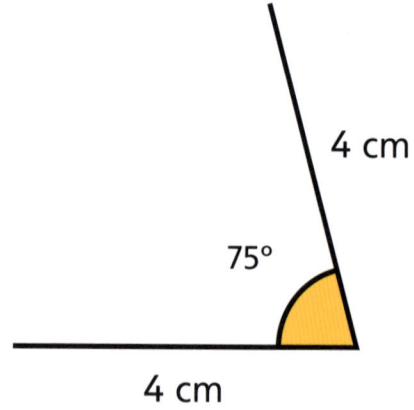

4 cm

75°

4 cm

2 Copy each angle.

a)

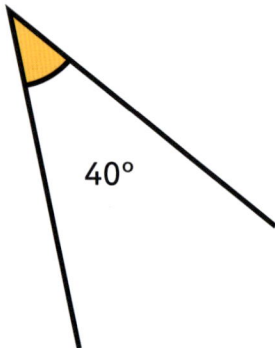

40°

b)

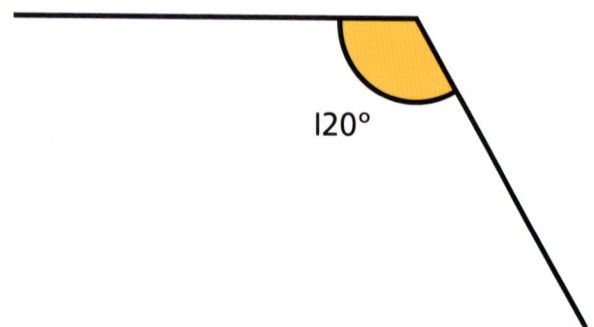

120°

CHALLENGE

3 **a)** Copy step I of the design.

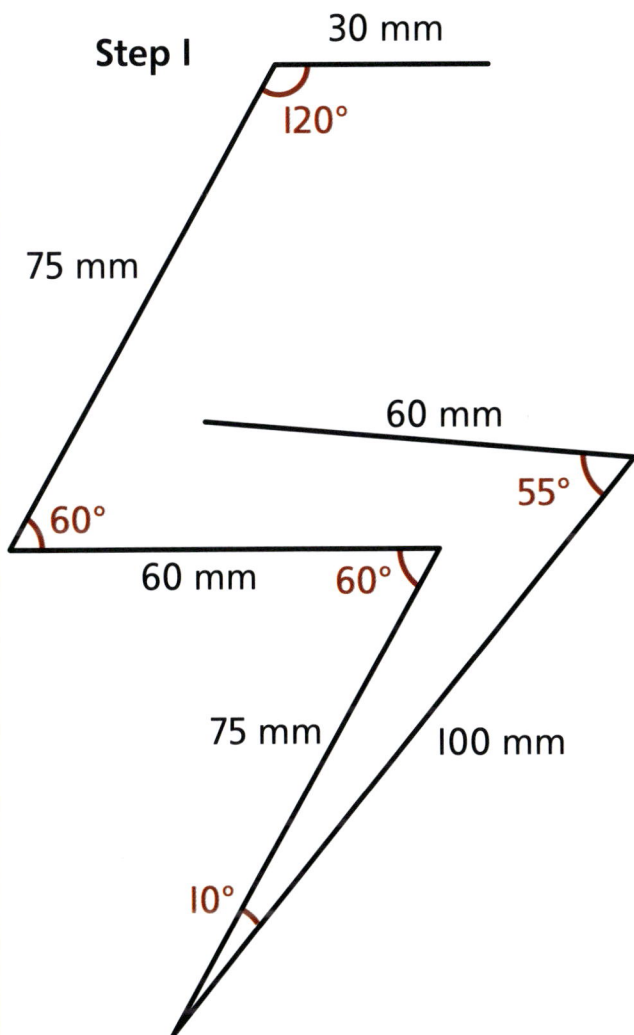

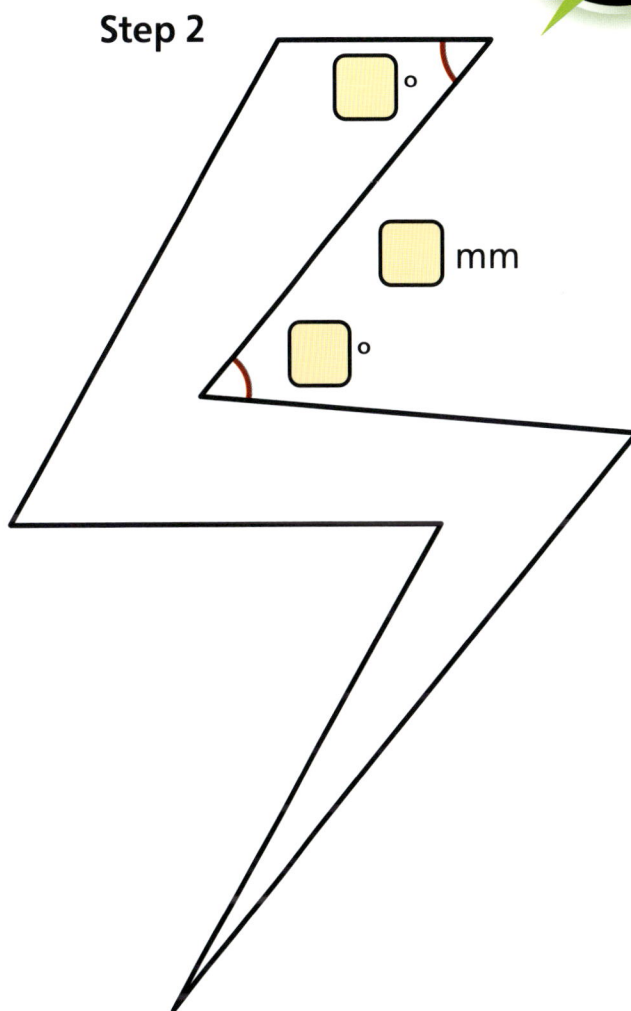

Step I

30 mm

120°

75 mm

60°

60 mm

60 mm 60°

55°

75 mm 100 mm

10°

Step 2

°

mm

°

b) Complete your shape by joining the lines as shown in step 2.

c) Measure the angles and the length of the line accurately.

Compare your measurements with a partner.

I wonder why some measurements are different.

23

→ Practice book 5C p15

Calculate angles around a point

Discover

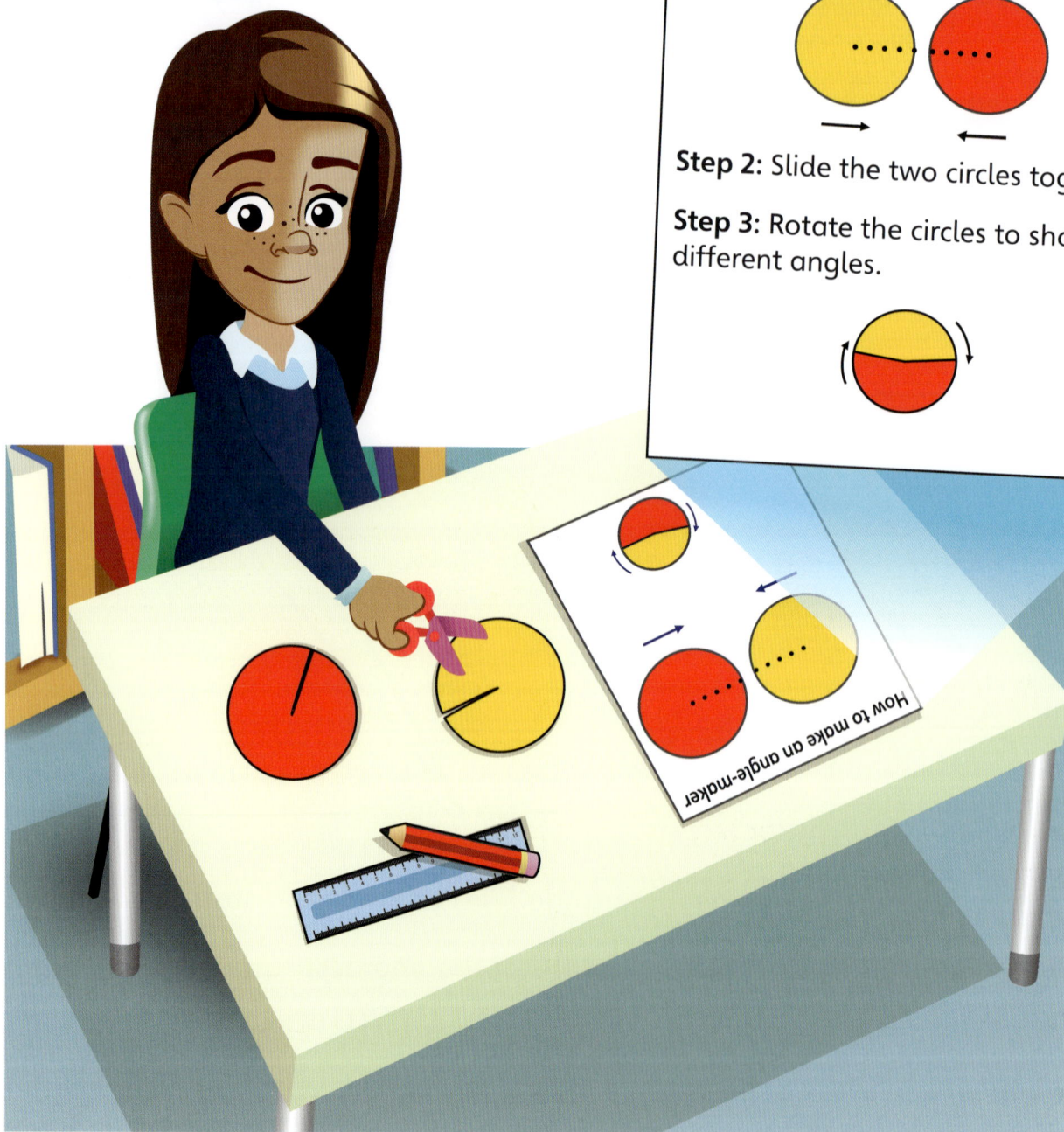

How to make an angle-maker

Step 1: Cut a line to the centre of each circle.

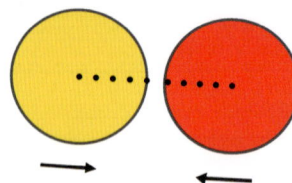

Step 2: Slide the two circles together.

Step 3: Rotate the circles to show different angles.

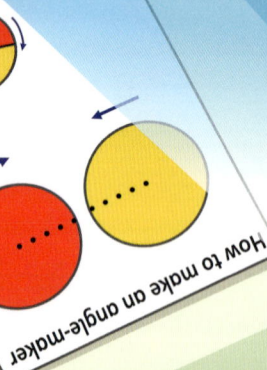

How to make an angle-maker

1 **a)** How can the angle-maker be used to show a 90° angle?

b) When the angle-maker shows a 90° angle, what is the other angle it shows?

Share

a) A whole turn is 360°. A 90° angle is a quarter turn.

The angle-maker can be used in any of these ways to show a 90° angle.

b) One right angle is a quarter turn, so there must be 3 quarter turns remaining.

$90° + 90° + 90° = 270°$

90°
90°   90°   270°
90°

270° is a three-quarter turn.

> I also know that a whole turn is 360° so I subtracted 90° from the whole turn.

$360° – 90° = 270°$

The other angle the angle-maker shows is 270°.

> I used these circles to investigate other pairs of angles.

25

Think together

1) What angles are shown on this angle-maker?

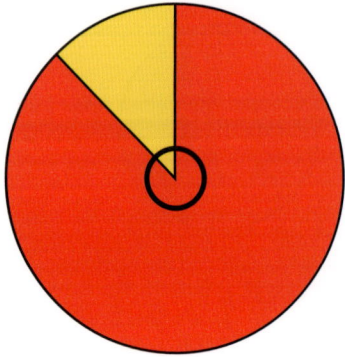

I will measure one angle, then calculate the other angle.

2) Find the missing angles.

a)

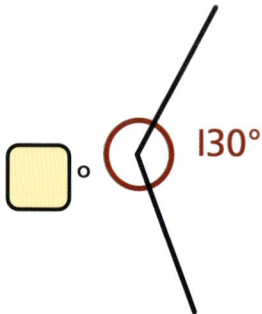

130°

b)

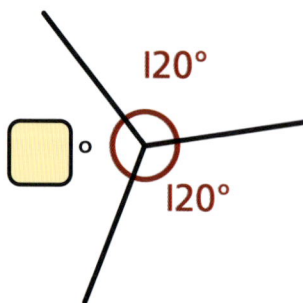

120°

120°

c)

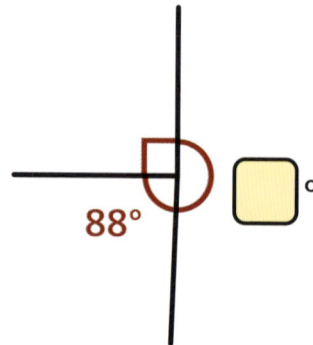

88°

3 Jamilla wants to copy this angle.

CHALLENGE

230°

Jamilla

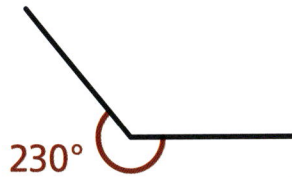

Angles bigger than 180° are called reflex angles.

a) Explain how Jamilla could use her protractor to draw an angle of 230°.

I think Jamilla can use what we have already learnt about angles to draw this angle.

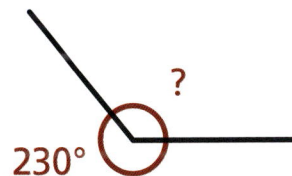

?

230°

b) Use this method to draw your own reflex angle of 230°.

Now draw an angle of 312°.

27

➜ **Practice book 5C p18**

Calculate angles on a straight line

Discover

Follow the instructions:

Step 1

Step 2

$80°$

Step 3

a $80°$

Max

1 a) What is the size of angle a?

b) Max does not measure the angles accurately.

He cuts two equal angles instead.

What angle does he cut?

Share

a)

I measured angle a with a protractor. It is 100°.

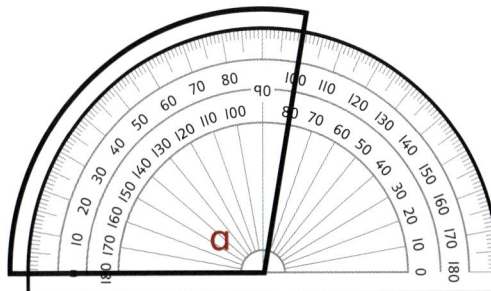

I calculated the missing angle. I know there are 180° in a half turn, so I worked out

$180° - 80° = 100°$.

180°

100° 80°

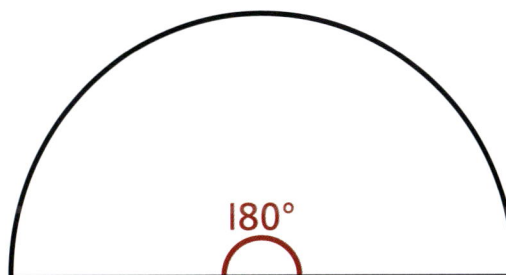

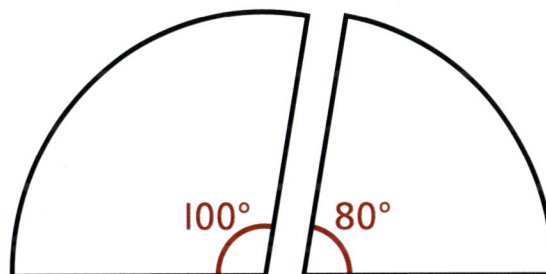

The two angles would make a half turn, so the complete angle is 180°.

$180° - 80° = 100°$

Angle a is 100°.

b) Half of 180° is 90°. The two equal angles must be right angles, or quarter turns.

Max cuts two 90° angles.

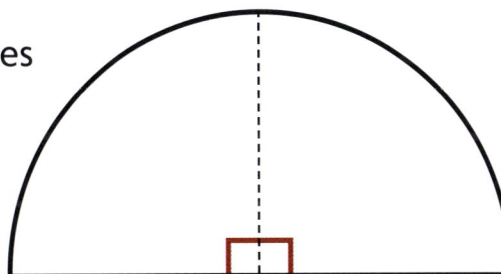

Think together

1 Predict the size of the missing angles. Then measure to check.

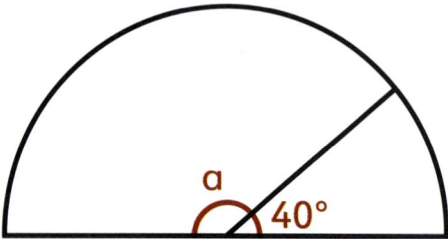 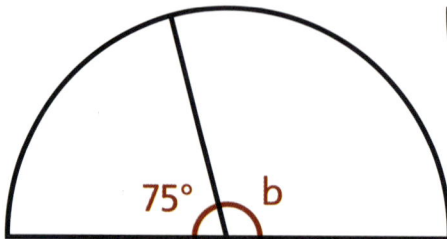 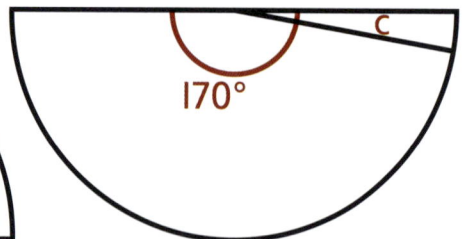

a = ☐°   b = ☐°   c = ☐°

2 Measure these angles. Which could fit together to make a straight line?

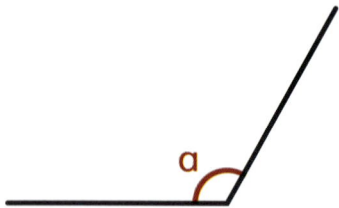 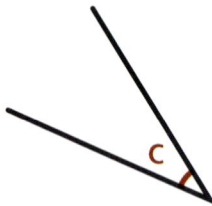 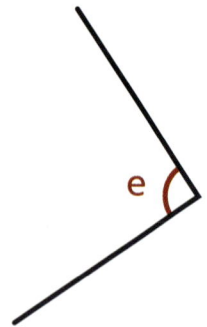

 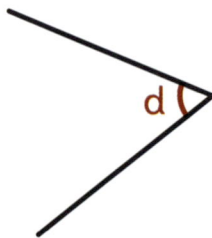 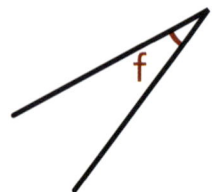

a = ☐°   b = ☐°   c = ☐°   d = ☐°   e = ☐°   f = ☐°

☐ and ☐ fit together to make a straight line.

☐ and ☐ fit together to make a straight line.

3 Max wants to split this angle into five equal parts. What is the size of each of the separate angles?

$a = \boxed{}°$

CHALLENGE

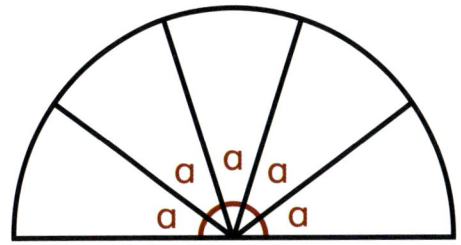

4 Isla rests a square on point P, which is on a straight line.

She measures the angles on either side as she rotates the square.

P

P

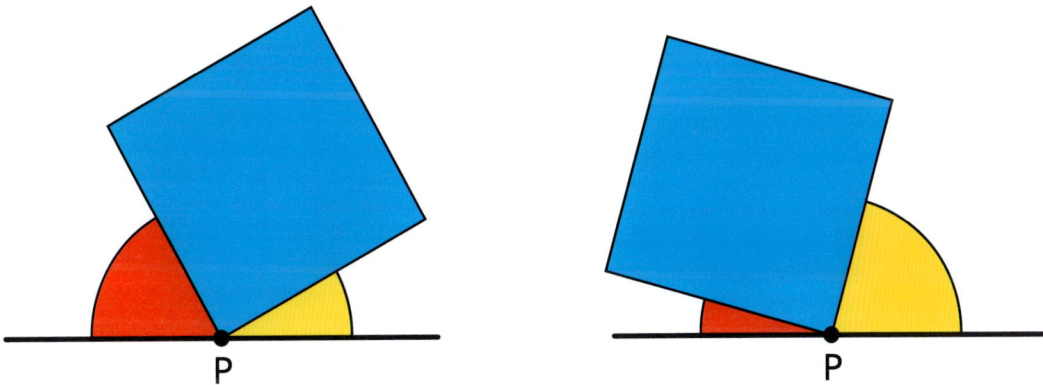

a) How can she make the left-hand angle and the right-hand angle equal?

b) Isla makes it so the left-hand angle is twice the size of the right-hand angle.

What is the size of each angle?

All three angles must total 180°. I already know the size of the **interior angles** of a square.

31

→ **Practice book 5C p21**

Lengths and angles in shapes

Discover

Lee

1 a) What are the interior angles of the parallelogram?

b) Lee thinks length A must be 20 cm and length B must be 10 cm.

Is he correct?

3 Max wants to split this angle into five equal parts. What is the size of each of the separate angles?

$a = \boxed{}°$

CHALLENGE

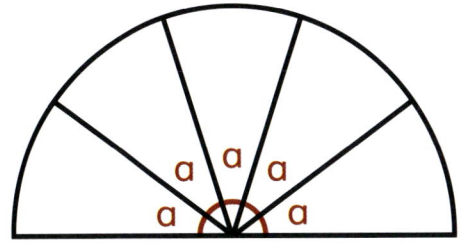

4 Isla rests a square on point P, which is on a straight line.

She measures the angles on either side as she rotates the square.

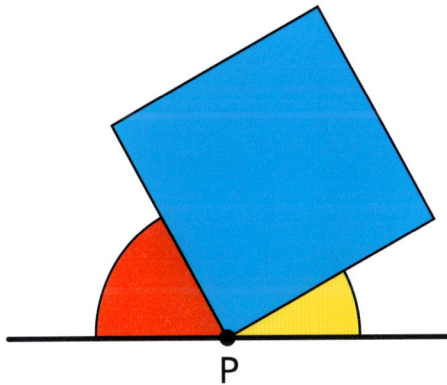

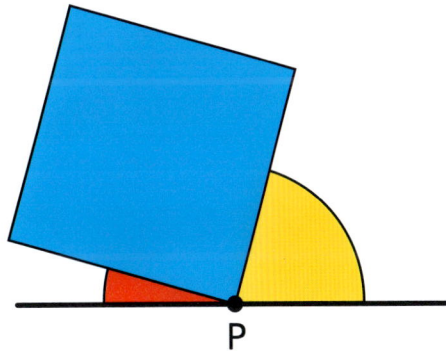

a) How can she make the left-hand angle and the right-hand angle equal?

b) Isla makes it so the left-hand angle is twice the size of the right-hand angle.

What is the size of each angle?

All three angles must total 180°. I already know the size of the **interior angles** of a square.

31

→ Practice book 5C p21

Lengths and angles in shapes

Discover

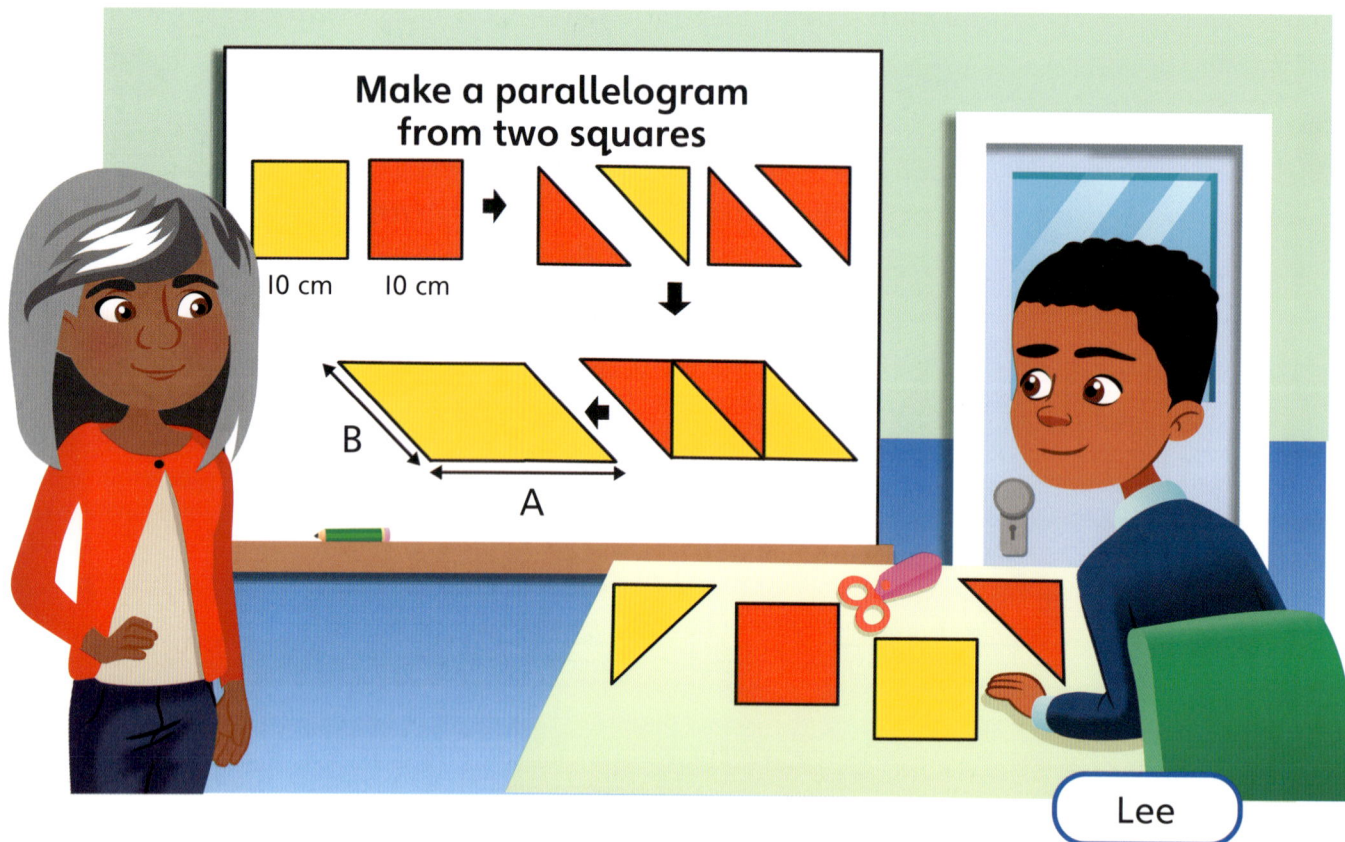

Make a parallelogram from two squares

10 cm   10 cm

B

A

Lee

1 a) What are the interior angles of the parallelogram?

b) Lee thinks length A must be 20 cm and length B must be 10 cm.

Is he correct?

Share

a) The four angles in a square are all 90°.

You can use this to calculate the angles of the triangles.

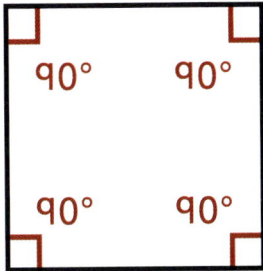

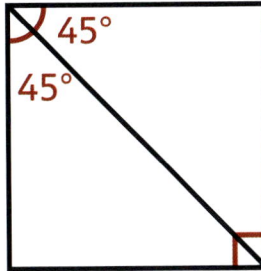

$$90° \div 2 = 45°$$

You can use this information to calculate the angles inside the parallelogram. We call these interior angles.

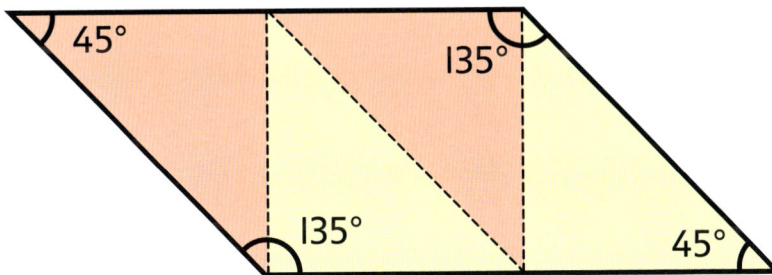

$$90° + 45° = 135°$$

The interior angles of the parallelogram are 45°, 135°, 45° and 135°.

b) Length A is two 10 cm lengths, so it must be 20 cm long.

Length B is the diagonal of one square. If you measure the length it is greater than 10 cm.

Lee is correct about length A, but incorrect about length B.

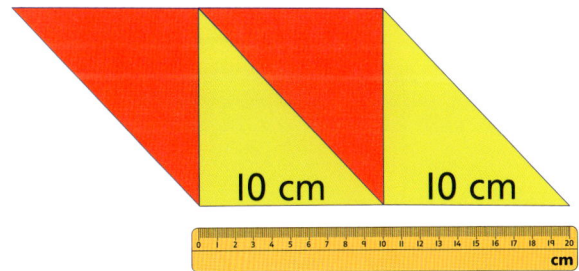

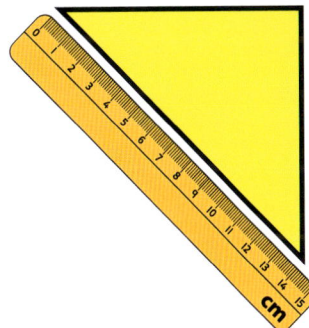

Think together

1 Lee fits together the four triangles he has made from two squares in different ways. What angles can you work out without measuring?

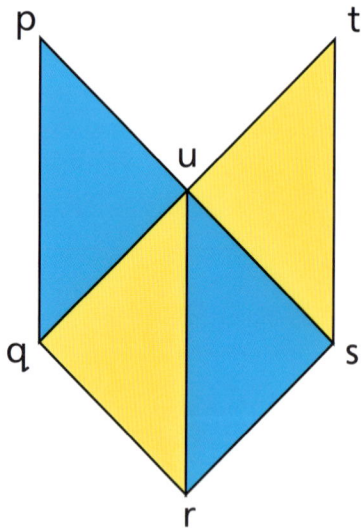

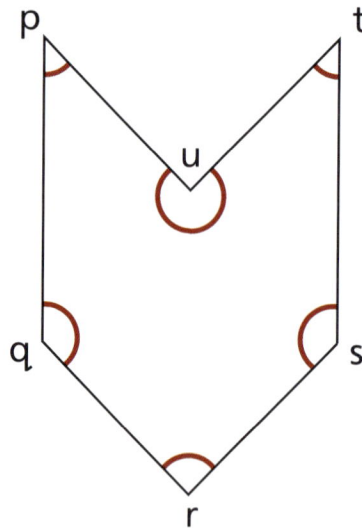

2 Work out the length and the width of Shape B.

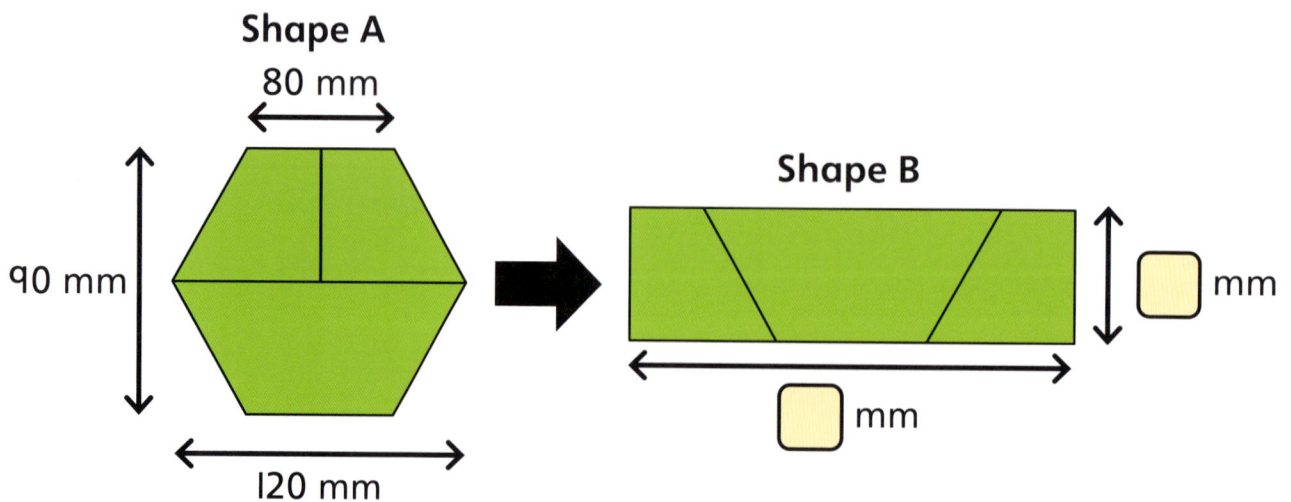

Shape A

80 mm

90 mm

120 mm

Shape B

☐ mm

☐ mm

CHALLENGE

3 Max splits a rectangle in half diagonally.

Each angle will be 45° because the rectangles are split exactly in half.

Max

Investigate Max's statement by checking what angles are produced when you split these shapes in half diagonally. Is he correct?

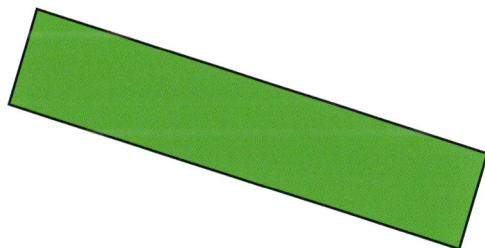

I will use trial and error and write my findings in a table.

→ **Practice book 5C p24**

Regular and irregular polygons

Discover

All of the interior angles are the same.

I think this is a regular octagon.

Isla

Richard

1 **a)** Is Isla correct? How do you know?

b) Is Richard correct? How do you know?

Share

a) There are different methods to check the size of the angles.

I measured them with a protractor. They all measured the same size.

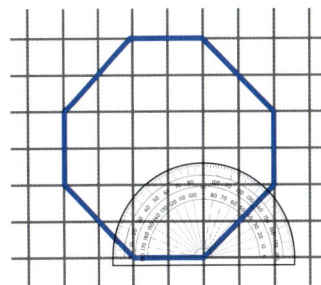

Each angle is made of a right angle and half a right angle. I saw this on the grid.

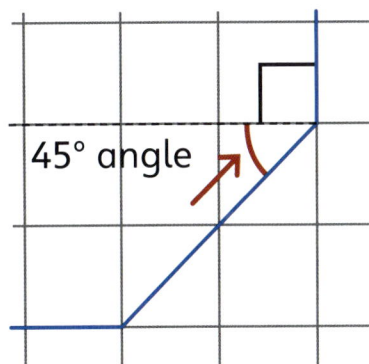

45° angle

$45° + 90° = 135°$

Every interior angle is 135°. Isla is correct.

b)

Regular shapes have: All angles equal **and** all sides the same length.

I know that if the angles are not all the same size, or the sides are not all the same length, then the shape is irregular.

2 cm

The sides are not all the same length.

Richard is not correct. This is an irregular octagon.

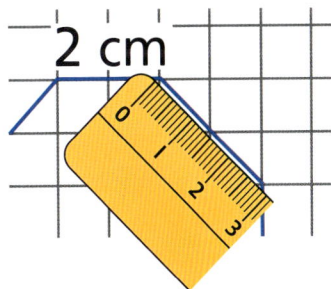

Think together

1 Explain why each shape is irregular.

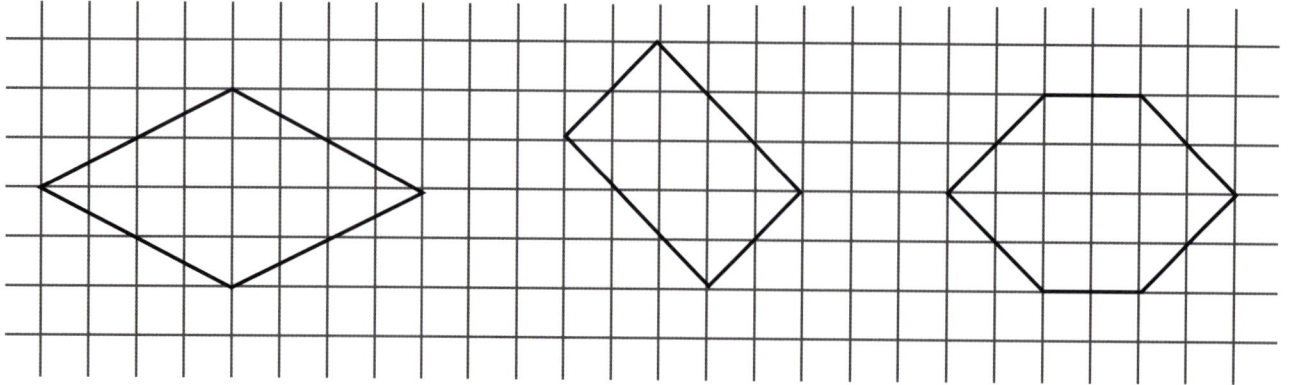

2 Measure the angles and the sides of the pentagons. Which one is regular? How do you know?

A

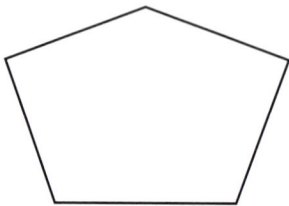

B

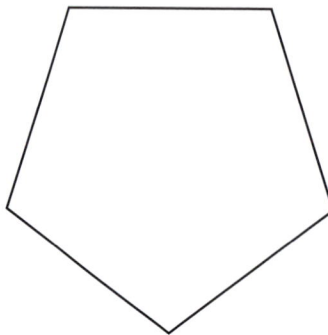

C

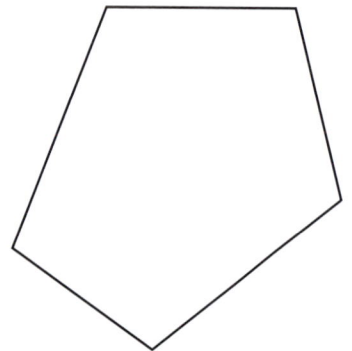

3 Max and Ambika are making shapes on different geoboards.

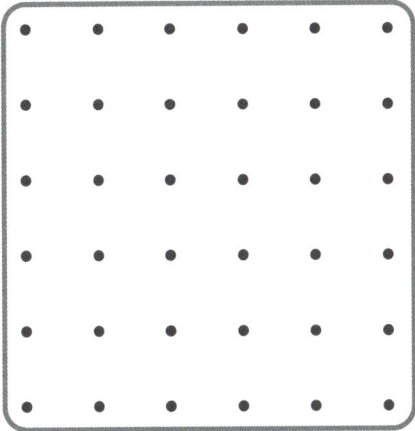

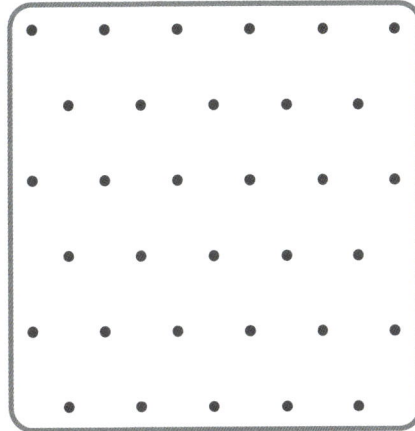

CHALLENGE

Max: I will make a regular quadrilateral.

Max

Ambika: I will make a regular hexagon.

Ambika

a) Which geoboard should each child use?

b) Which other regular shapes could Max and Ambika make on the different boards?

c) Which regular shapes cannot be made on either board?

I will make a list of all the regular shapes I know and try to make them on a geoboard.

39

Parallel lines

Discover

I **a)** Which lines on the gates are parallel?

b) Explain why the diagonal lines on the gates are not parallel.

Share

a) All the horizontal and all the vertical lines on the gates are parallel.

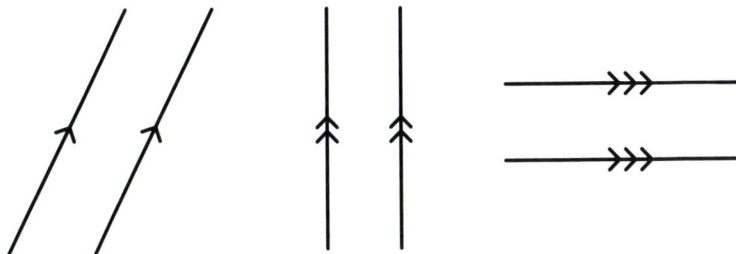

We can show parallel lines with arrow markings.

We can mark the parallel lines on the gates with arrows.

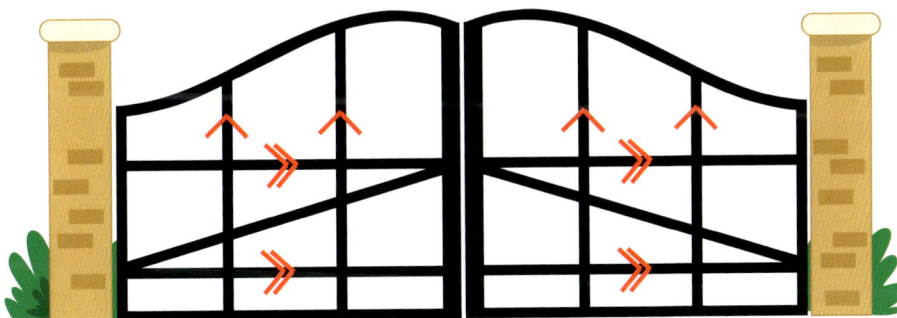

I think there are different numbers of arrows on the horizontal and vertical lines to show the pairs.

b) The diagonal lines on the gates are not parallel because if they continued they would cross over.

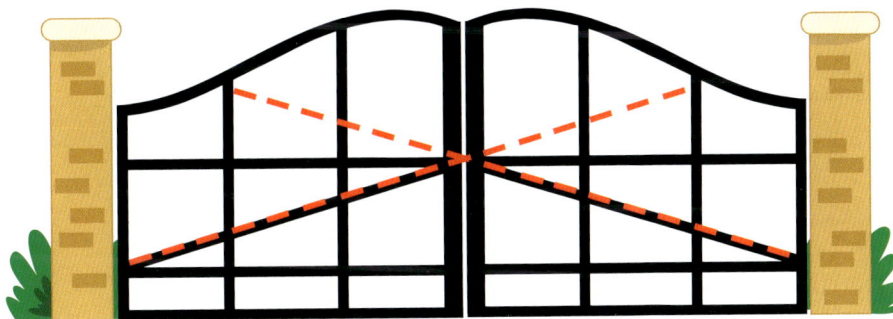

Think together

1 One of the gates has rusted from its hinges.

How many sets of parallel lines are there now?

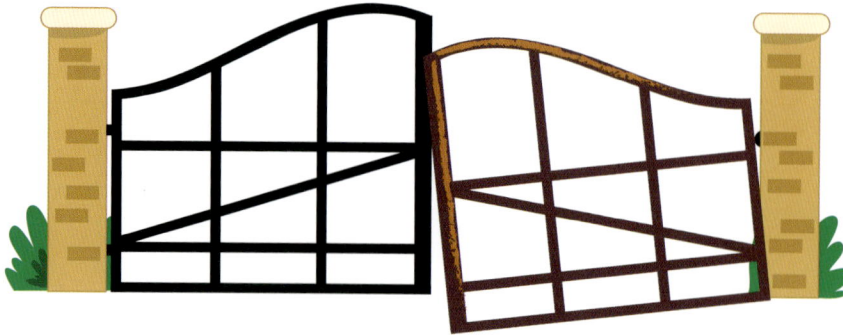

2 Which sides should have arrow markings on to show that they are parallel?

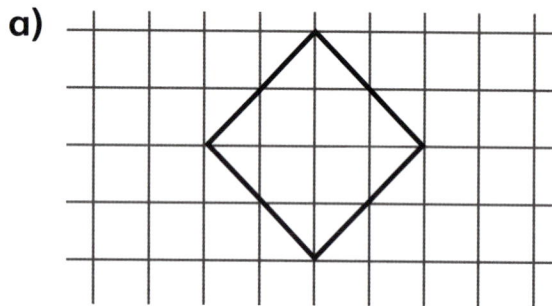

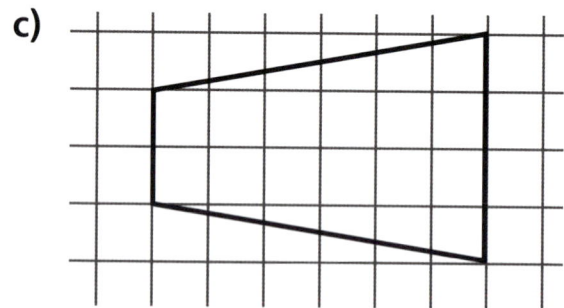

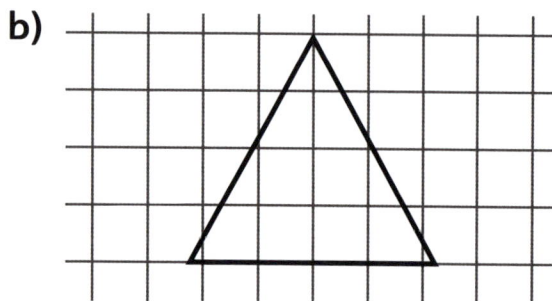

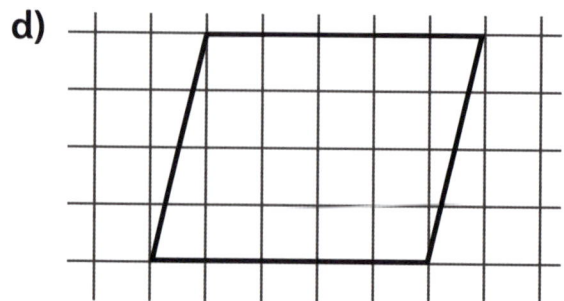

a)

c)

b)

d)

I wonder if parallel lines must be exactly the same length.

CHALLENGE

3 Aki has drawn a shape and labelled every vertex.

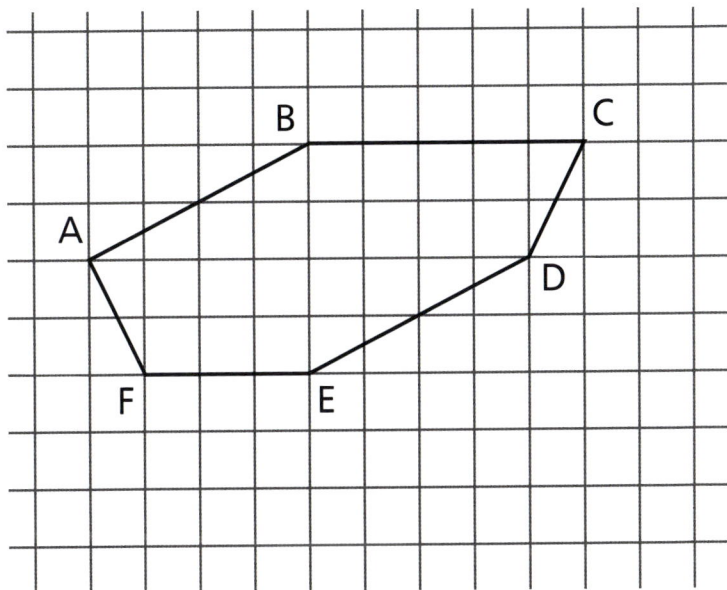

Line BC is parallel to line EF.

Aki

a) Point to the lines Aki is describing.

b) Which other lines are parallel? How do you know?

c) How would you draw lines parallel to AB or to BC on the grid below?

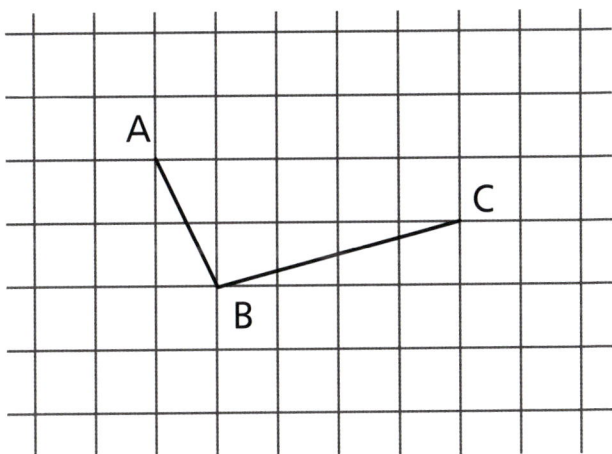

I will use the grid pattern to help me.

→ Practice book 5C p30

Perpendicular lines

Discover

Sofia

They need to be vertical.

I made them perpendicular.

Toshi

1 **a)** Which streetlamps are perpendicular to the road?

b) Which streetlamps are both vertical and perpendicular to the road?

Can you prove they are perpendicular?

Share

a) Perpendicular lines cross or meet at a 90° angle.

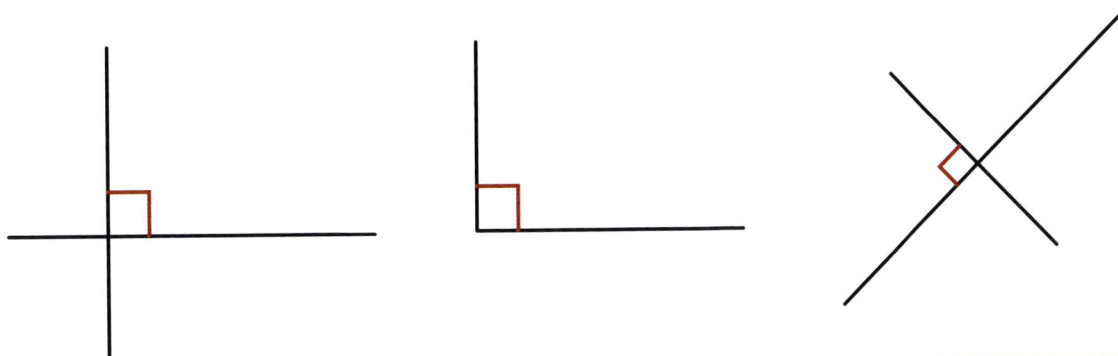

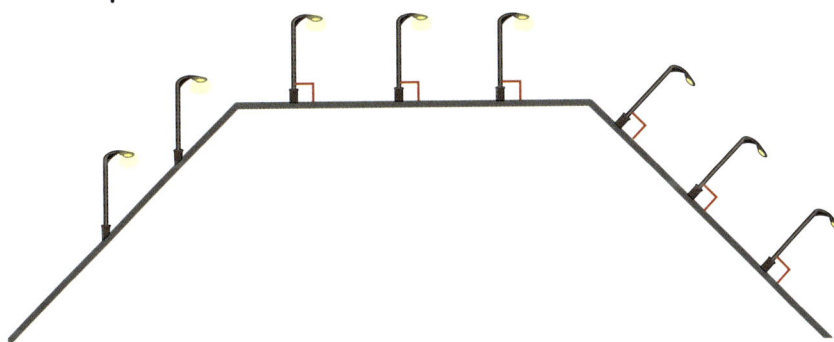

The streetlamps on the top of the hill and on the right are perpendicular to the road because they make right angles.

> Remember, a 90° angle is also called a right angle. We show it with a box marking.

b) The road on top of the hill is horizontal, which is perpendicular to any vertical line.

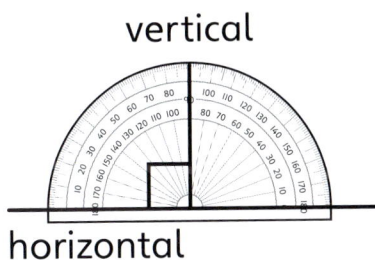

vertical

horizontal

The streetlamps on the top of the hill are both vertical and perpendicular to the road, as they make right angles.

> I proved this with a protractor.

45

Think together

1 Which of these diagrams show perpendicular lines?

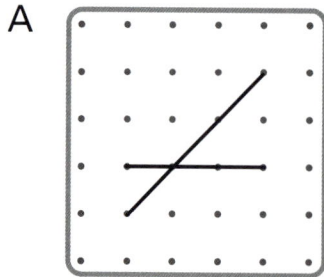

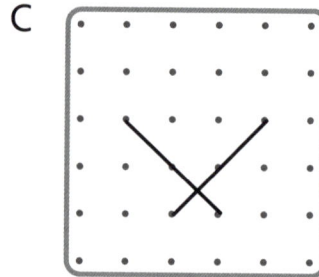

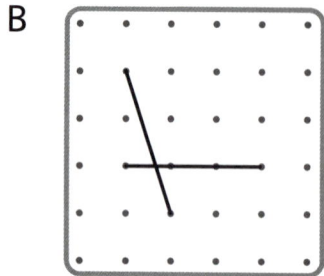

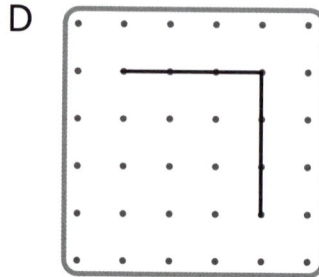

A

C

B

D

2 **a)** Name the lines that are perpendicular to the line AB.

b) Point to the lines that are perpendicular to the line HI.

Think about what would happen if AB or HI was extended to meet the other lines in the diagrams. Which would cross at a right angle?

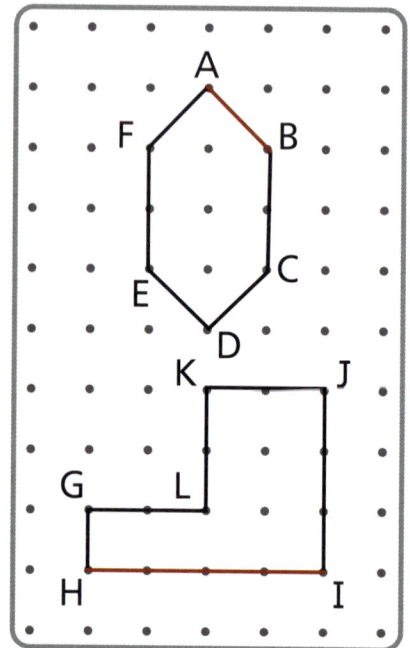

CHALLENGE

3 **a)** Bella thinks she has made rectangles on her geoboards. Is she correct? Explain your answer.

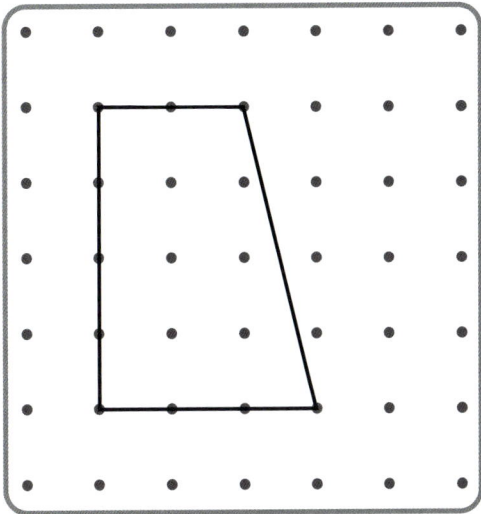

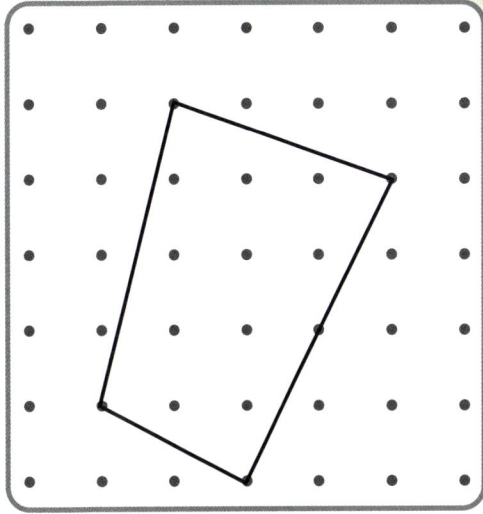

b) Explain how to complete the rectangles.

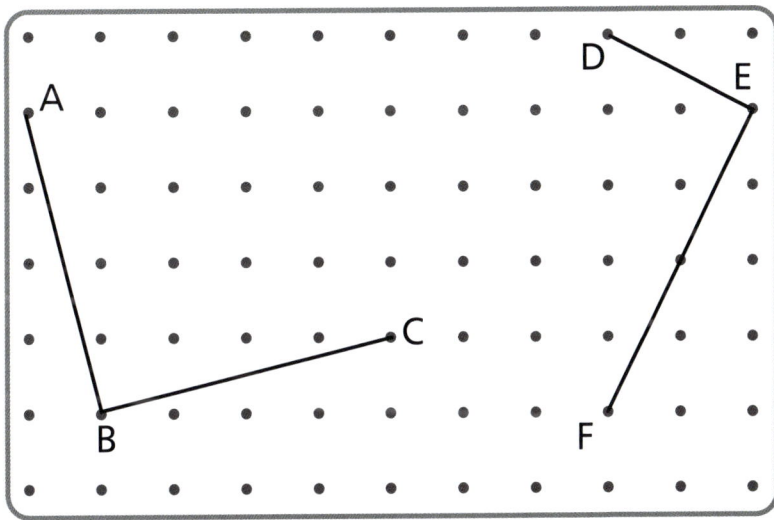

> I wonder how I can make perpendicular lines to complete the rectangles.

> I will look at the grid to help me make the perpendicular lines accurate.

47

Investigate lines

Discover

1 **a)** Measure the angle where the plain red strip of paper crosses a dotted strip.

Is it the same each time?

b) How can you move the plain red strip of paper so that it is parallel to the stripy blue strip of paper?

Does it help to notice if there are any perpendicular lines?

Share

a) Use a protractor to measure the angle where the plain red strip of paper crosses each dotted strip of paper.

> I measured the other side of the line and each angle was 30°.

All the dotted strips of paper are parallel. The plain red strip crosses each dotted strip of paper at an angle of 150°. The angle is the same each time.

b) The stripy blue strip of paper is perpendicular to every dotted strip of paper. Move the plain red strip so it is also perpendicular to the dotted strips. The plain red strip will then be parallel to the stripy blue strip of paper.

> I used a protractor to check the angle of the stripy blue strip.

49

Think together

1 How could you place a strip of paper parallel to the plain red strip?

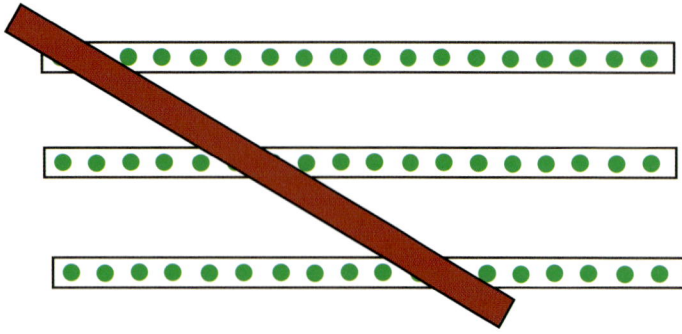

2 Isla folds a piece of paper. Identify any parallel and perpendicular lines.

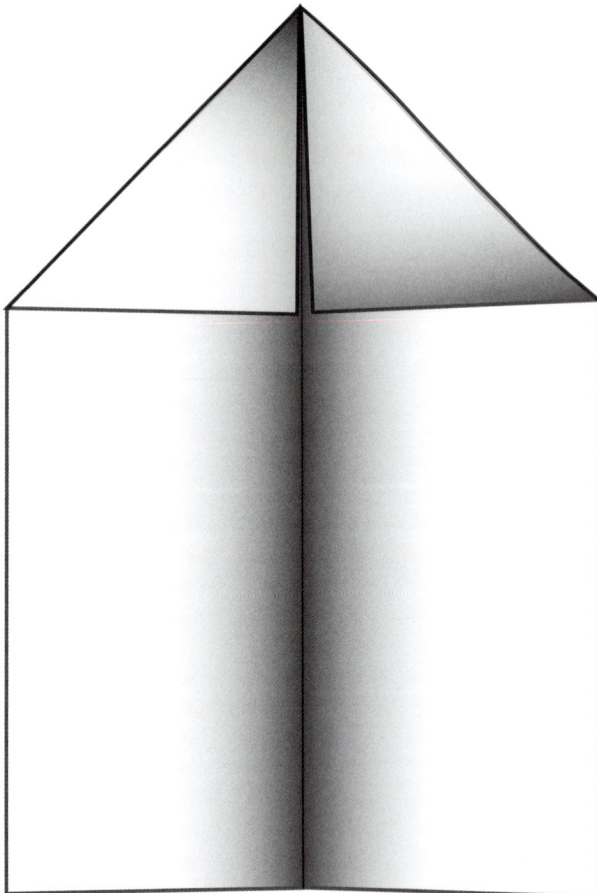

CHALLENGE

3 Max draws lines to join opposite corners of these shapes.

a) Which shapes have diagonals that are perpendicular?

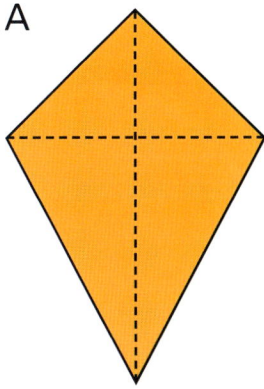

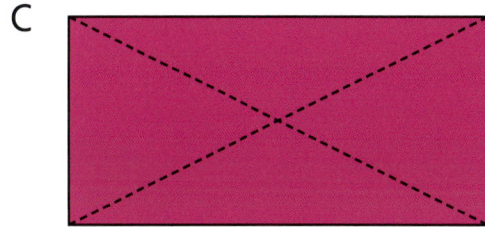

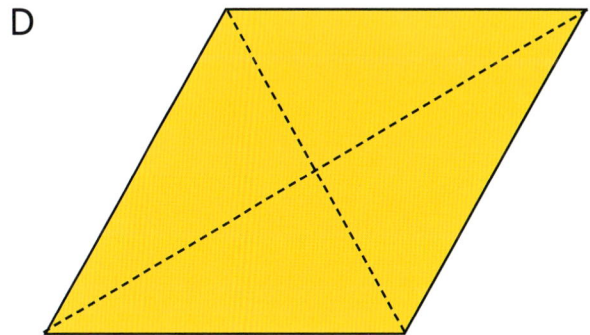

A

C

B

D

> I think the diagonals of squares are always perpendicular.

b) Do you agree with Astrid? Explain your answer.

51

→ Practice book 5C p36

3D shapes

Discover

① **a)** Emma looks at the shape from position A. What can she see?

b) Bella looks at the shape from position B and Aki looks at the shape from position C. What do they each see?

Share

a) Position A is a **top view**.

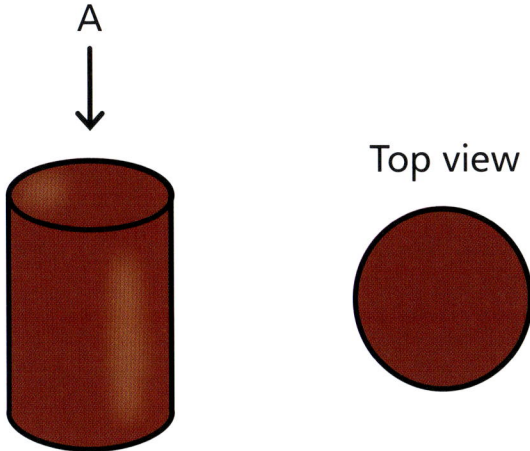

A

Top view

> We sometimes call this view the **plan view**.

From position A, Emma can see only one face of the cylinder. The face is a circle.

b) Bella and Aki both have a **side view**. For this cylinder, each side view is a rectangle.

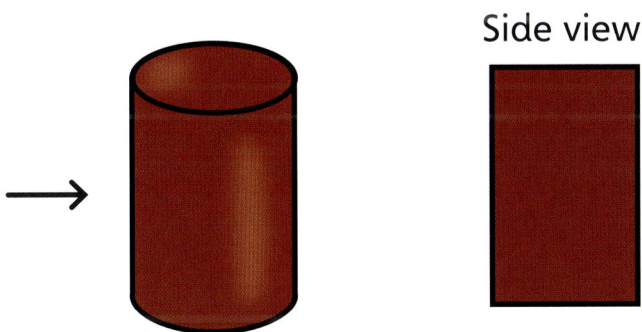

Side view

> I think I know why the side view of a cylinder is a rectangle, even though it has a curved surface.

Bella and Aki each see the same side view of the cylinder. They both see a rectangle.

Think together

1 Which of the shapes A, B and C could not be a view of this cube? Explain to a partner why.

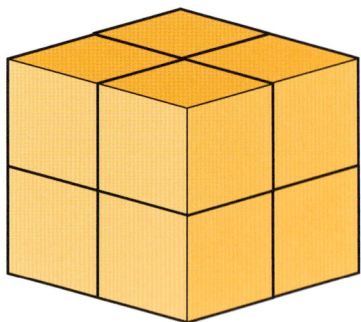

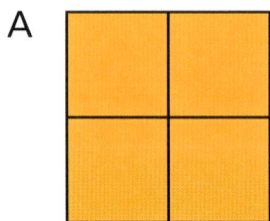

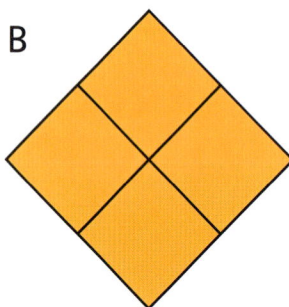

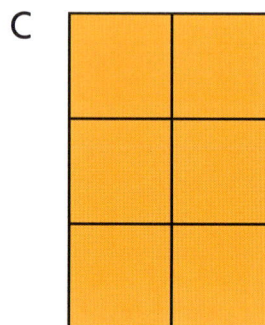

A   B   C

2 Luis, Andy and Jamie look at this prism from different positions. Describe and draw what they can each see.

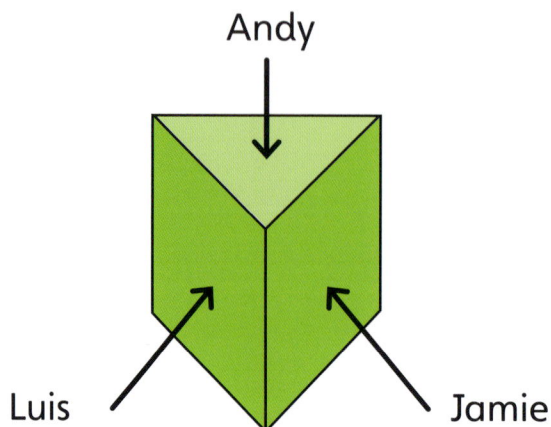

Andy

Luis   Jamie

CHALLENGE

3 Max looks at this collection of 3D shapes from above.

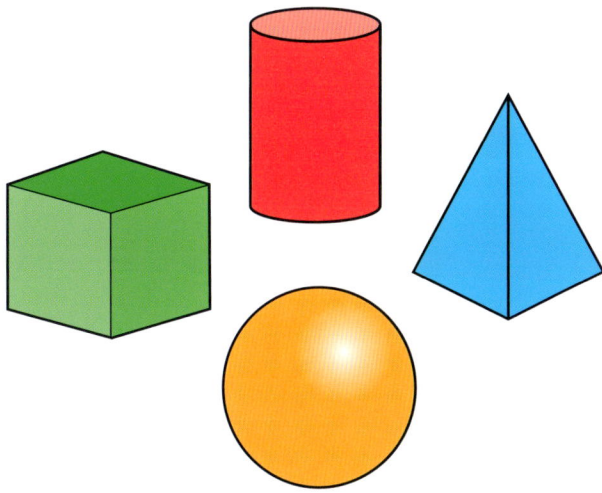

Which of these could be what he sees?

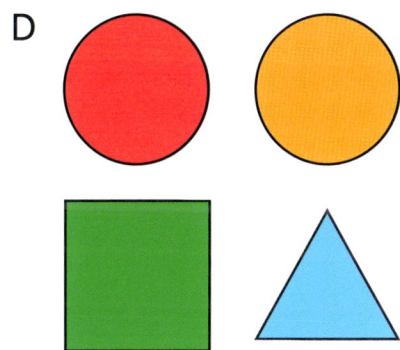

A

C

B

D

I will think carefully about which shapes are next to each other.

55

End of unit check

1 Which shows a 180° turn?

A    B 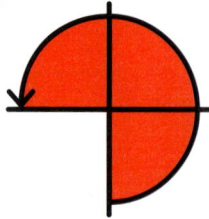   C 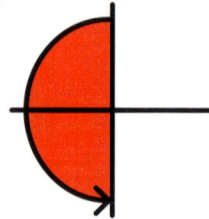   D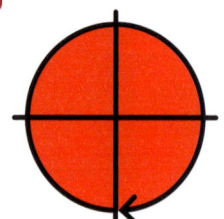

2 What angle does this show?

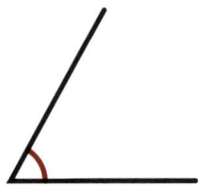

A 60°   B 45°   C 120°   D 30°

3 Explain the mistake.

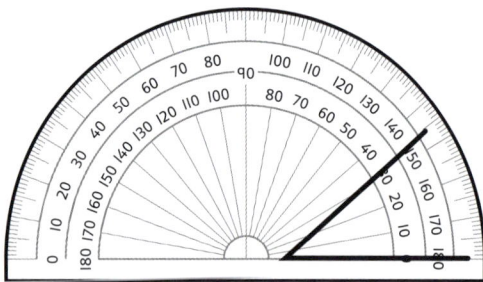

A The protractor is upside down.

B The centre is not lined up with the turn.

C The angle is obtuse so the protractor is not big enough.

D The base line is not lined up with one line of the angle.

4 Which missing angle is not 50°?

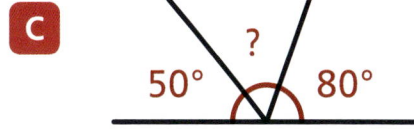

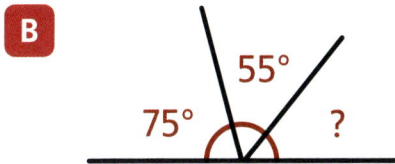

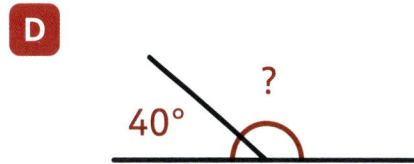

A

130° ?

B

55°
75° ?

C

?
50° 80°

D

?
40°

5 Which shape does not have a view that is a rectangle?

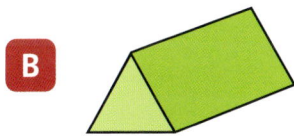

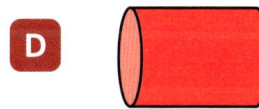

A

B

C

D

6 Which shape has one pair of parallel lines and no perpendicular lines?

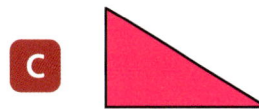

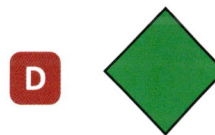

A

B

C

D

→ Practice book 5C p42

Unit 13
Geometry – position and direction

In this unit we will …

⚡ Read and plot coordinates on a grid

⚡ Find the coordinates of vertices of shapes on a grid

⚡ Learn to reflect simple 2D shapes in vertical and horizontal lines

⚡ Plot and find coordinates of a reflected point on a grid

⚡ Use coordinates to calculate new points of a reflected shape

⚡ Translate 2D shapes on grid paper

⚡ Use coordinates to find translations

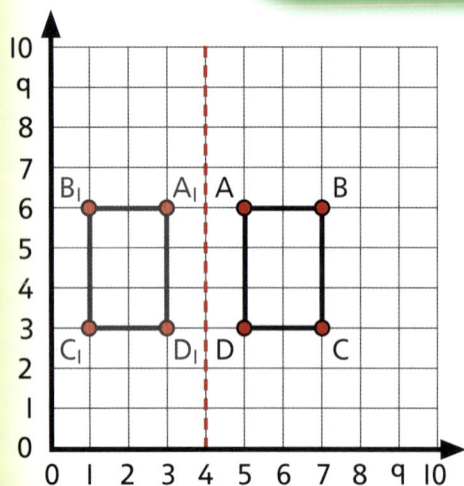

We will be reflecting shapes in a mirror line. What are the coordinates of this reflected shape? Do you notice anything about the reflection?

Here are some maths words we will be using. Are any of these words new?

reflection translation vertex

vertices coordinates mirror line

horizontal vertical

We need to be able to work out the distance between coordinates on a grid. How far apart are the coordinates A and B?

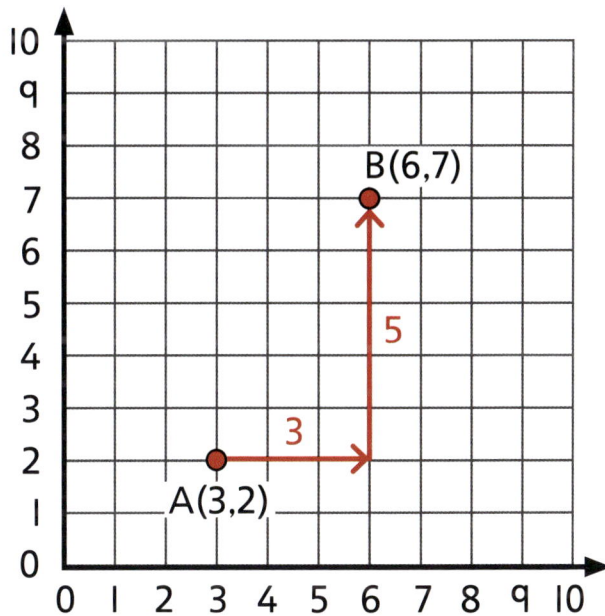

Read and plot coordinates

Discover

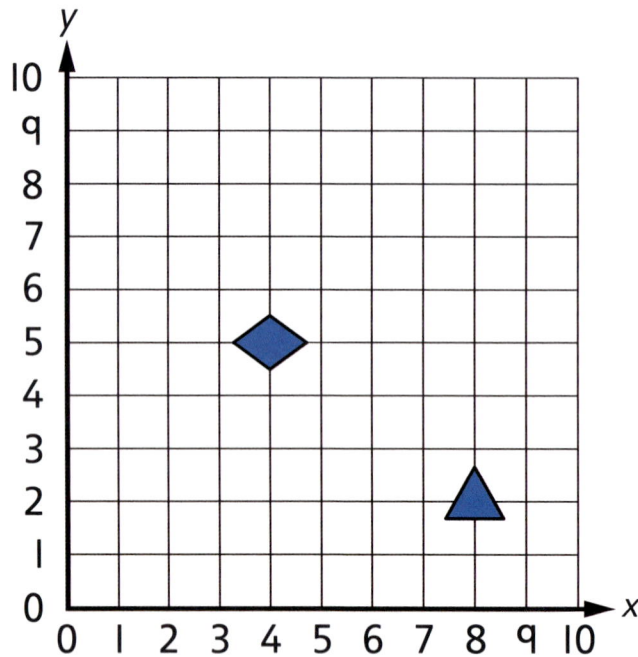

1) a) What are the **coordinates** of the centre of the triangle?

b) Reena says, 'The rhombus is at (5,4).'

Discuss her thinking.

Share

a)

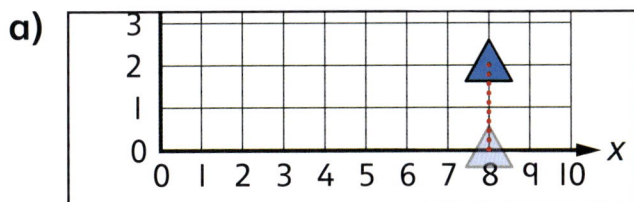

The *x*-coordinate is 8.

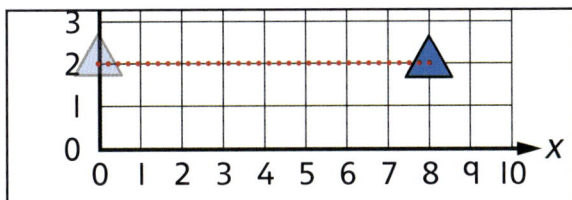

The *y*-coordinate is 2.

The triangle is at (8,2).

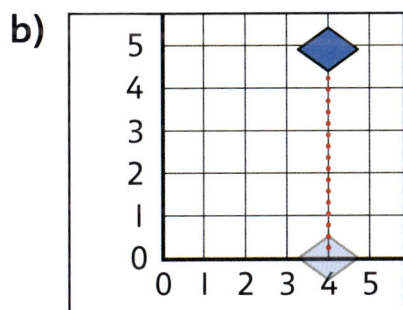

b)

The *x*-coordinate is 4.

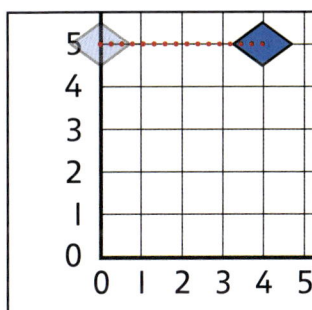

The *y*-coordinate is 5.

Reena has written the coordinates in the wrong order.

The centre of the rhombus is at (4,5).

Remember we always write the *x*-coordinate first and then the *y*-coordinate.

Think together

1 Place a counter at each coordinate on the grid.

a) (5,4)

b) (2,3)

c) (0,6)

d) (4,0)

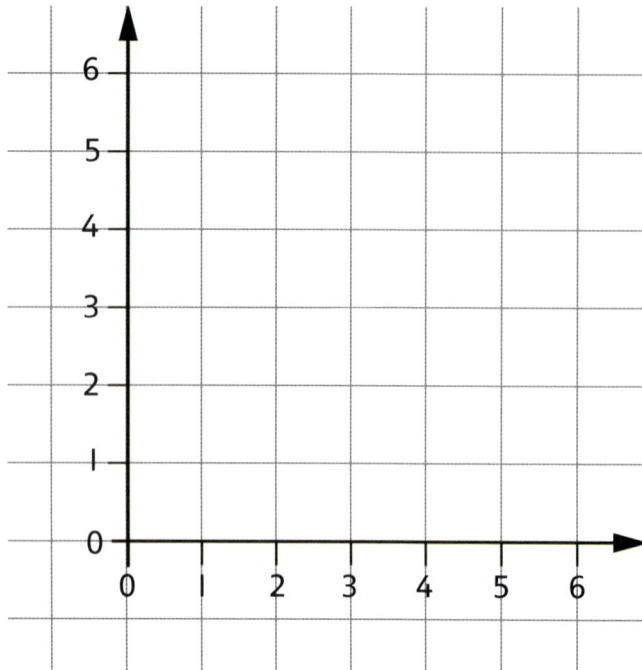

2 Write the coordinates of each point. What do you notice?

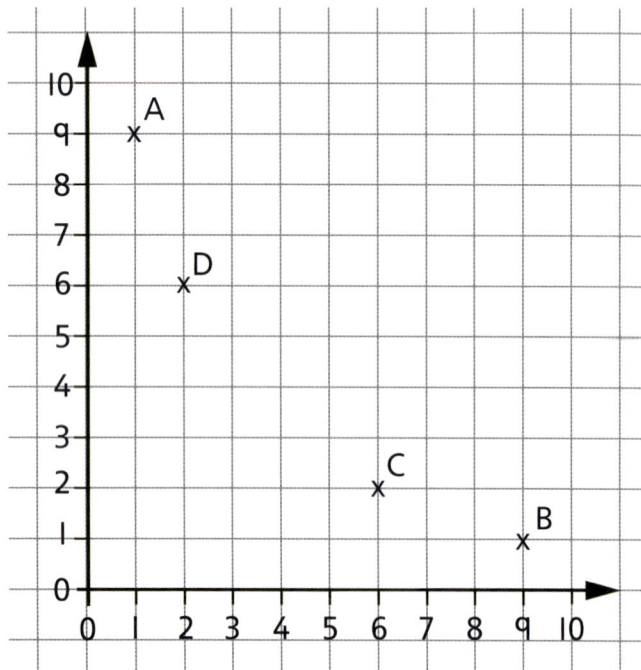

A(☐ , ☐)

B(☐ , ☐)

C(☐ , ☐)

D(☐ , ☐)

CHALLENGE

3 Draw your own treasure map, like the one shown.

Mark 5 or more treasure chests.

Keep your map hidden.

A partner should guess where your treasure chests are, by saying coordinates.

They should use another grid to record their guesses.

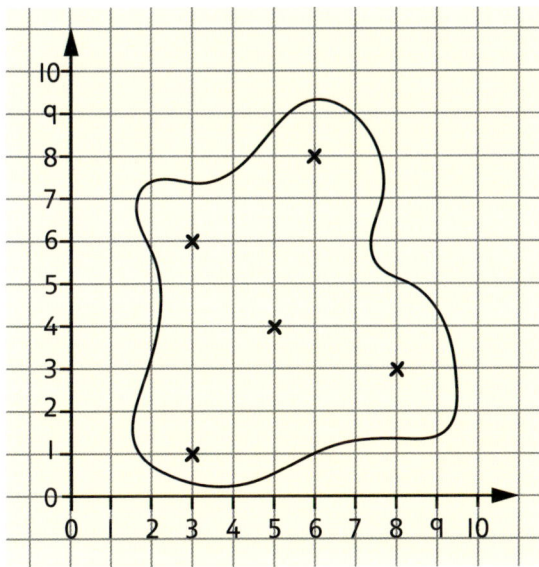

I guess (4,1).

That point is next to a treasure chest.

I guess (8,6).

That point is not near a treasure chest.

→ Practice book 5C p45

Problem solving with coordinates

Discover

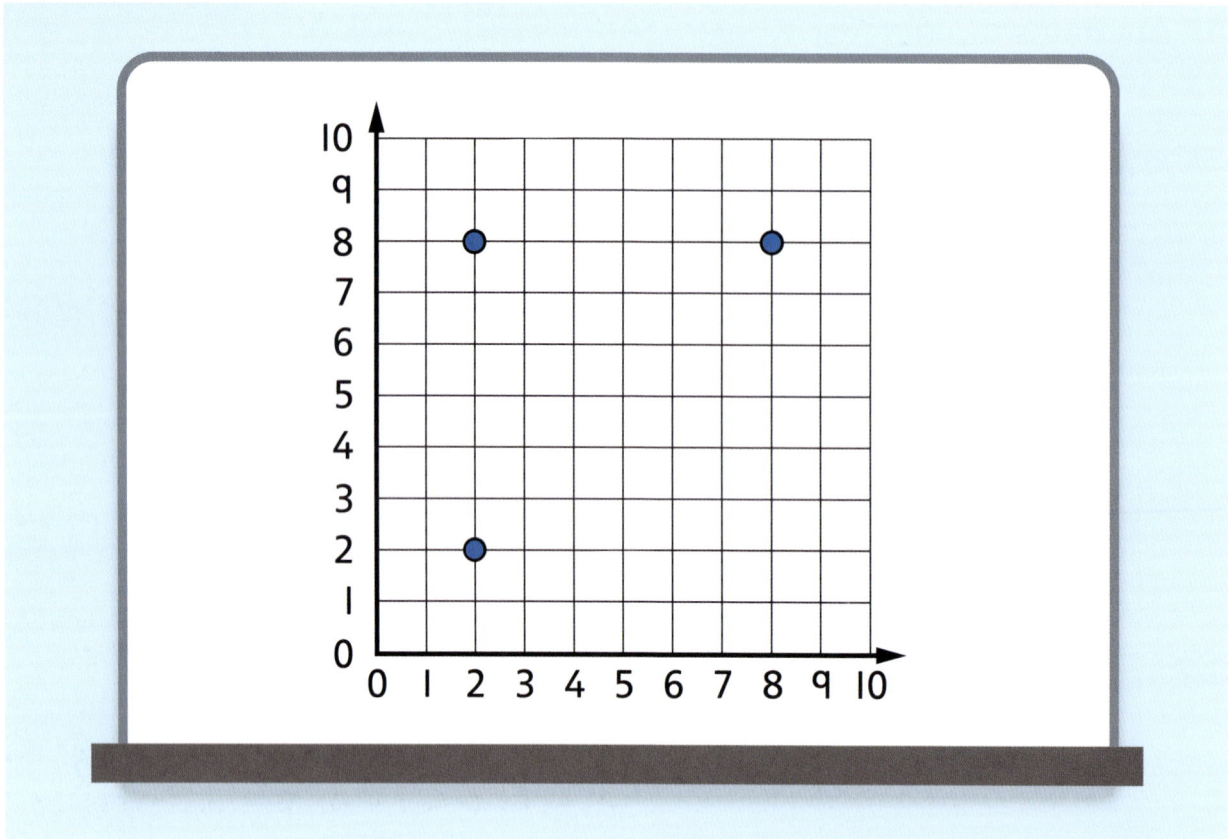

1 **a)** Three vertices of a shape have been marked.

Describe the shape fully.

b) Add one more vertex to form a square.

What are the coordinates of the four vertices?

Share

a)

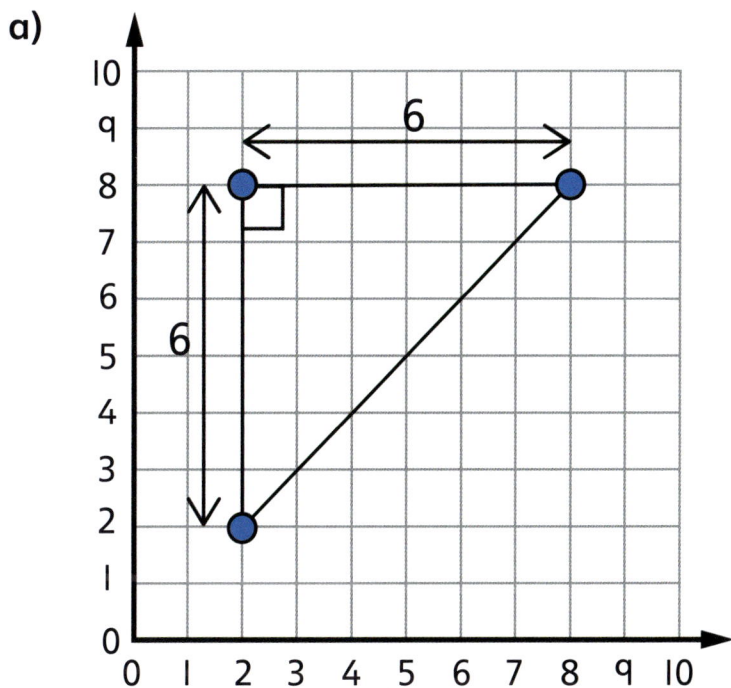

This is a right-angled triangle.

It is isosceles because two sides are the same length.

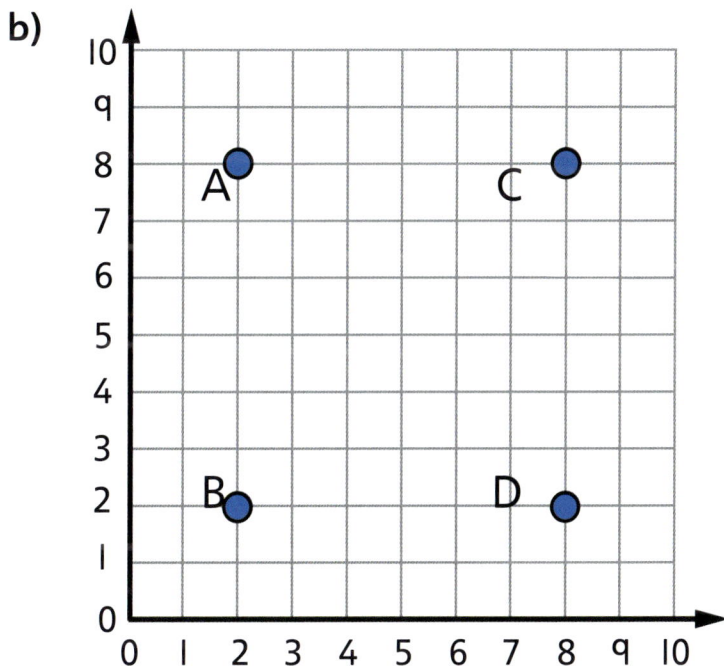

b)

A(2,8)

B(2,2)

C(8,8)

D(8,2)

> I looked at where the *x*- and *y*-coordinates of the other points are.

65

Think together

1 These points are two vertices of a rectangle.

They are diagonally opposite each other in the rectangle.

What are the coordinates of the other vertices?

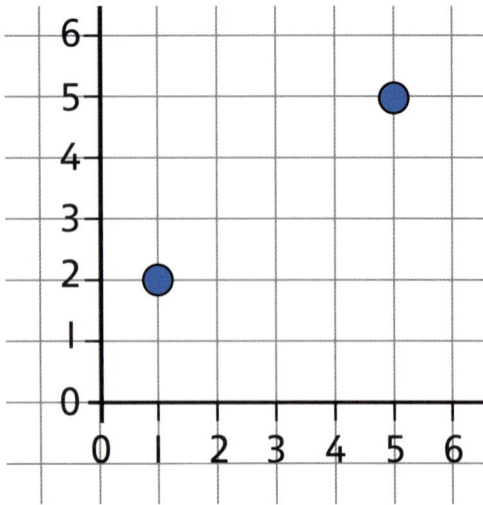

2 These points are three vertices of a rhombus.

What are the coordinates of the fourth vertex?

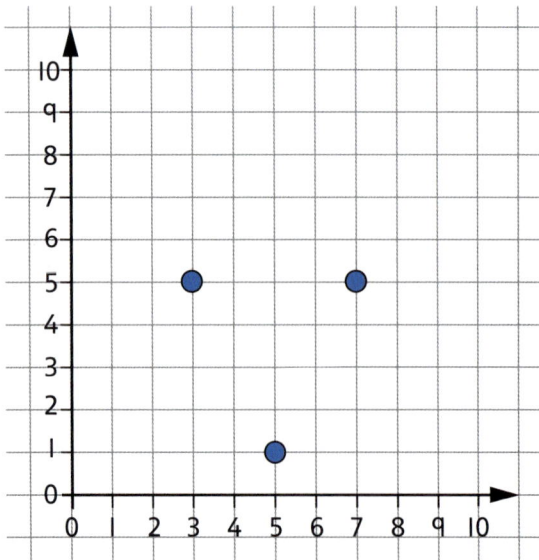

3 Work out the coordinates of the vertices of this square.

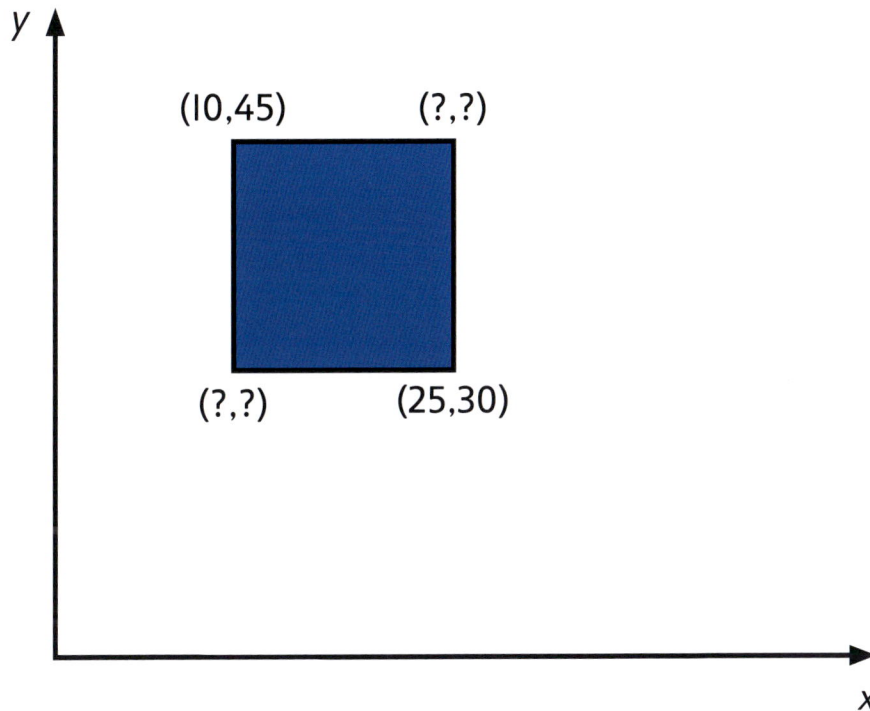

CHALLENGE

(10,45)   (?,?)

(?,?)   (25,30)

There are no grid lines or labels on the axes. This is impossible!

I think I can start this by thinking about the coordinates I DO know.

→ Practice book 5C p48

Translate shapes

Discover

I will slide my bed 5 squares to the left.

Bella

1 a) Describe the new position of Bella's bed.

b) Bella decides to move the table. She slides it 8 squares to the right, then 6 squares down. Where will the table be now?

Share

a) When a shape slides across a grid, this is called a **translation**.

> I know that each vertex moves 5 squares to the left.

Point A moves 5 squares to the left.

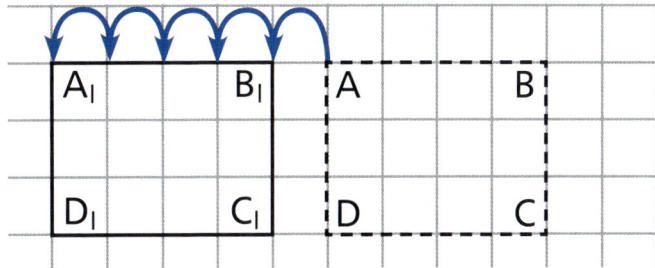

Each vertex moves 5 squares to the left.

> A common mistake is to think that there must be a gap of 5 between the old position and the new position.

The new position of Bella's bed will be above the table.

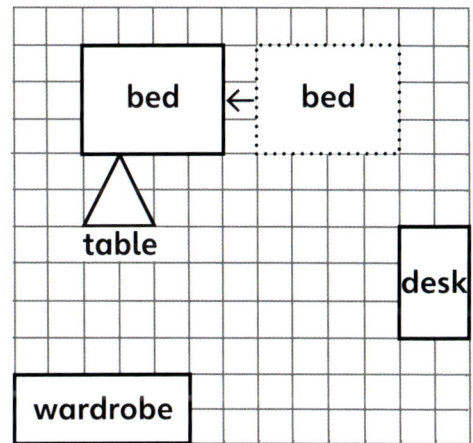

b) Bella moves the table 8 squares to the right. Then she moves it 6 squares down.

> A translation moves left or right first, then up or down. This is like coordinates.

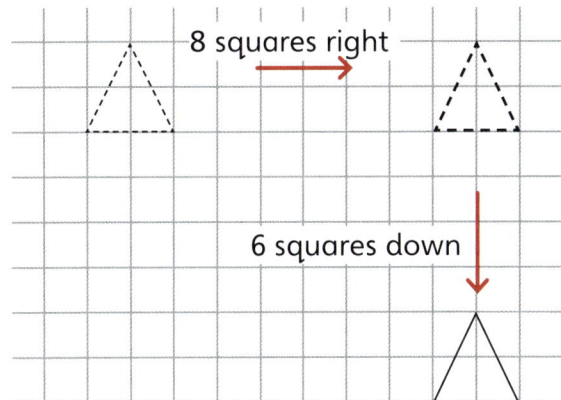

The table will now be in the bottom right corner of her room, near the desk.

Think together

1 This desk is translated to a new position, shown by the dotted lines. Describe the translation.

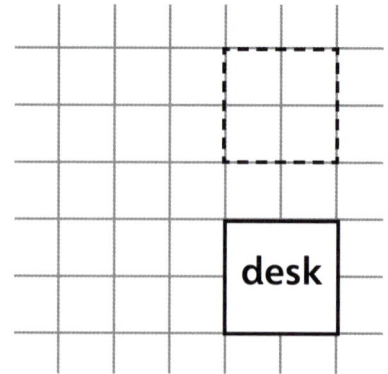

The desk has moved ☐ squares

_____ .

2 a) Describe the translation from square A to square B, and from B to A.

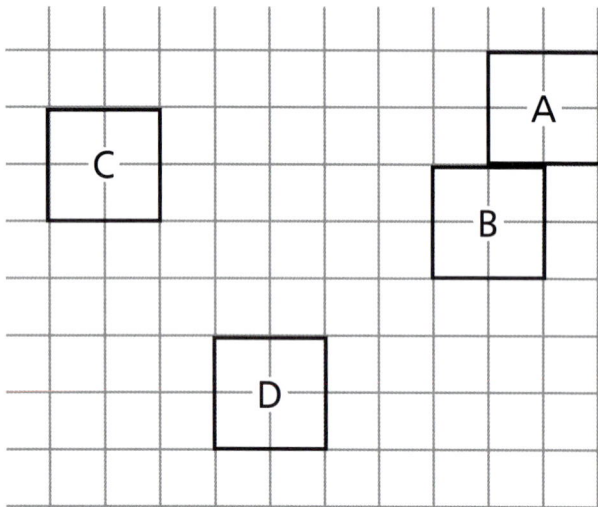

> Your answer must show how many squares each vertex has moved left or right first, then up or down.

A to B: ☐ left and 2 _____

B to A: ☐ _____ and ☐ _____

b) Describe the translation from C to D and from D to C.

c) What do you notice?

3 **a)** The shaded triangle, A, is translated and reflected. Which of the other triangles show **reflections** and which show translations? How can you tell?

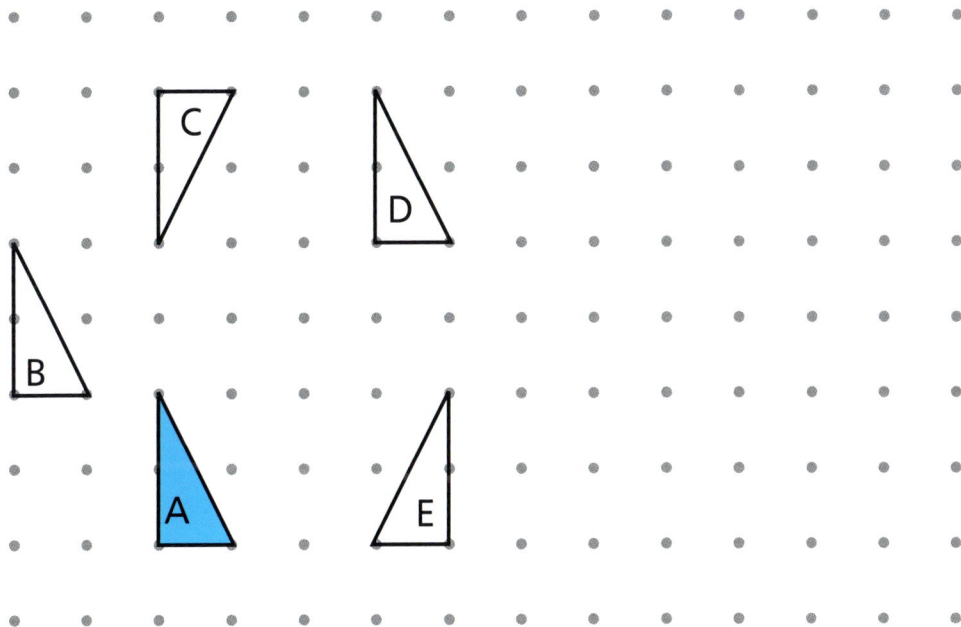

CHALLENGE

> I can spot translations by imagining the shape sliding smoothly.

b) Describe each translation.

c) Where are the **mirror lines** for the reflections?

> I can test for reflections by using a mirror.

d) Triangle A is translated 10 right and 3 up. Point to its new position on the grid.

→ **Practice book 5C p51**

Translate points

Discover

Alex

Andy

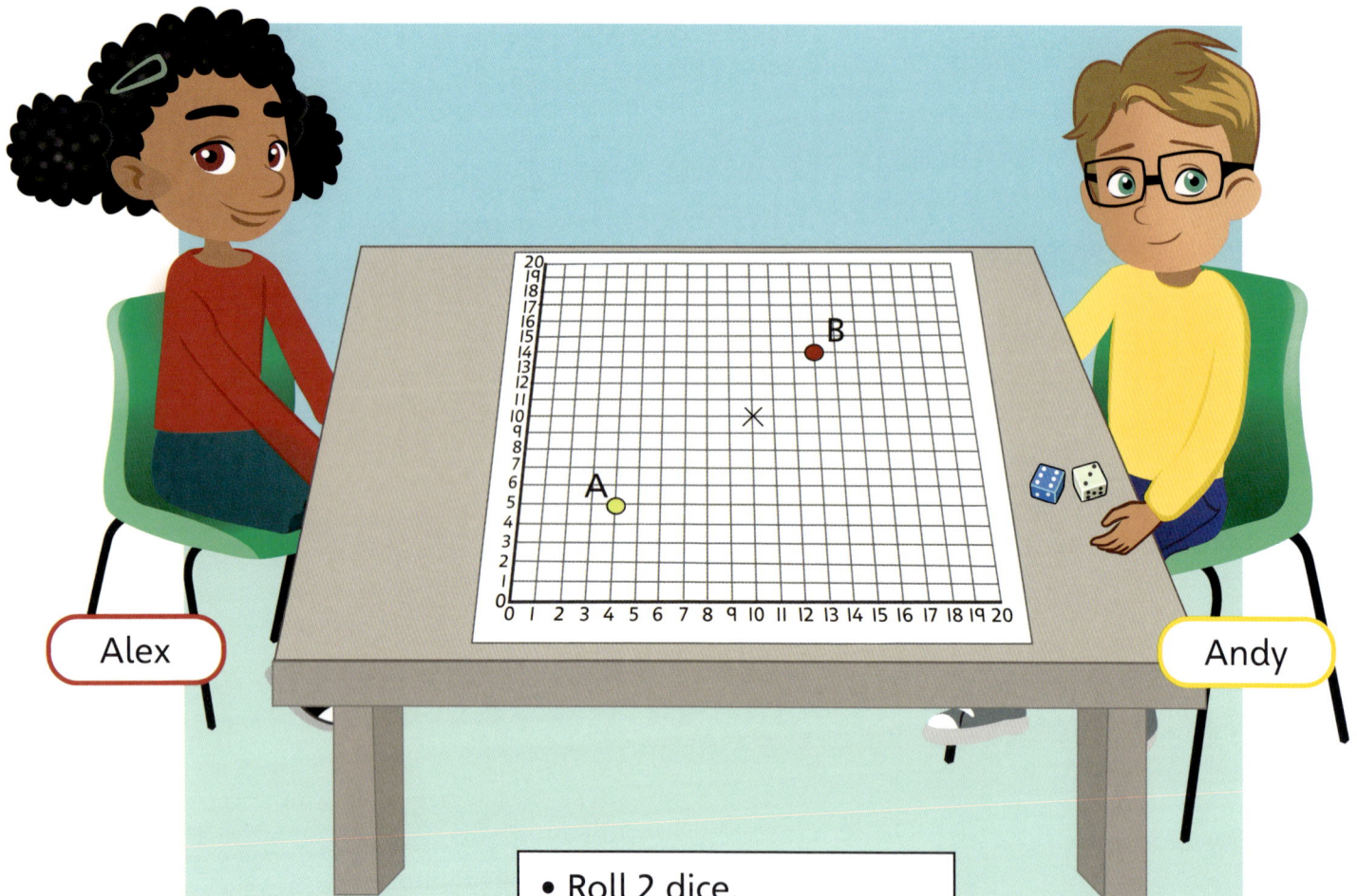

- Roll 2 dice.
- Use your scores to translate your counter.
- The aim is to land on the X.

1 **a)** Andy has the yellow counter (A). He chooses to translate 6 right and 3 up. What are the coordinates of his new position?

b) What translation of Alex's counter (B) would win?

Share

a) Andy's counter is at (4,5).

> I counted the grid squares to find the new position.

> I used the coordinates to calculate the new position. This is more efficient.

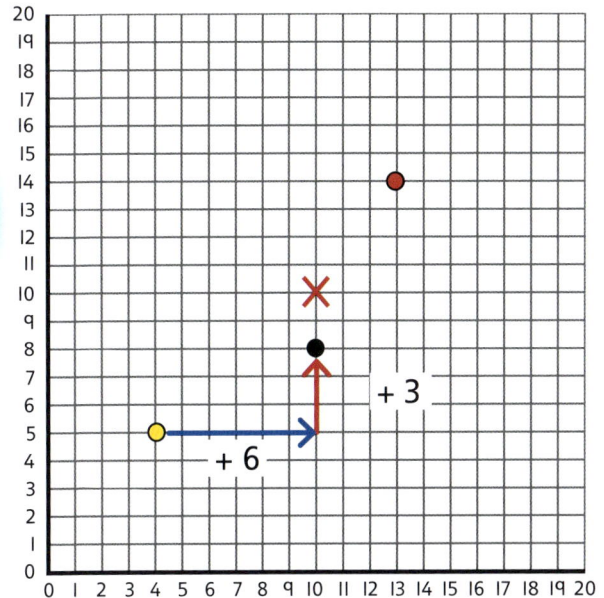

The starting position is (4,5).

A translation 6 right increases the horizontal coordinate by 6.

$4 + 6 = 10$

A translation 3 up increases the vertical coordinate by 3.

$5 + 3 = 8$

The coordinates of Andy's new position are (10,8).

b) Alex is on position (13,14). She wants to land on (10,10).

She needs to decrease the horizontal coordinate by 3. $13 - 3 = 10$. This is a translation 3 left.

She needs to decrease the vertical coordinate by 4. $14 - 4 = 10$. This is a translation 4 down.

A translation of Alex's counter 3 left, 4 down would win.

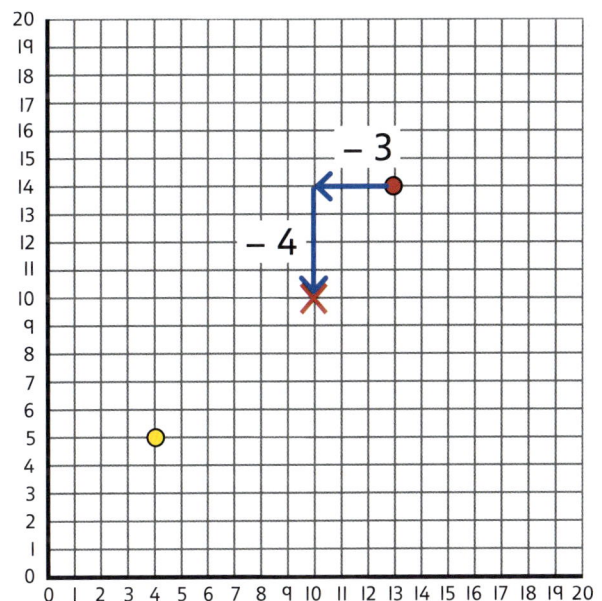

Think together

When a point A is translated, the new point is named A₁.

1 The boat is translated 6 right, then 3 down. What are the coordinates of A and B after each translation?

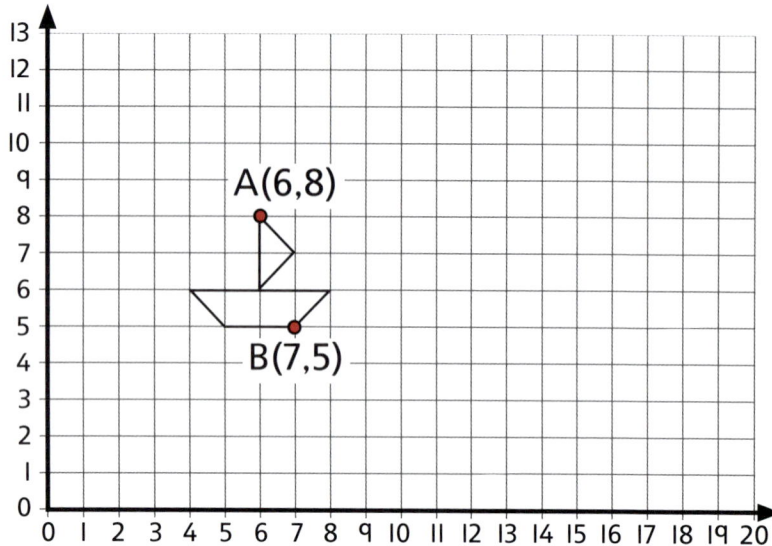

After translating 6 right:

$A_1($ ☐ , ☐ $)$

$B_1($ ☐ , ☐ $)$

After translating 3 down:

$A_2($ ☐ , ☐ $)$

$B_2($ ☐ , ☐ $)$

2 What are the coordinates of this square after a translation 10 right and 8 up?

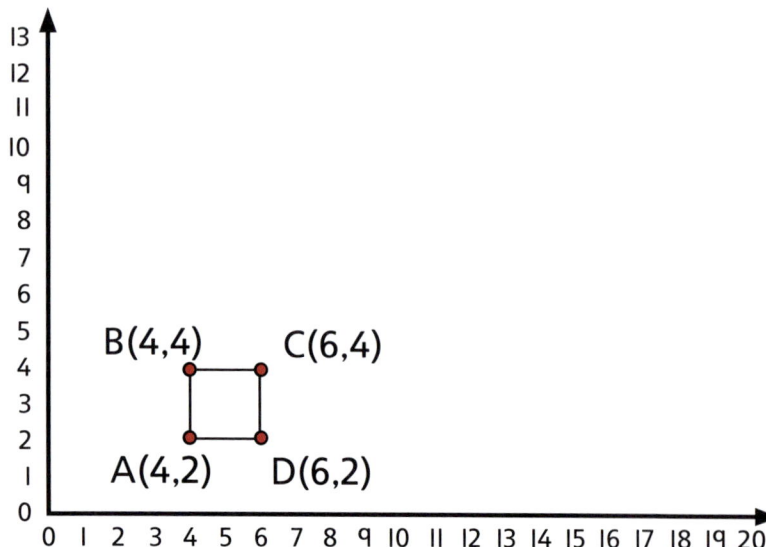

$A_1($ ☐ , ☐ $)$

$B_1($ ☐ , ☐ $)$

$C_1($ ☐ , ☐ $)$

$D_1($ ☐ , ☐ $)$

CHALLENGE

3 **a)** A triangle has been translated 6 right and 6 up.

What were the vertices of its starting position?

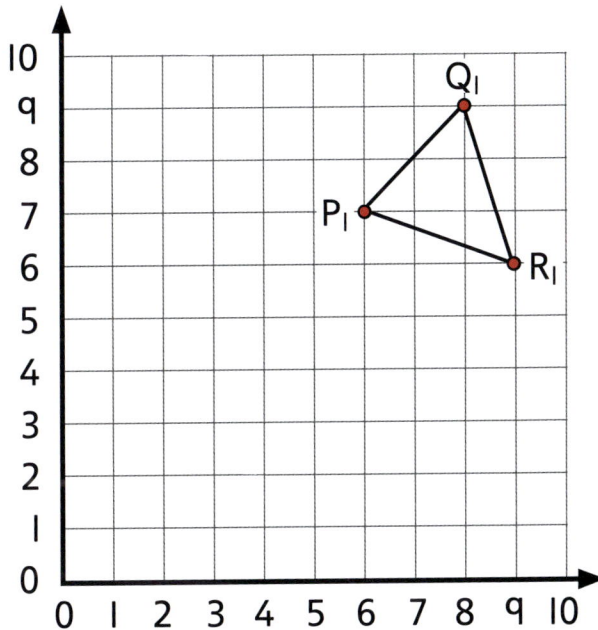

P(☐ , ☐)

Q(☐ , ☐)

R(☐ , ☐)

b) A triangle has been translated 11 left and 9 down.

What were the coordinates of the original triangle?

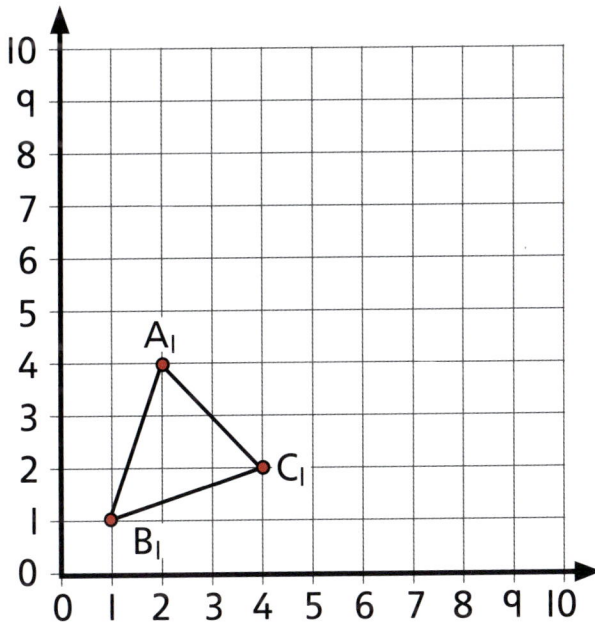

I will have to use the coordinates because the original triangle will be off this grid.

A(☐ , ☐)   B(☐ , ☐)   C(☐ , ☐)

→ **Practice book 5C p54**

Reflection

Discover

What will this triangle look like in a mirror? Reflect the shape by placing a mirror on each line.

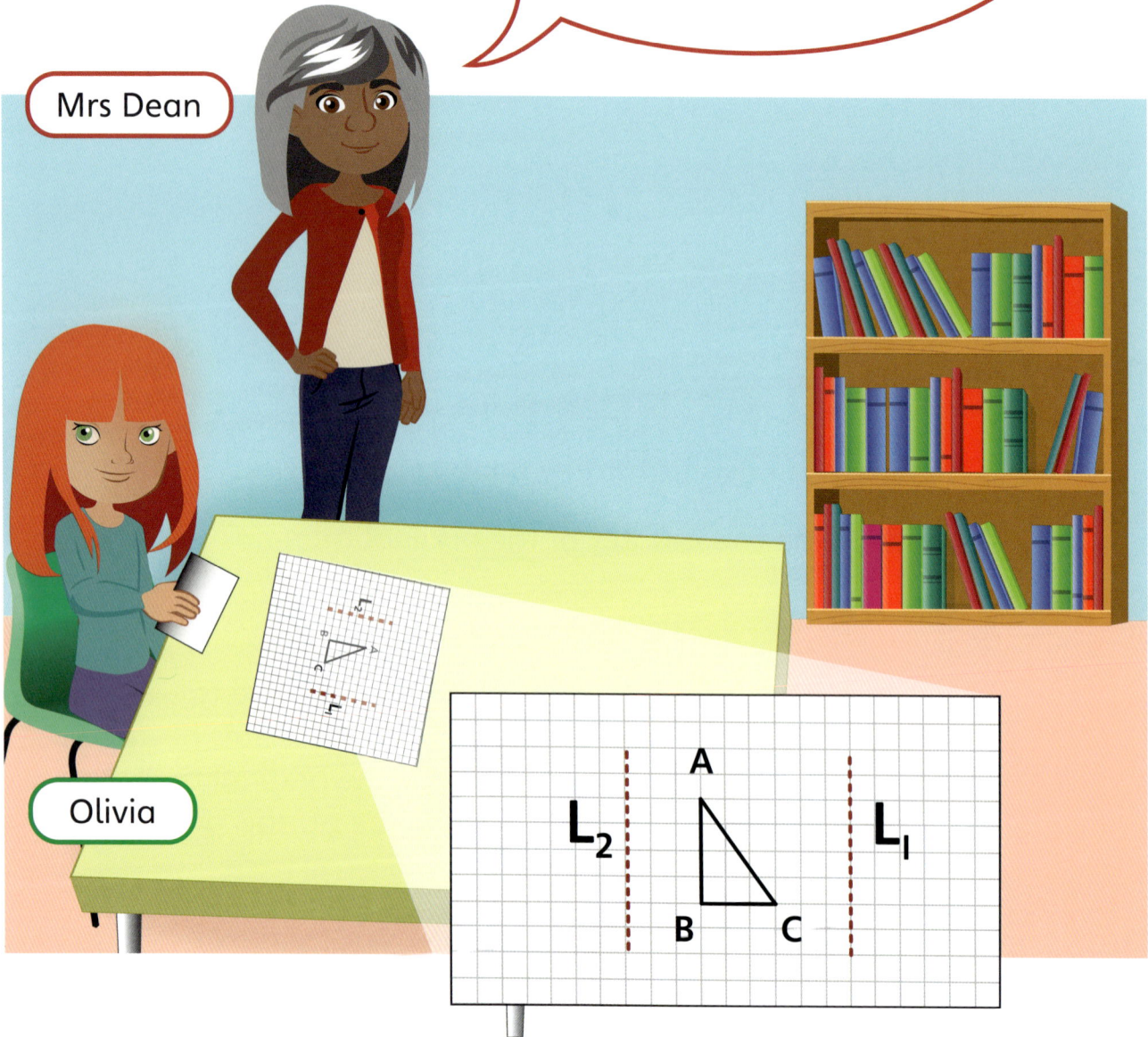

Mrs Dean

Olivia

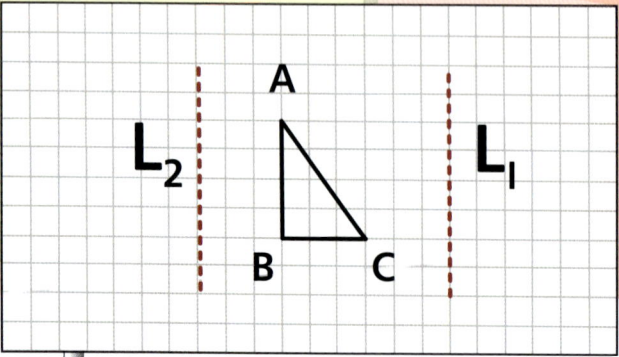

1 a) What will the reflection be when the mirror is placed on line L_1?

b) Draw the reflection when the mirror is placed on line L_2.

Share

a) Each vertex must be the same distance from the mirror line.

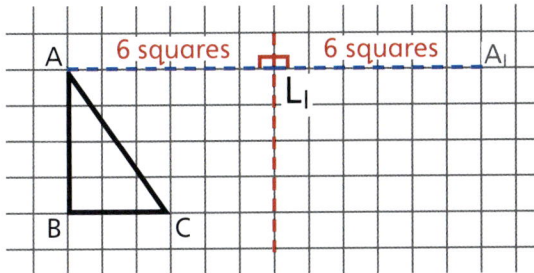

Vertex A is 6 squares from the mirror line, so I needed to count 6 squares on the other side of the line.

Vertex C is 3 squares from the line, so the new vertex C_1 must be 3 squares from the mirror line too.

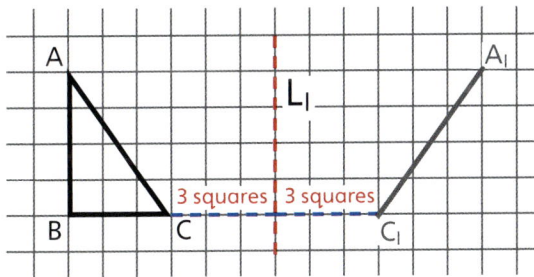

I could see where vertex B_1 should go because it is below vertex A_1 and level with vertex C_1.

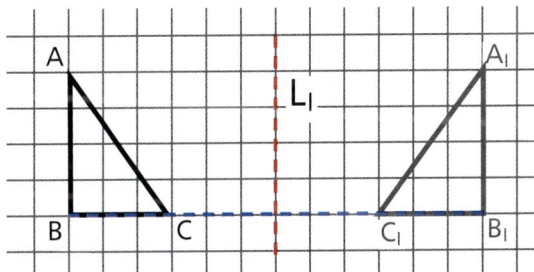

b)

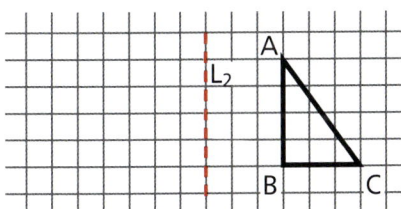

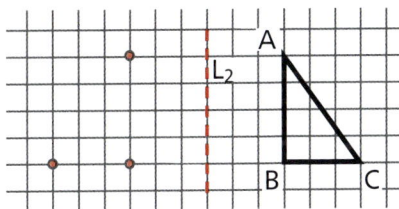

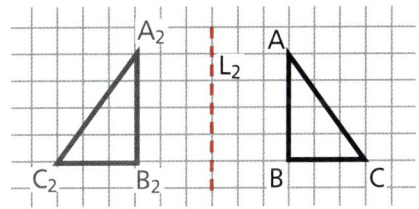

Think together

1 Complete the reflection of the triangle in the dotted line.

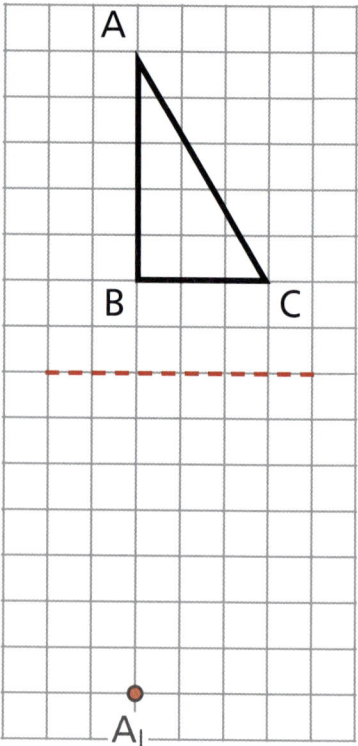

2 Bella drew the image of ABC, reflected in the dotted mirror line.

Explain her mistake. Then draw the correct reflection on squared paper.

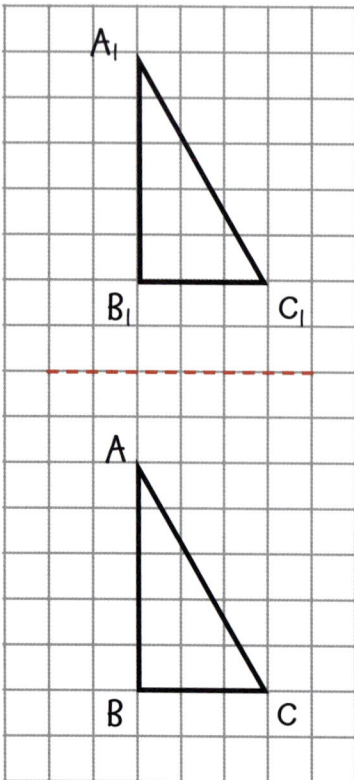

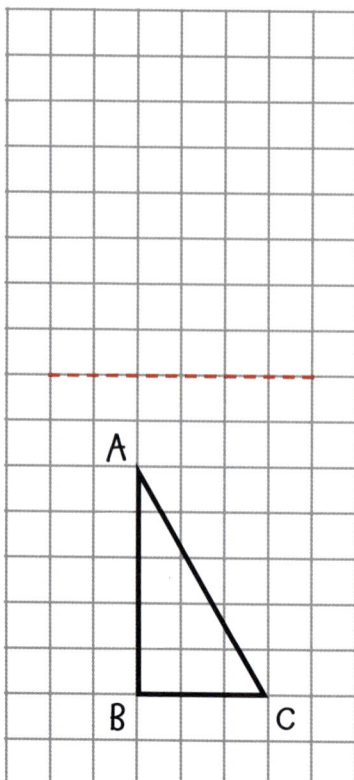

CHALLENGE

3 **a)** Max has used reflection to turn 'M' into 'W'.

Explain how to use reflection to turn '9' into '6'.
Where would you put the mirror line or lines?

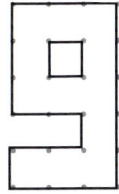

I wonder if you have to reflect the shape more than once.

I will try more than one way to turn 9 into 6.

b) Predict what the letter V will look like when it is reflected in the mirror line. Then use the isometric grid to draw the reflection of the letter V.

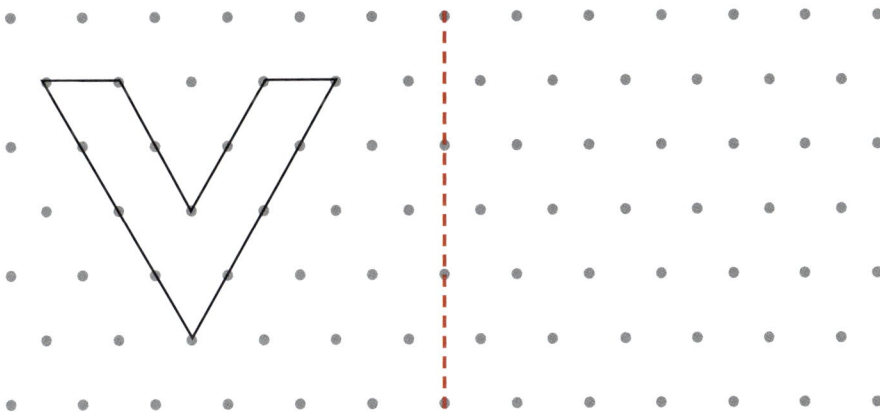

79

→ Practice book 5C p57

Reflection in horizontal and vertical lines

Discover

T marks the spot, but the real location of the treasure is the reflection of point T in the line L.

Jen

Toshi

1. a) Reflect the point T in the mirror line. What are the true coordinates of the treasure?

   b) There is a secret cave at the reflection of coordinates (6,8). What are the coordinates of the secret cave?

Share

a) T is at the coordinates (2,3).

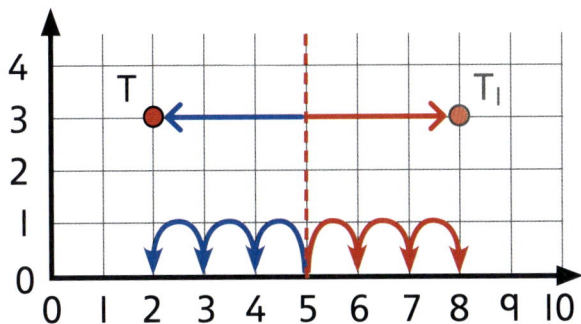

Remember, we always put the number across first, so (2,3) means 2 along and 3 up.

The new horizontal coordinate must be $5 + 3 = 8$.

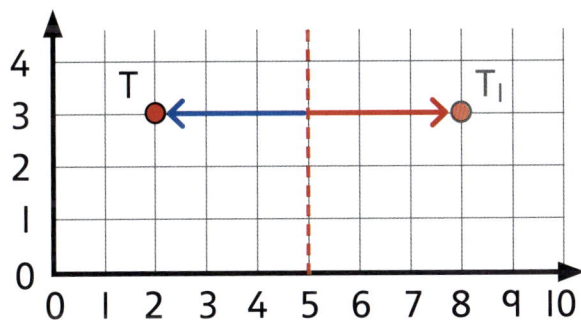

I counted how many squares T is from the mirror line. The reflected point must be the same distance away on the other side.

The true coordinates of the treasure, T_1, are (8,3).

I noticed that the second part of the coordinates does not change.

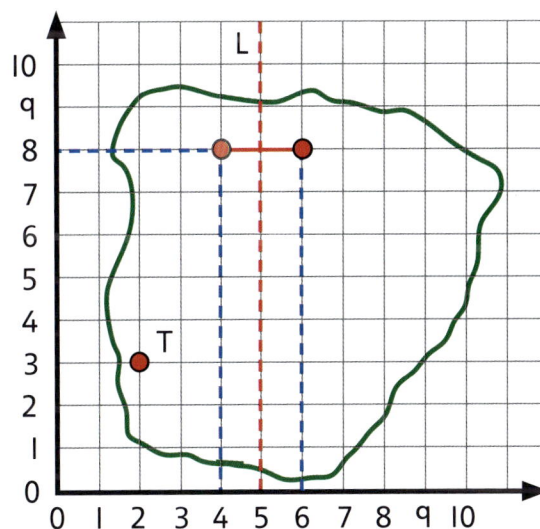

b) The first part of the coordinates is 1 to the right of the mirror line: $5 + 1 = 6$.

The reflected coordinate must be 1 to the left of the mirror line: $5 - 1 = 4$.

The second part of the coordinates stays the same (**8**).

The coordinates of the secret cave are (4,8).

Think together

1 Max marks three points with counters. Aki reflects the points in a mirror line (L) and places a counter on each of the reflected points.

What are the coordinates of each reflected point?

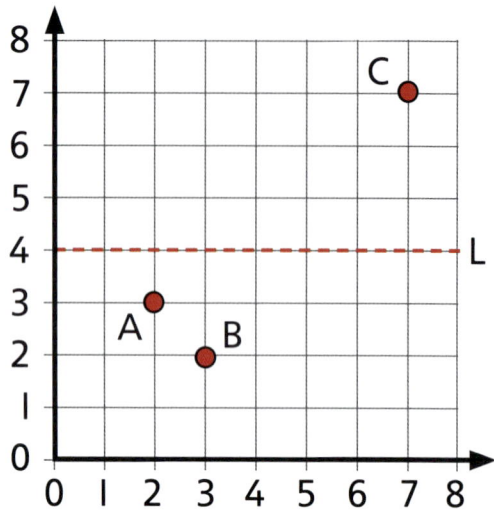

Max's counters are placed at:

A(2,3)

B(3,2)

C(7,7)

Aki's counters will be placed at:

A_l(⬜ , ⬜)

B_l(⬜ , ⬜)

C_l(⬜ , ⬜)

2 The rectangle on this grid is reflected in the dotted mirror line.

Write the coordinates of the reflected rectangle.

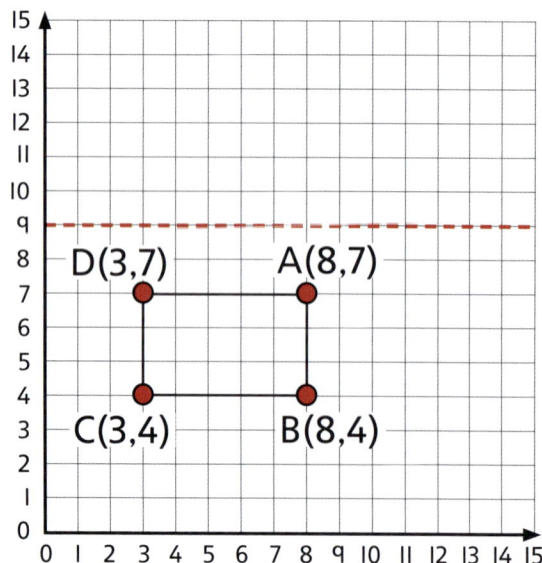

D(3,7)   A(8,7)

C(3,4)   B(8,4)

> I wonder which part of the coordinates will not change.

A_l(⬜ , ⬜)

B_l(⬜ , ⬜)

C_l(⬜ , ⬜)

D_l(⬜ , ⬜)

3 **a)** The rectangle is reflected in the mirror line. What are the coordinates of the reflected vertices?

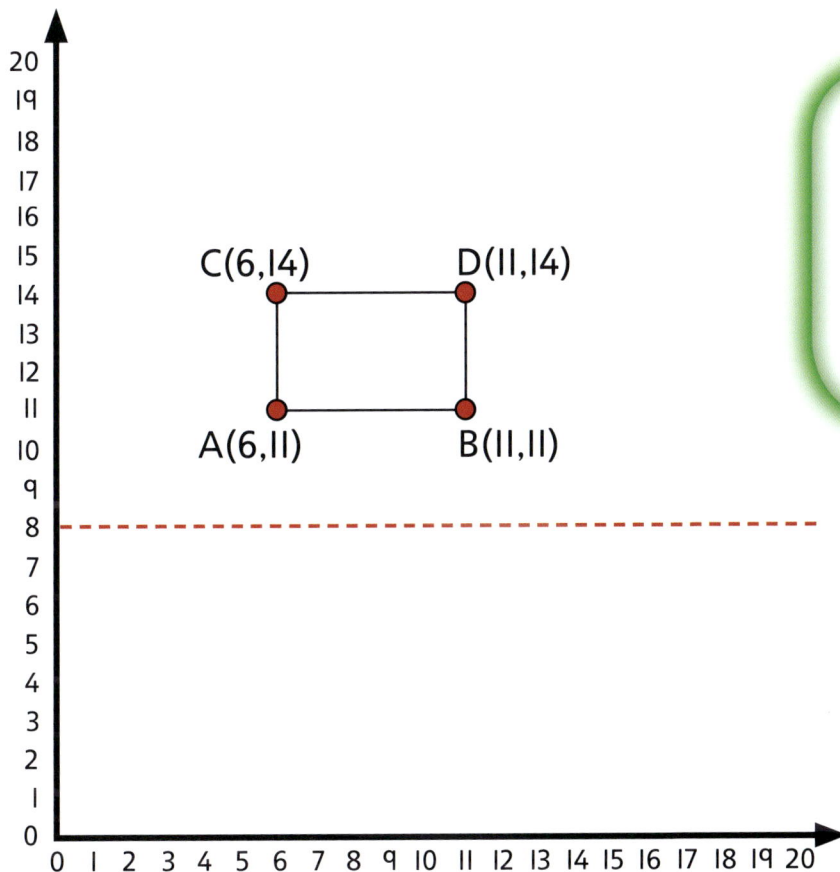

CHALLENGE

I cannot see the grid lines so I will use the coordinates to calculate the new position.

C(6,14)   D(11,14)

A(6,11)   B(11,11)

b) Write the coordinates of the triangle and of the reflected triangle.

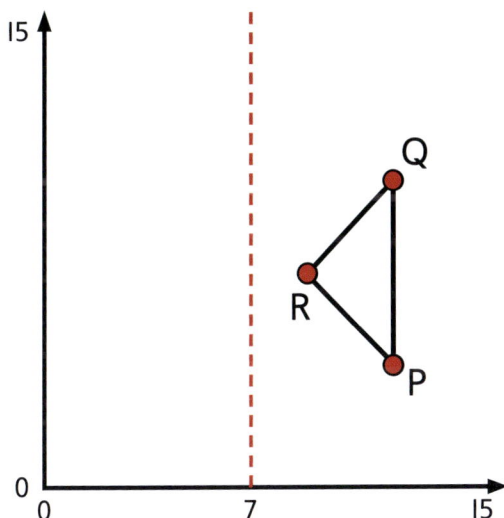

Q

R

P

83

→ **Practice book 5C p60**

End of unit check

1 What are the coordinates of point P?

A (3,5)

B (5,3)

C (4,5)

D (5,5)

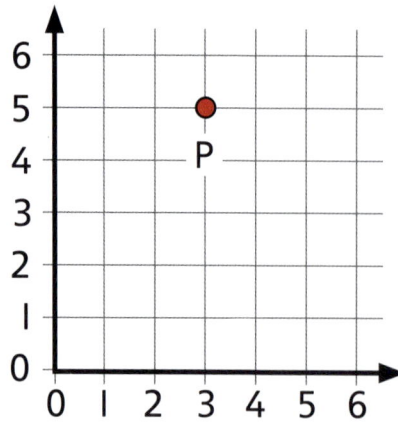

2 What are the coordinates of the missing vertex of the rectangle?

A (2, 2)

B (4, 2)

C (2, 4)

D (4, 4)

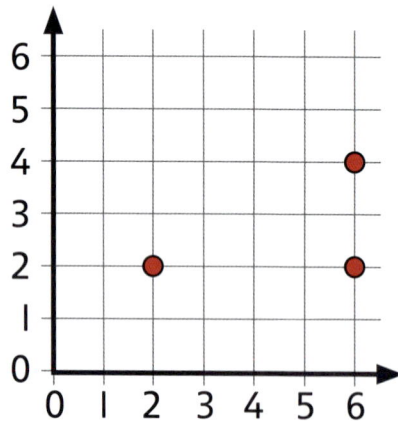

3 Which reflection is correct?

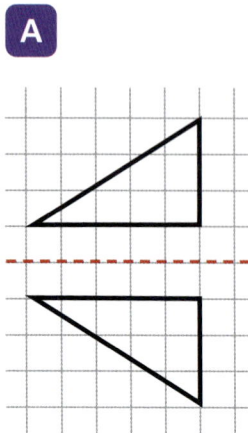

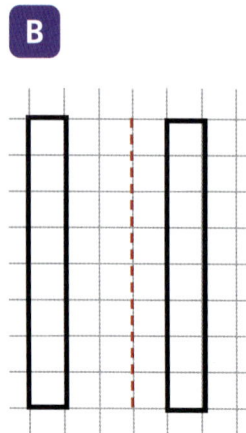

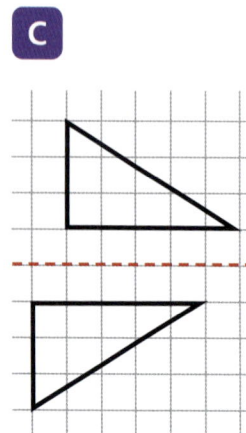

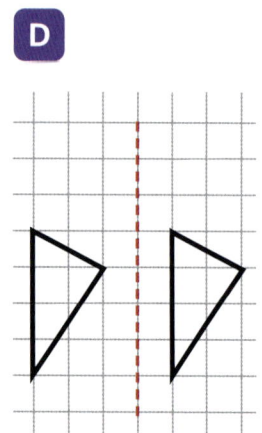

A   B   C   D

4 Which diagram shows shape A translated by 4 right and 3 up?

A

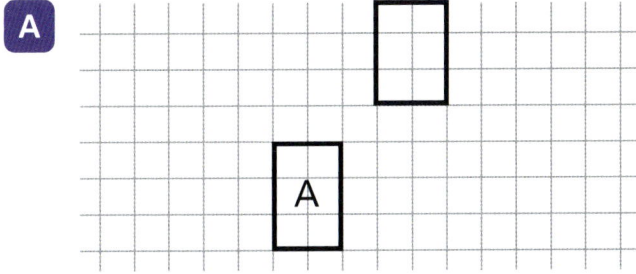

B

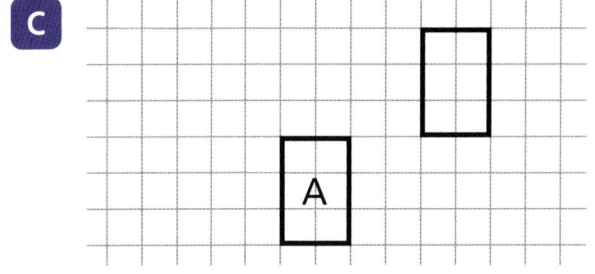

C

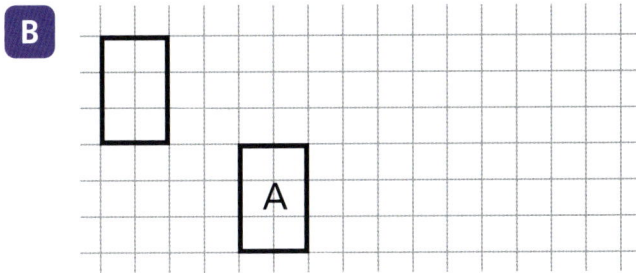

D

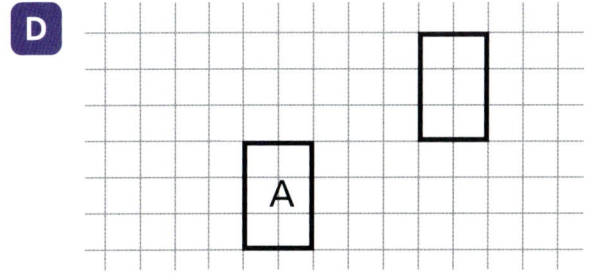

5 The isosceles triangle is reflected in the mirror line. What are the coordinates of the reflected point P?

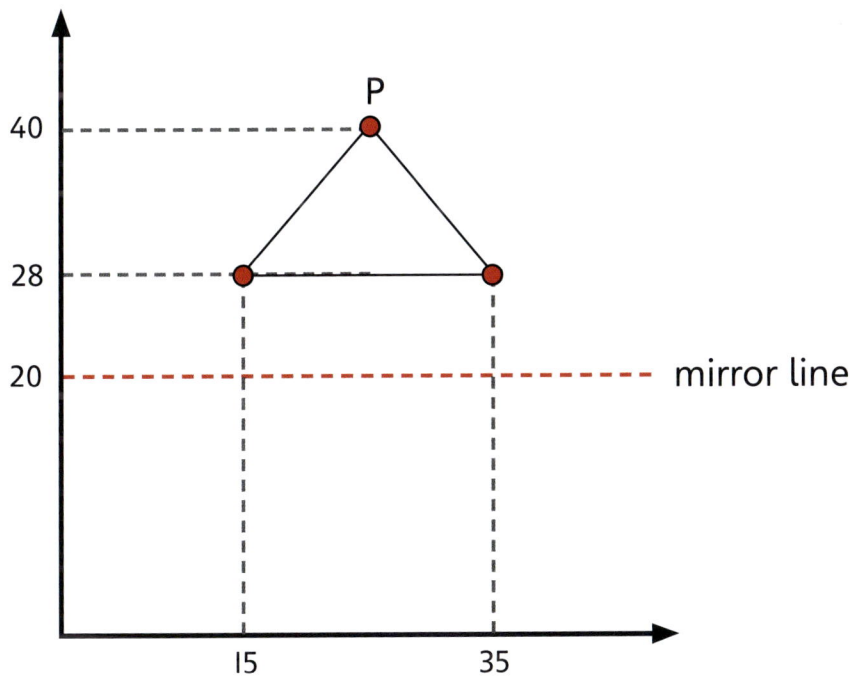

85

→ Practice book 5C p63

Unit 14
Decimals

In this unit we will ...

⚡ Add and subtract decimals with the same number of digits after the decimal point

⚡ Add and subtract decimals with a different number of digits after the decimal point

⚡ Add whole numbers to decimals

⚡ Find decimal complements to 1

⚡ Subtract decimals from whole numbers

⚡ Solve problems involving addition and subtraction of decimals, including money problems

⚡ Multiply and divide decimals and whole numbers by 10, 100 and 1,000

We will need to use column methods. How can we add these two numbers?

H	T	O
100	10 10	1 1 1 1 1 1 1
	10 10 10 10 10 10 10	1 1 1 1 1 1

	H	T	O
		1	2	6
+		7	5

We will need some maths words.
Do you know what they all mean?

add   subtract   decimal   tenths

hundredths   thousandths   complement

divide   decimal point   whole   multiply

column   exchange   place value

decimal place   digit

We also need to be able to subtract numbers.

Can you remember a way of making 500 – 367 easier?

Why are these two calculations the same?

	H	T	O
	5	0	0
−	3	6	7

	H	T	O
	4	9	9
−	3	6	6

Add and subtract decimals within 1 ①

Discover

Isla: We have lots of each different length of track.

Richard: I used three pieces of different lengths to make the straight section.

0·1 m
0·2 m
0·3 m
0·4 m

0·8 m

① a) Which pieces of track could Richard have used to make the straight section?

b) Isla chooses from all of the pieces of track.

What other ways could she have made a straight section of track 0·8 m long?

Share

a) There are track pieces 0·1 m, 0·2 m, 0·3 m and 0·4 m long.

You need to find three pieces of different lengths that add up to 0·8 m.

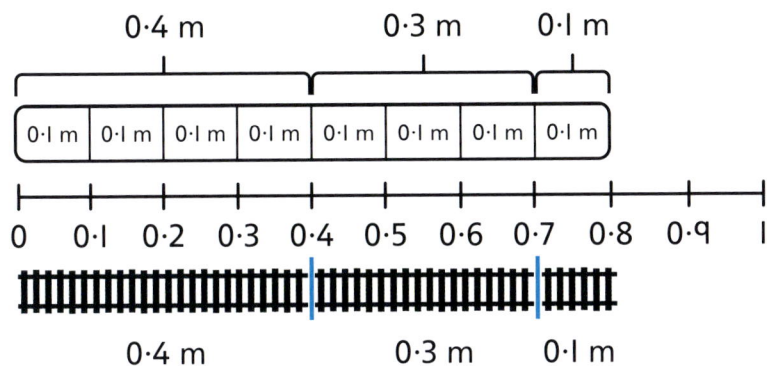

I used a bar model to work out the possible pieces.

$$0·4 \text{ m} + 0·3 \text{ m} + 0·1 \text{ m} = 0·8 \text{ m}$$

Richard could have used 0·4 m, 0·3 m and 0·1 m track pieces to make the straight section.

b) There are several possible answers. Here are 2 ways:

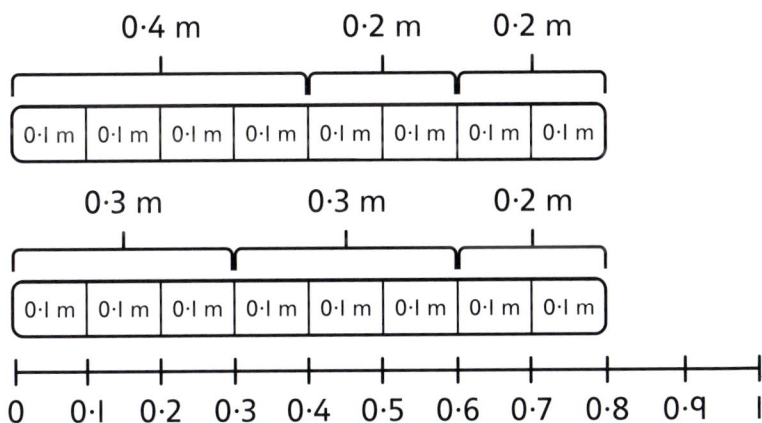

$$0·4 + 0·2 + 0·2 = 0·8$$

Isla could have used one 0·4 m and two 0·2 m pieces.

Or she could have used two 0·3 m and one 0·2 m pieces to make a track of 0·8 m.

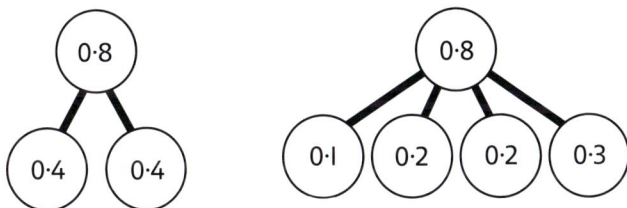

I have found other answers that add to 8 tenths.

Think together

1 **a)** These pieces of track (A and B) are put together.

How long is the track in total?

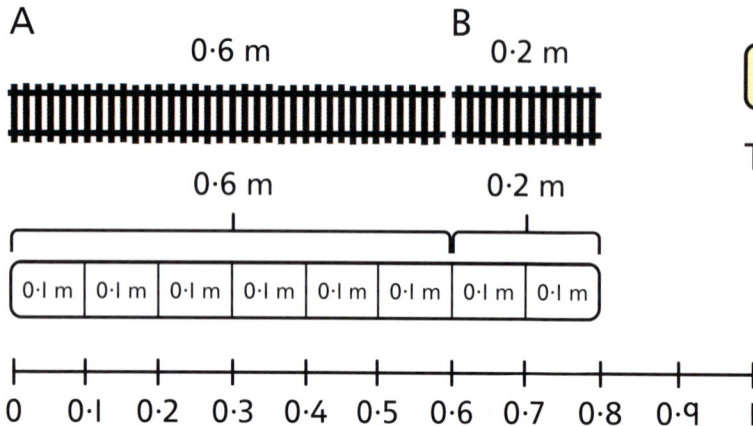

A
0·6 m

B
0·2 m

0·6 m   0·2 m

| 0·1 m | 0·1 m | 0·1 m | 0·1 m | 0·1 m | 0·1 m | 0·1 m | 0·1 m |

0   0·1   0·2   0·3   0·4   0·5   0·6   0·7   0·8   0·9   1

☐ m + ☐ m = ☐ m

The track is ☐ m in total.

b) How much longer is track piece C than track piece D?

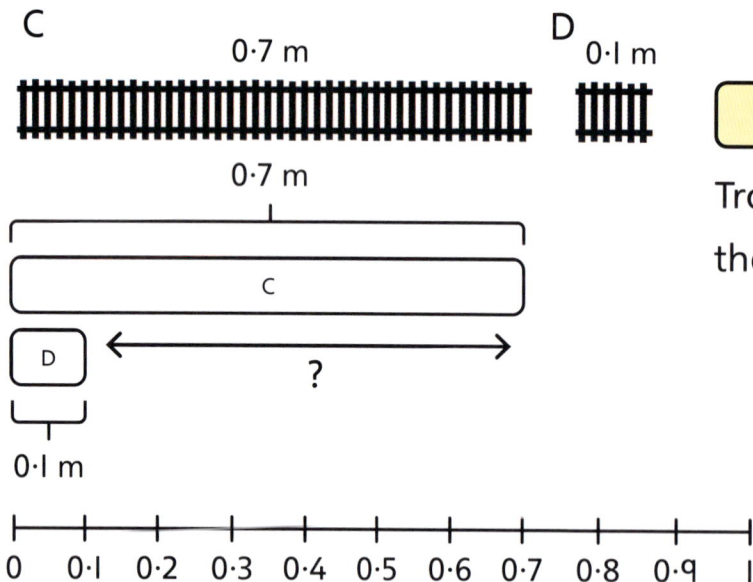

C
0·7 m

D
0·1 m

0·7 m

C

D

?

0·1 m

0   0·1   0·2   0·3   0·4   0·5   0·6   0·7   0·8   0·9   1

☐ m − ☐ m = ☐ m

Track piece C is ☐ m longer than track piece D.

2 **a)** Which two numbers add up to 0·9?

b) Which numbers have a difference of 0·1?

c) Which two numbers add up to 0·6 and have a difference of 0·2?

0·1   0·3   0·5
0·2   0·4

3 Here are some more pieces of track.

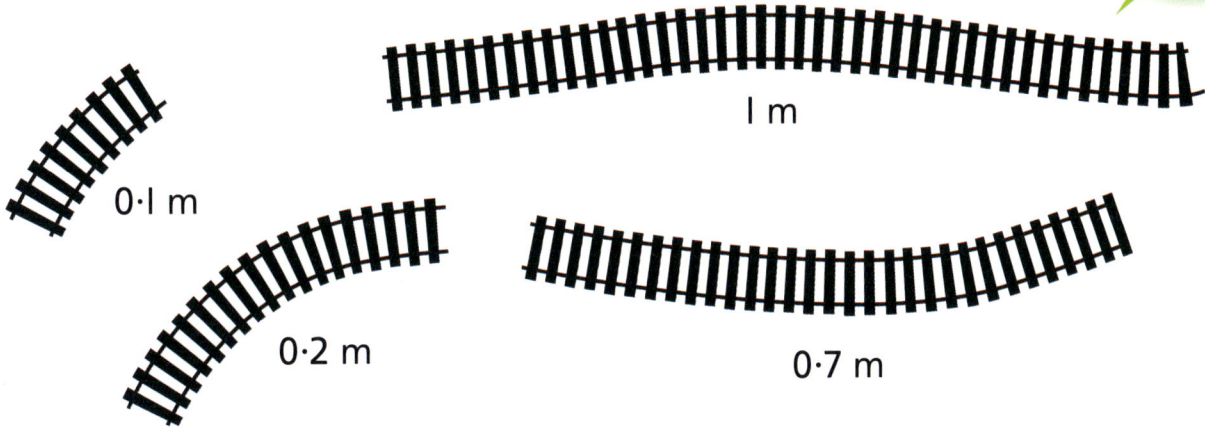

CHALLENGE

0·1 m

1 m

0·2 m

0·7 m

a) Isla puts the 0·1 m, 0·2 m and 0·7 m pieces of track together.

What mistake has Isla made in her calculation?

> The total length of my track is 0·10 m, because 1 + 2 + 7 = 10.

Isla

b) Richard puts the 0·7 m and 1 m pieces of track together.

What is the difference in length between the two pieces?

> I will use a number line and add on to find the difference.

> I will subtract 0·7 m from 1 m.

→ **Practice book 5C p66**

Add and subtract decimals within 1 ❷

Discover

1 **a)** How much orange paint can Olivia and Luis make?

b) How much **more** orange paint do they have to make to get the amount they need?

Share

> I used column addition, just like when adding whole numbers.

a) Olivia and Luis can add 0·23 l of yellow paint to 0·45 l of red paint.

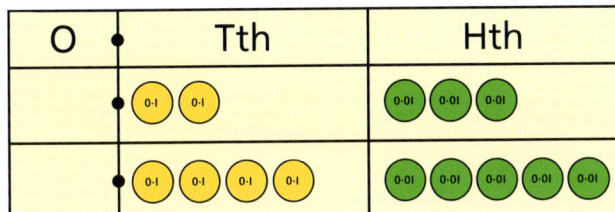

O	•	Tth	Hth
	0 •	2	3
+	0 •	4	5
	0 •	6	8

0·23 + 0·45 = 0·68   Olivia and Luis can make 0·68 l of orange paint.

b) A subtraction will show how much more orange paint they need to make.

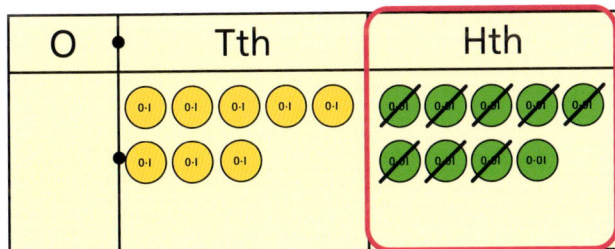

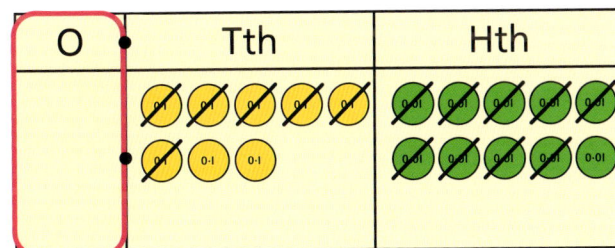

O	•	Tth	Hth
	0 •	8	9
–	0 •	6	8
	0 •	2	1

Subtract the hundredths.

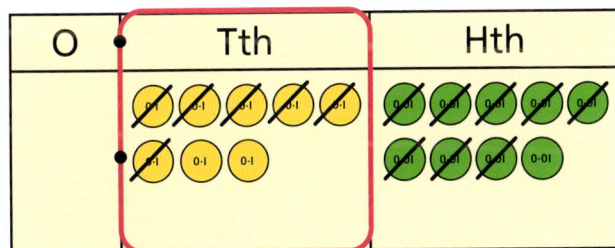

O	•	Tth	Hth
	0 •	8	9
–	0 •	6	8
	0 •	2	1

Subtract the tenths.

0·89 – 0·68 = 0·21 l

Olivia and Luis need to make 0·21 l more orange paint.

O	•	Tth	Hth
	0 •	8	9
–	0 •	6	8
	0 •	2	1

Think together

1 **a)** Look at the containers. How much orange paint can be made?

Yellow 0·41 l

Red 0·42 l

Orange

O	•	Tth	Hth
	•	0·1 0·1 0·1 0·1	0·01
	•	0·1 0·1 0·1 0·1	0·01 0·01

	O	•	Tth	Hth
	0	•	4	1
+	0	•	4	2
		•		

b) Bronwyn adds the water to the blackcurrant to make blackcurrant squash.

How much squash can be made?

0·25 l   0·22 l

c) How much more soup is in the larger can?

Soup 0·55 l

Soup 0·32 l

2 Complete the missing numbers in these column additions.

a)

	O	•	Tth	Hth
	0	•	6	3
+	0	•	0	5
		•		

b)

	O	•	Tth	Hth	Thth
	0	•	3	1	
+	0	•		6	3
	0	•	5		9

c)

	O	•	Tth	Hth
	0	•	5	
+	0	•		6
	0	•	9	9

CHALLENGE

3 Kate and Ebo each have a bucket of slime.

Ebo: My bucket has 0·305 l in it.

Kate: My bucket has 0·221 l more than Ebo's in it.

a) How much slime do they have altogether?

b) They each get rid of 0·102 litres of slime.
How much slime do they have altogether now?

To find 'altogether', I need to work out how much Kate has first.

I think there are different ways to work out the second part.

95

→ Practice book 5C p69

Complements to 1

Discover

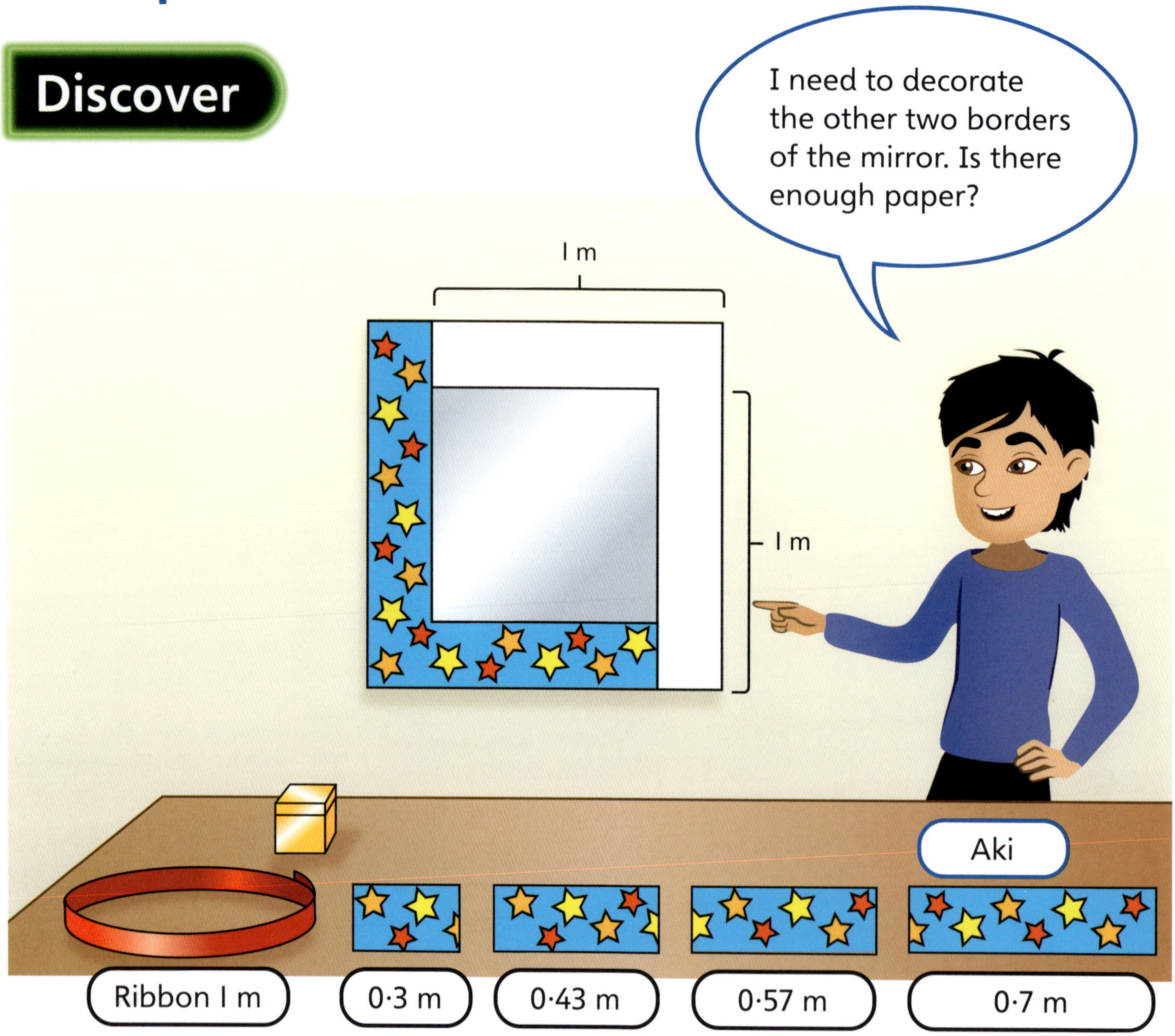

I need to decorate the other two borders of the mirror. Is there enough paper?

1 m

1 m

Aki

Ribbon 1 m

0·3 m

0·43 m

0·57 m

0·7 m

1 **a)** How can Aki use the paper to decorate the other two borders of the mirror?

b) Aki bought 1 m of ribbon. He used 0·235 m to go around the outside of his treasure box.

How much ribbon does Aki have left?

Share

a) Aki has two I m borders to cover. He needs to find two lots of paper pieces that make I m.

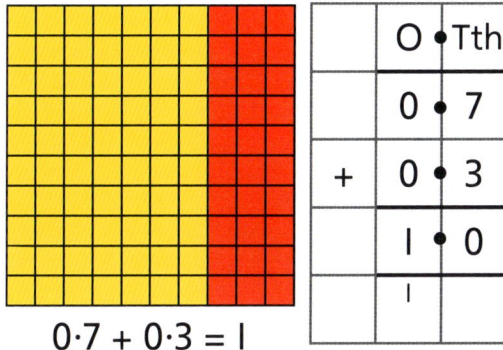

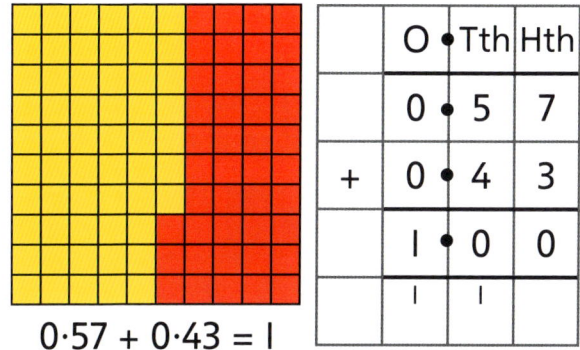

O	•	Tth
0	•	7
+ 0	•	3
I	•	0
I		

0·7 + 0·3 = I

O	•	Tth	Hth
0	•	5	7
+ 0	•	4	3
I	•	0	0
I		I	

0·57 + 0·43 = I

> I remembered that on a hundredths grid, I column is equal to I tenth (0·I) or 10 hundredths (0·10).

> I used number bonds to 10 and 100 to work out which numbers add to one whole.

Aki can use the 0·7 m and 0·3 m pieces to decorate one border of the mirror, and 0·57 m and 0·43 m pieces to decorate the other.

b) You need to do a subtraction to work how much ribbon Aki has left.

I m ribbon

0·765 m	0·235 m

> I used number bonds to 1,000 to check my answer.
>
> 235 + 765 = 1,000

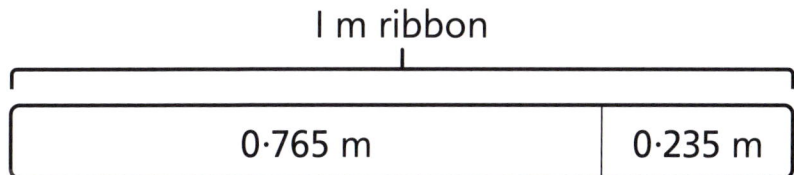

O	•	Tth	Hth	Thth
0	•	9	9	10
− 0	•	2	3	5
0	•	7	6	5

Write I as I·000 and subtract 0·235.

Aki has 0·765 m of ribbon left.

Think together

1. These pieces of decorative paper have been cut from 1 m strips.

   Find the amount left from each original strip.

   a) 0·4 m

   b) 0·49 m

   c) 0·68 m

   A **complement** to 1 is the number that will make a total of 1 when it is added.

2. Copy and write the missing numbers.

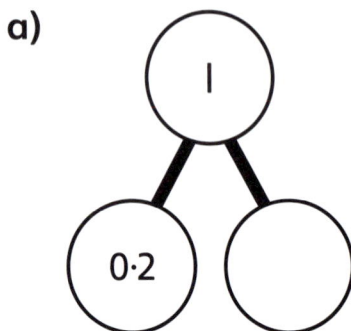

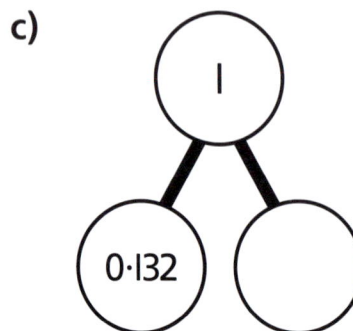

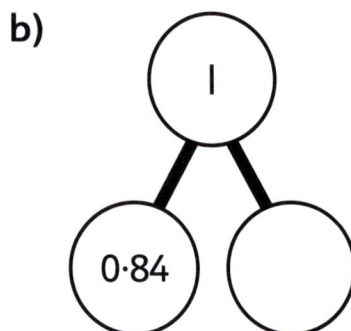

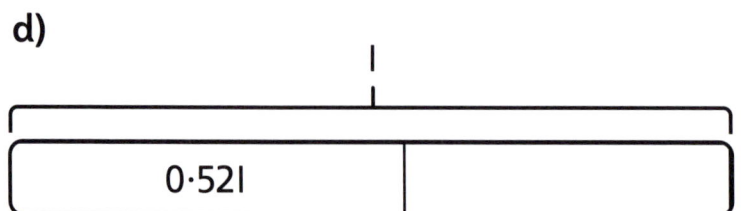

   a) 1 → 0·2, ☐

   b) 1 → 0·84, ☐

   c) 1 → 0·132, ☐

   d) 0·521 ☐

CHALLENGE

3 Look at the place value grids.

O	Tth	Hth
	0·1 0·1	0·01 0·01 0·01 0·01 0·01 0·01 0·01 0·01 0·01

O	Tth	Hth	Thth
	0·1 0·1 0·1 0·1 0·1 0·1 0·1	0·01 0·01	0·001 0·001 0·001 0·001

Use more counters to work out the missing numbers.

a) $0.29 + \boxed{} = 1$

b) $0.724 + \boxed{} = 1$

> For the first one, I think I need to add 1 hundredth and 8 tenths counters so there are 10 in each column. Then I can exchange.

> I do not think that is right. When you add the hundredth you need to do an exchange before you add some tenths.

c) Work out the missing numbers so that each calculation is true.

$0.34 + 0.21 + \boxed{} = 1$

$0.34 - 0.21 + \boxed{} = 1$

$0.234 + \boxed{} + \boxed{} = 1$

→ **Practice book 5C p72**

Add and subtract decimals across 1

Discover

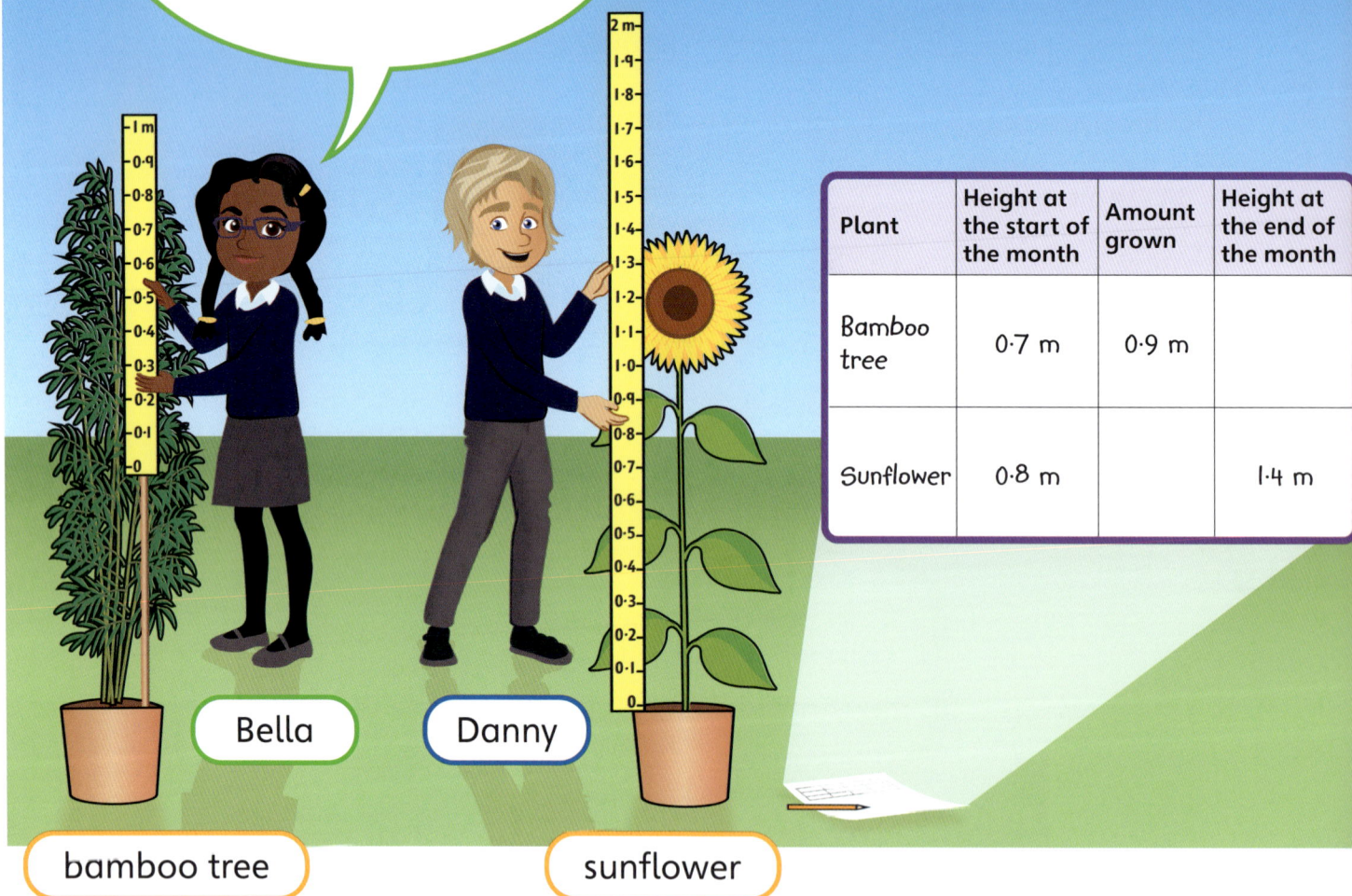

We recorded how high each plant has grown since the start of the month.

Plant	Height at the start of the month	Amount grown	Height at the end of the month
Bamboo tree	0·7 m	0·9 m	
Sunflower	0·8 m		1·4 m

Bella

Danny

bamboo tree

sunflower

1. **a)** How tall was the bamboo tree at the end of the month? Try and work it out in your head.

   b) How much has the sunflower grown?

Share

a) At the start of the month the bamboo tree was 0·7 m tall. It grows by 0·9 m. You need to add 0·7 and 0·9.

I worked out 2 jumps in my head.

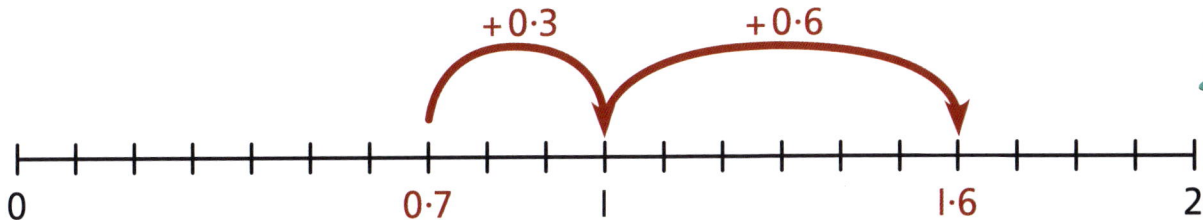

$0·7 + 0·9 = 1·6$

At the end of the month the height of the bamboo tree is 1·6 m.

b) The height of the sunflower at the start of the month was 0·8 m.

By the end it was 1·4 m.

Subtract to find out how much it grew.

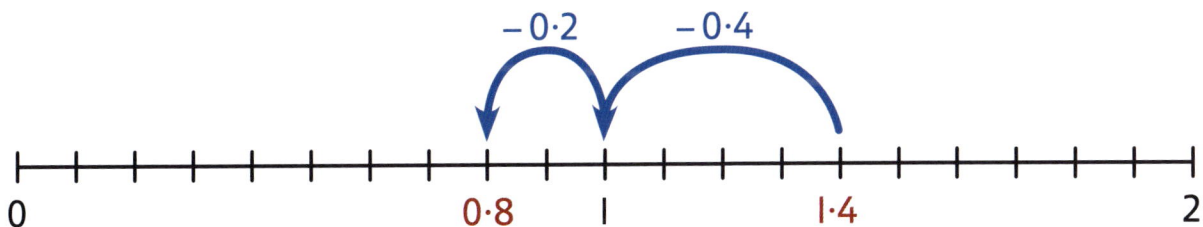

The difference is 0·6.

The sunflower has grown by 0·6 m.

Think together

1 **a)** Bella and Danny measured another sunflower.

What is the height of this sunflower at the end of the month?

Plant	Height at the start of the month	Amount grown	Height at the end of the month
Sunflower	1·7 m	0·8 m	

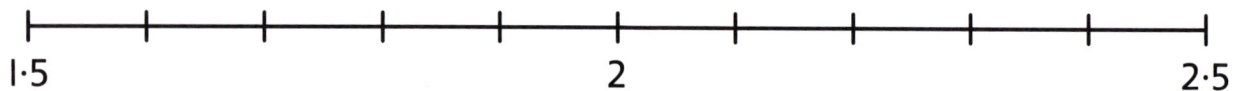

```
├──┼──┼──┼──┼──┼──┼──┼──┼──┼──┤
1·5                 2                 2·5
```

b) Emma collects 0·5 kg of apples from her apple tree. She then collects 0·7 kg of plums.

I collected 0·12 kg of fruit in total.

Emma

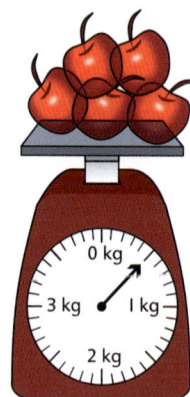

Explain why Emma is wrong.

2 Work out the following calculations.

a) 7 + 8 = ☐

0·7 + 0·8 = ☐

0·07 + 0·08 = ☐

1·7 + 0·8 = ☐

b) 12 − 8 = ☐

1·2 − 0·8 = ☐

0·12 − 0·08 = ☐

I will use a number line to help me.

What patterns did you notice?

3 Max is working out the following calculations in his head.

CHALLENGE

0·7 + 0·8 + 0·3

10 − 1·5

0·99 + 0·99

0·36 + 0·25

Max

Discuss with a partner how you might work them out.

I wonder what I would do if the decimal point was not there.

103

Add decimals with the same number of decimal places

Discover

Menu
Pizza £2·96
Juice £1·04
...ghetti
...n & chip...

I only have £4.

My meal costs £1·35 more than yours.

Max

Jamie

1 **a)** Max wants to buy a pizza and a juice. Does he have enough money?

b) What is the total cost of Jamie's meal?

Share

a) Add £2·96 and £1·04 to work out the total cost of a pizza and a juice.

Add the hundredths first.

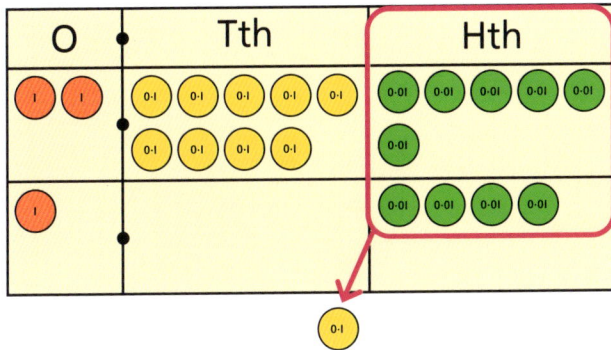

O	•	Tth	Hth
		2 • 9	6
+		1 • 0	4
		•	0
		1	

Add the tenths next.

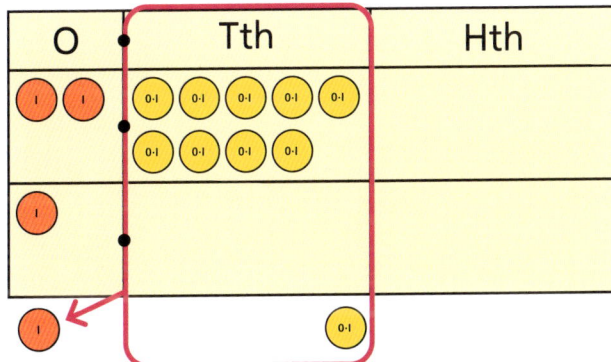

O	•	Tth	Hth
		2 • 9	6
+		1 • 0	4
		• 0	0
		1 • 1	

Finally, add the 1s.

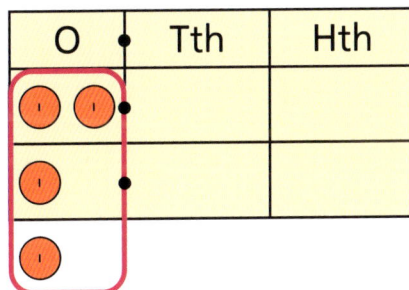

O	•	Tth	Hth
		2 • 9	6
+		1 • 0	4
		4 • 0	0
		1 • 1	

Max's meal costs £4 in total, so he has enough money.

I used the column method to add the two amounts.

b) Jamie's meal costs £1·35 more than Max's.

You need to work out £4 + £1·35.

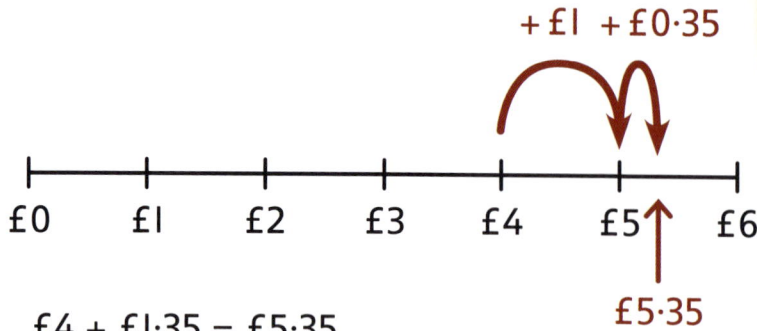

+£1 +£0·35

£0   £1   £2   £3   £4   £5   £6

£5·35

£4 + £1·35 = £5·35

The total cost of Jamie's meal is £5·35.

> I used a number line and added on the whole pounds first and then the part of the whole.

Think together

1 Here are some items for sale in a supermarket.

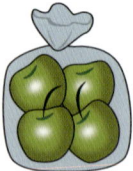

| Bag of apples £1·99 | Bananas £2·34 | Melon £3·75 | Bag of pears £1·70 | Bag of cherries £3·57 |

 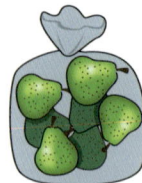 

How much do these items cost in total?

a) bananas and melon

	O	•	Tth	Hth
	2	•	3	4
+	3	•	7	5
		•		

b) pears and cherries

	O	•	Tth	Hth
	1	•	7	0
+	3	•	5	7
		•		

2 Work out the additions.

a)

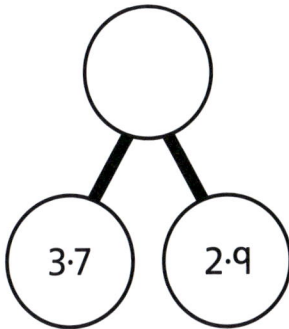

3·7   2·9

c) What is 6 ones, 3 tenths and 4 hundredths plus 7 ones, 2 tenths and 9 hundredths?

b)

2·453	5·232

CHALLENGE

3 Jamilla buys three items. She pays exactly £12.

a) Which items did she choose?

I am going to add the last digits and see if any add up to 10.

£0·94   £3·15

£2·38   £4·26   £6·47

b) When added together, two of the items cost exactly the same as another two items.

Which items are they?

I wonder how I can check that my answers are correct.

107

→ **Practice book 5C p78**

Subtract decimals with the same number of decimal places

Discover

I would like a pineapple and a watermelon please.

That will be £5·74 in total.

Pineapples £2·25 each

Amelia

Toshi

1 a) How much does the watermelon cost?

b) Amelia gives Toshi £6·00. How much change does she get?

Share

I used the column method. I started from the right-hand column.

a) To find the cost of the watermelon you need to subtract £2·25 from £5·74.

£5·74	
£2·25	?

Subtract the 5 hundredths first.
There are not enough hundredths.

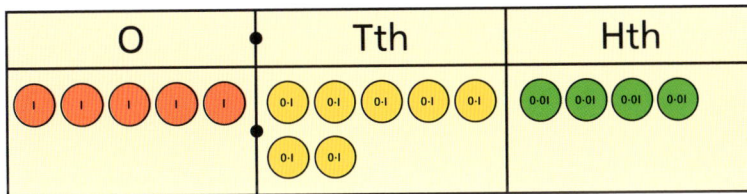

O		Tth	Hth

O	•Tth	Hth
5	• 7	4
− 2	• 2	5
	•	

Exchange 1 tenth for 10 hundredths.

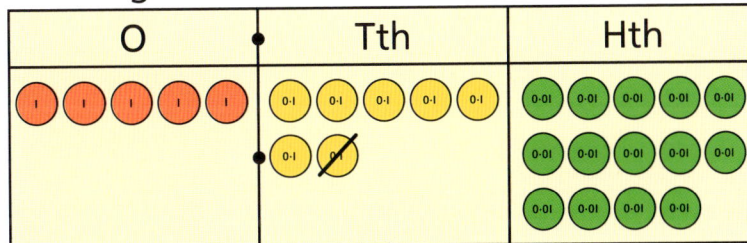

O		Tth	Hth

O	•Tth	Hth
5	• ^{6}7	^{1}4
− 2	• 2	5
	•	

Now subtract the 5 hundredths.

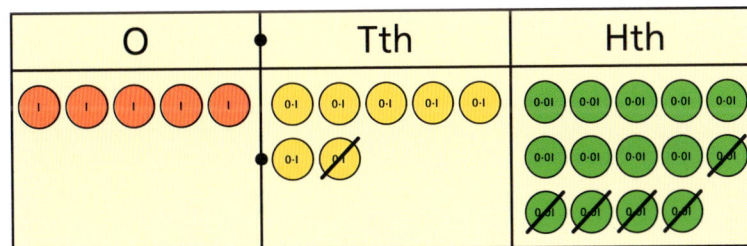

O		Tth	Hth

O	•Tth	Hth
5	• ^{6}7	^{1}4
− 2	• 2	5
	•	9

Now subtract the 2 tenths, then the 2 ones.

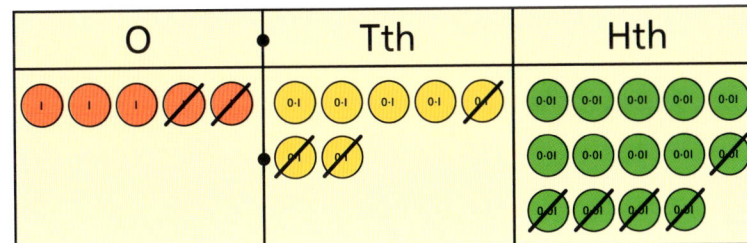

O		Tth	Hth

O	•Tth	Hth
5	• ^{6}7	^{1}4
− 2	• 2	5
3	• 4	9

The watermelon costs £3·49.

b) To find the change you need to subtract.

£6·00 − £5·74 = £0·26

> I used a number line to count on to find the difference. I think this is an efficient way to find change.

+0·06   +0·20

£5·00 £5·10 £5·20 £5·30 £5·40 £5·50 £5·60 £5·70 £5·80 £5·90 £6·00

£5·74

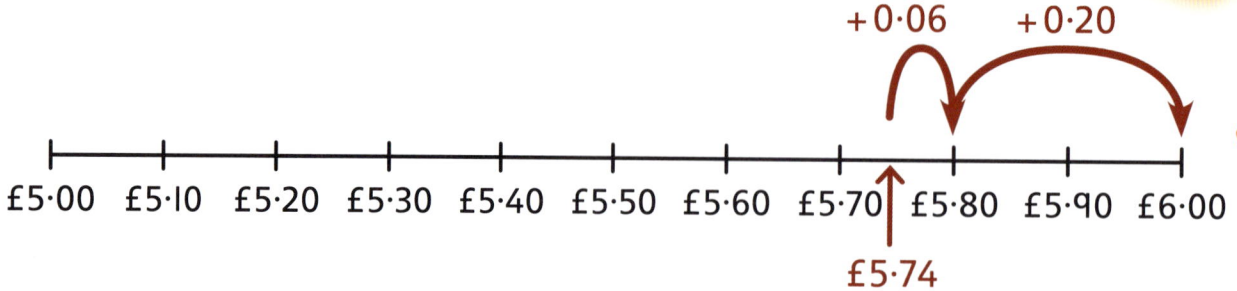

Amelia gets 26p change.

Think together

1 A shop sells some socks and hats.

How much cheaper is the hat than the socks?

£3·52   £5·15

O	•	Tth	Hth
	1 1 1 1 1	0·1	0·01 0·01 0·01 0·01 0·01

	O	•	Tth	Hth
	5	•	1	5
−	3	•	5	2
		•		

2 Write these as column subtractions and complete them.

a) 0·82 − 0·38 = ☐

b) 3·25 − 1·73 = ☐

c) 37·5 − 13·9 = ☐

d) 2·054 − 1·375 = ☐

CHALLENGE

3 Lexi, Reena and Ebo are thinking of numbers.

Lexi: If I add 2·7 to my number I get 7·3.

Reena: If I add 1·23 to my number and then add 3·57, my answer is 12·04.

Ebo: I started with 12·65 and subtracted 3·92 to get to my number.

Ebo says that to work out Lexi's number you need to subtract. He does the following calculation.

a) What mistake has Ebo made?

b) What are Ebo and Reena's numbers?

	O	•Tth
	7	• 3
−	2	• 7
	5	• 4

I wonder why I have to subtract to find Lexi's number.

I think it is because you have to do the inverse since Lexi has already added on 2·7 to get 7·3.

111

→ Practice book 5C p81

Add decimals with a different number of decimal places

Discover

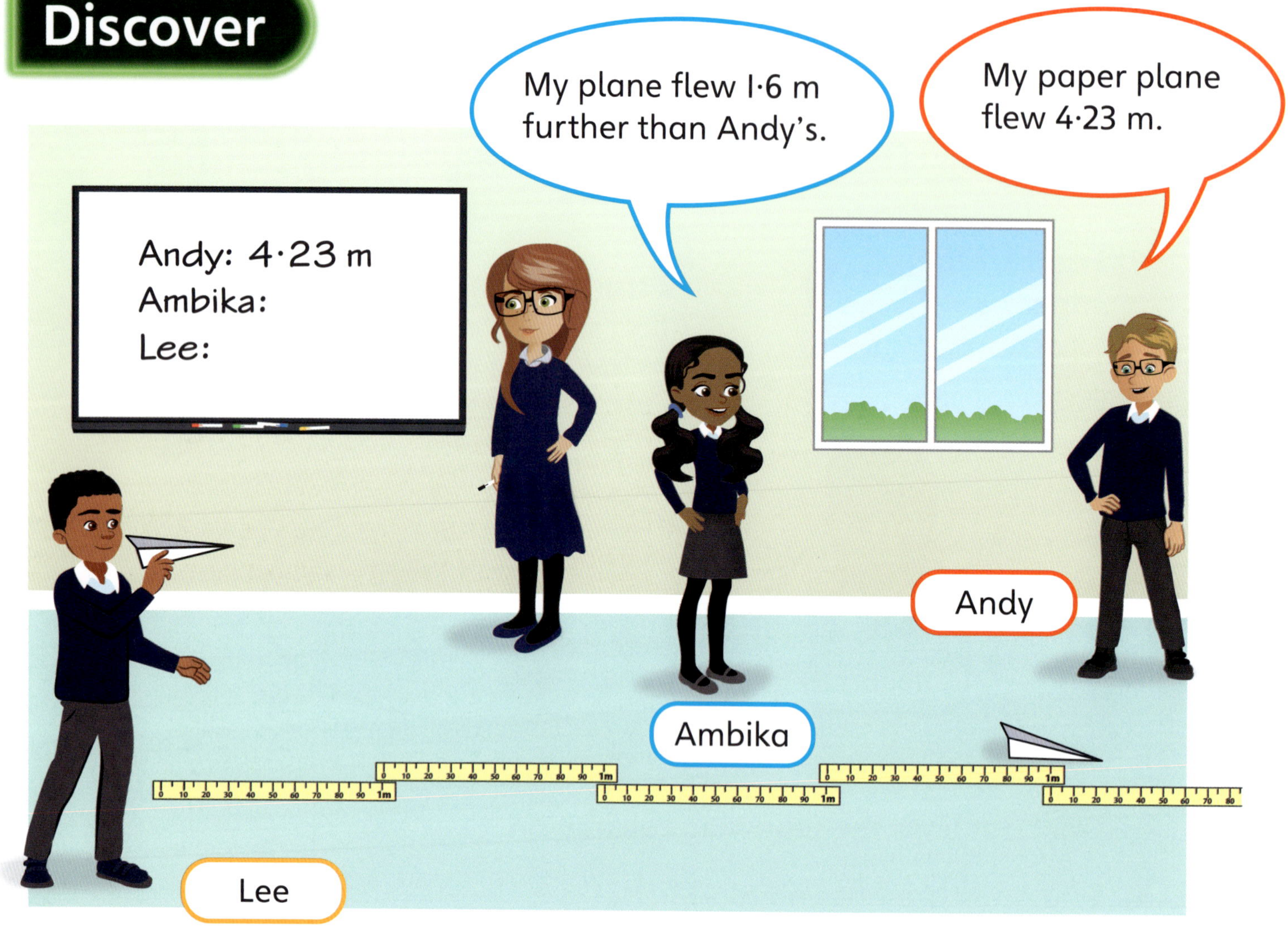

My plane flew 1·6 m further than Andy's.

My paper plane flew 4·23 m.

Andy: 4·23 m
Ambika:
Lee:

Andy

Ambika

Lee

1 **a)** How far did Ambika's paper plane fly?

b) Lee throws his paper plane. It goes the shortest distance, flying 0·42 m less than Andy's plane. How far does Lee's paper plane fly?

Share

a) Andy's plane flew 4·23 m. Ambika's plane flew 1·6 m further.

You need to add 4·23 and 1·6.

O		Tth	Hth
① ① ① ①	•	0·1 0·1	0·01 0·01 0·01

	O	•	Tth	Hth
	4	•	2	3
−	1	•	6	0
	5	•	8	3

4·23 + 1·6 = 5·83

Ambika's paper plane flew 5·83 m.

> I used the column method to add. I lined the numbers up at the decimal point. I added an extra 0 in the hundredths column to make the same number of digits after the decimal point.

b) Lee's plane flies 0·42 m less than Andy's plane.

Method 1

	O	•	Tth	Hth
	$^3\cancel{4}$	•	$^1 2$	3
−	0	•	4	2
	3	•	8	1

Method 2

4·23 m = 423 cm

0·42 m = 42 cm

423 cm − 42 cm = 381 cm = 3·81 m

> I converted all the measurements into centimetres and then subtracted.

Lee's paper plane flies 3·81 m.

Think together

1 More of the class took part in the paper plane throwing competition.

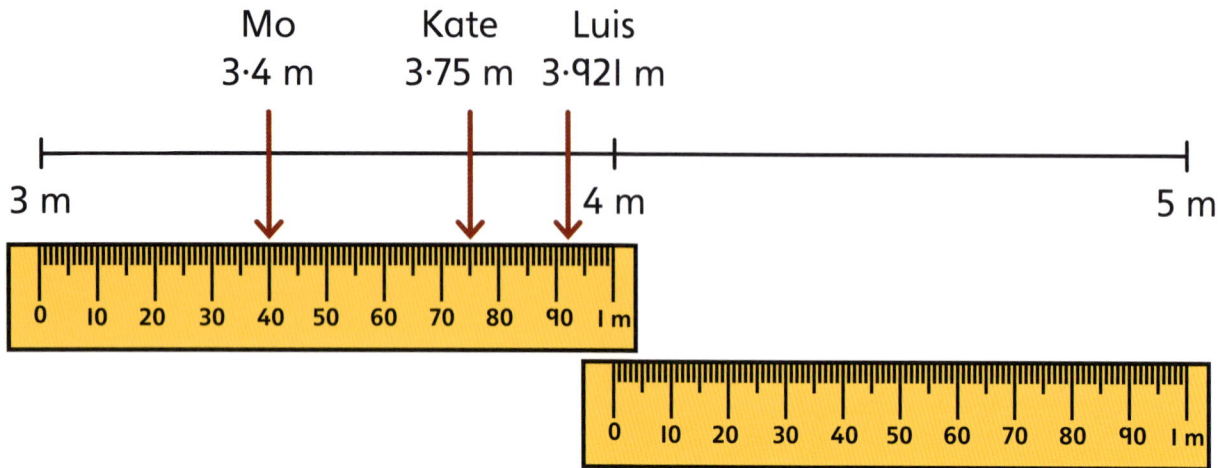

Mo	Kate	Luis
3·4 m	3·75 m	3·921 m

3 m   4 m   5 m

a) Mo had a second throw. He threw 0·65 m further than his first throw. How far did his second throw fly?

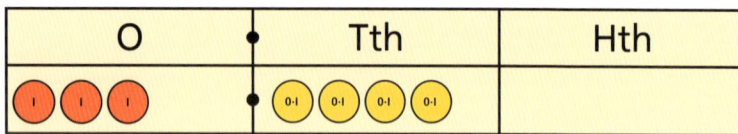

O	•	Tth	Hth
① ① ①	•	0·1 0·1 0·1 0·1	

	O	•	Tth	Hth
	3	•	4	0
+	0	•	6	5
		•		

b) Josh throws a plane.

His plane lands 1·6 m further than Luis's plane.

How far does Josh's plane fly?

	O	•	Tth	Hth	Thth
	3	•	9	2	1
+	1	•	6	0	0
		•			

2   Complete this addition pyramid.

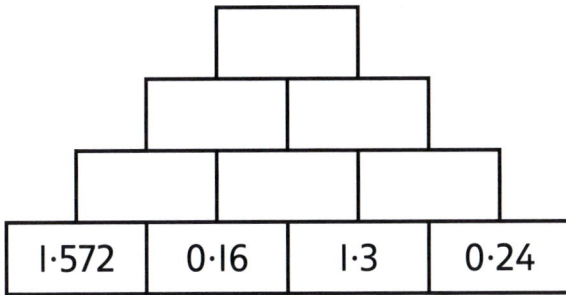

1·572	0·16	1·3	0·24

Remember, in an addition pyramid each pair of numbers adds up to the number above it.

3   **a)**   What mistakes have been made in these calculations?

CHALLENGE

$4·5 + 1·34$

	O	•Tth	Hth
	•	4	5
+	1 •	3	4
	1 •	7	9

$82·43 + 1·89$

	T	O •Tth	Hth
	8	2 • 4	3
+		1 • 8	9
	8	3 • 2	2

b)   What does the correct working out look like?

I think one of these calculations has been lined up incorrectly.

I wonder if I could do calculations to check the answers.

→ **Practice book 5C p84**

Subtract decimals with a different number of decimal places

Discover

1 **a)** How much juice is in the two bottles in total?

b) Jamilla started with a full bag of flour. How much is left in the bag now some flour is on the scales?

Share

I did a column addition.

a) There is one 5 l bottle and one 1·25 l bottle of juice.

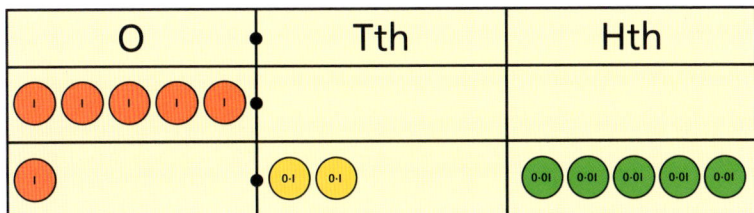

O		Tth	Hth

	O	•Tth	Hth
	5	• 0	0
+	1	• 2	5
	6	• 2	5

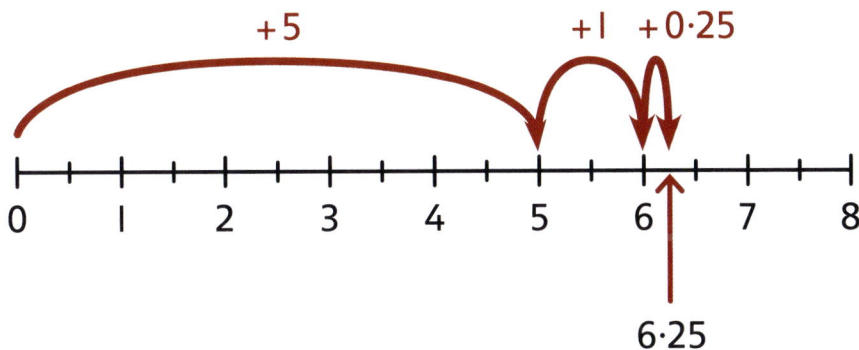

+5   +1   +0·25

0   1   2   3   4   5   6   7   8

6·25

I added the wholes and then added the part.

There is 6·25 l of juice in the two bottles in total.

b) The full bag of flour weighed 2 kg. Jamilla tipped 0·296 kg onto the scales.

The amount of flour left in the bag is 2 kg – 0·296 kg.

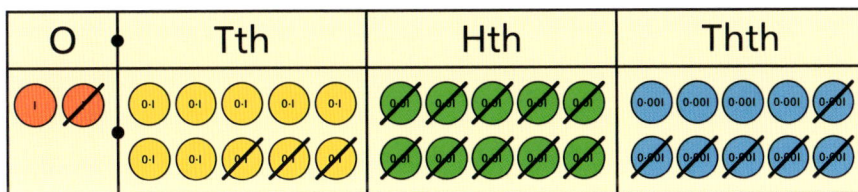

O	•	Tth	Hth	Thth

	O	•Tth	Hth	Thth
	$^1\cancel{2}$	$•^9\cancel{0}$	$^9\cancel{0}$	$^1 0$
–	0	• 2	9	6
	1	• 7	0	4

2 kg – 0·296 kg = 1·704 kg.

There is 1·704 kg of flour left in the bag.

Remember that 2 can be written as 2·000 so that there are the same number of digits after the decimal point.

Think together

1 **a)** How much more pasta is in the large bag than in the small bag?

	O	•Tth
	5	0
−	2	8

b) How much more cereal is in the large box than in the small box?

	O	•Tth	Hth
	2	0	0
−	0	6	5

c) Zac pours some milk from the full bottle into the glass.
The glass holds 0·358 l of milk.

How much milk is left in the bottle?

	O	•Tth	Hth	Thth
	3			
−	0	3	5	8

2 Work out the subtractions.

a) 7·6 – 3·52

b) 7·68 – 3·5

c) 7·68 – 3·9

d) 17·68 – 3·5

e) 4·2 – 1·79

f) 4·25 – 1·795

CHALLENGE

3 Jamilla uses two different methods to work out 2 – 0·296.

Method 1

	O	•Tth	Hth	Thth
	1	• 9	9	9
–	0	• 2	9	6
	1	• 7	0	3

1·703 + 0·001 = 1·704

Method 2

	O	•Tth	Hth	Thth
	1	• 9	9	9
–	0	• 2	9	5
	1	• 7	0	4

a) Why do Jamilla's methods work? Which method do you prefer?

This makes the subtraction easier. I wonder why it shows the same answer as 2 – 0·296 though.

I could use a number line to prove that 2 – 0·296 is the same as 1·999 – 0·295.

b) Use your preferred method to work out these calculations.

| 6 – 3·45 | 3 – 0·914 | 26 – 2·8 |

Problem solving with decimals ❶

Discover

Life support mass:

Spacesuit mass: 49·89 kg

Fact:
An astronaut who weighs 76·8 kg on Earth, weighs only 12·75 kg on the moon!

Life support   Spacesuit

❶ **a)** How much greater is the weight of the astronaut on Earth than on the moon?

b) The mass of the life support is 90·2 kg heavier than the spacesuit.

What is the total mass of the spacesuit and life support?

Share

a) moon

12·75 kg

? →

Earth

76·8 kg

> I used a bar model to help me. I saw that I needed to do a subtraction as I was finding a difference.

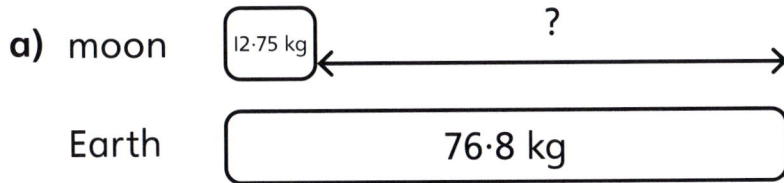

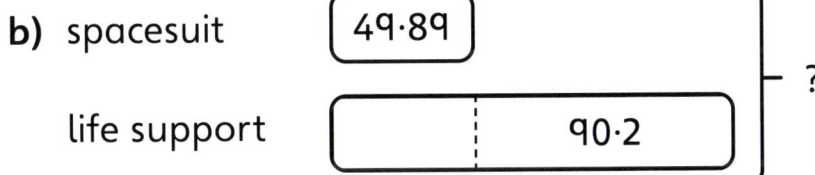

	T	O	•	Tth	Hth
	7	6	•	⁷8̸	¹0
−	1	2	•	7	5
	6	4	•	0	5

$76·8 - 12·75 = 64·05$

The weight of the astronaut on Earth is 64·05 kg more than on the moon.

b) spacesuit

49·89

life support

	90·2

?

> I found the mass of the life support first.

The mass of the life support is

$49·89 \text{ kg} + 90·2 \text{ kg} = 140·09 \text{ kg}.$

The total mass of the spacesuit and the life support is

$140·09 \text{ kg} + 49·89 \text{ kg} = 189·98 \text{ kg}.$

	H	T	O	•	Tth	Hth
		4	9	•	8	9
+		9	0	•	2	0
	1	4	0	•	0	9
		1	1			

	H	T	O	•	Tth	Hth
	1	4	0	•	0	9
+		4	9	•	8	9
	1	8	9	•	9	8
					1	

The total mass of the spacesuit and the life support is 189·98 kg.

Think together

1 Lexi can jump up to 1·5 m on Earth. The same jump would be 9·144 m on the moon because the gravity is different.

How much further could Lexi jump on the moon?

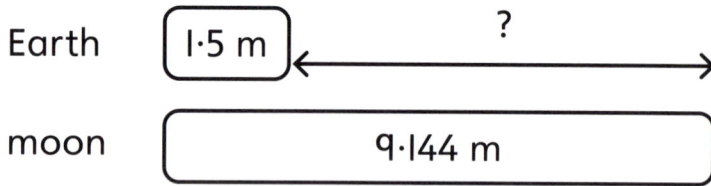

Earth | 1·5 m

?

moon | 9·144 m

	O	•	Tth	Hth	Thth
	9	•	1	4	4
−	1	•	5		
		•			

2 How much do the science magazines cost in total?

Explain your method.

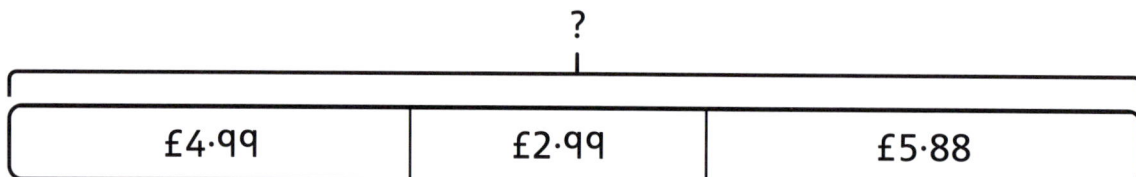

SCIENCE £4·99   SCIENCE £2·99   SCIENCE £5·88

?

£4·99 | £2·99 | £5·88

3 Astronauts bring three rocks back from the moon.

CHALLENGE

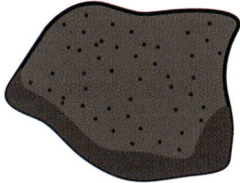

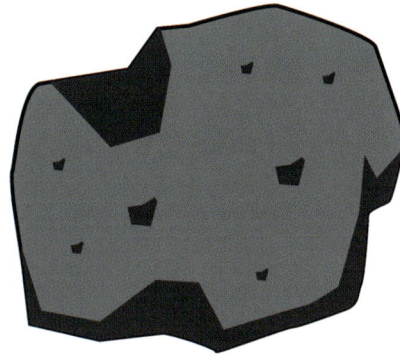

Rock A   Rock B   Rock C
                12 kg

The mass of rock A is 3·6 kg less than rock B.

The mass of rock C is 4·75 kg greater than rock B.

a) Work out the total mass of the three rocks.

b) How much more does rock C weigh than rock A?

I am going to work out the mass of each of the rocks.

I am not sure that you need to. There might be a more efficient way. A bar model will help you to work it out.

123

Problem solving with decimals ❷

Discover

① **a)** What will happen to the balance scale when Ebo puts the bag of sugar in the empty balance pan?

b) By adding or removing some sugar or oats to or from the bags, how can Emma and Ebo get the scales to balance?

Share

a) First, find the mass of the oats.

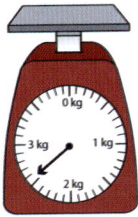

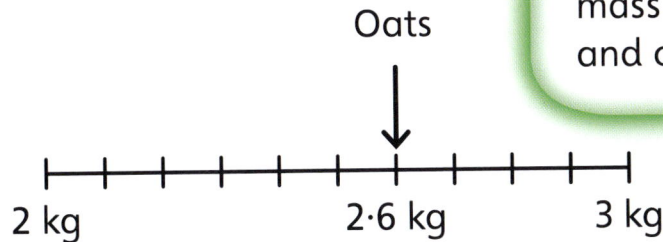

Oats

2 kg   2·6 kg   3 kg

I worked out the mass of the pears and oats altogether.

The mass of the oats is 2·6 kg.

The mass of the pears is 0·89 kg.

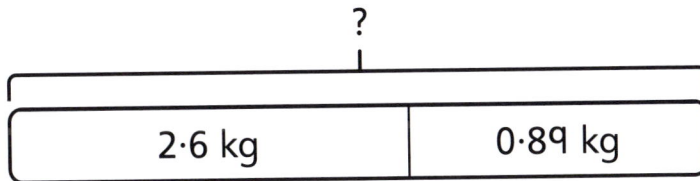

?

| | 2·6 kg | 0·89 kg |

O	•	Tth	Hth
2	•	6	0
+ 0	•	8	9
3	•	4	9
1			

2·6 kg + 0·89 kg = 3·49 kg

3·49 kg > 3 kg, so the balance scale will not move enough to tip the balance.

SUGAR 3 kg

OATS

b)

To balance, the scales need to be the same mass either side. So, I had to either reduce the amount of oats or add more sugar.

3·49 kg − 3 kg = 0·49 kg

Emma and Ebo can add 0·49 kg of sugar to the bag of sugar.

Or they can remove 0·49 kg of oats from the bag of oats.

O	•	Tth	Hth
3	•	4	9
− 3	•	0	0
0	•	4	9

Think together

1 Emma weighs out some sugar from the 3 kg bag into two scales.

How much sugar is left in the bag?

0·74 kg   SUGAR 3 kg   0·65 kg

3 kg

| 0·74 kg | 0·65 kg | ? |

> I think there is more than one way to work this out.

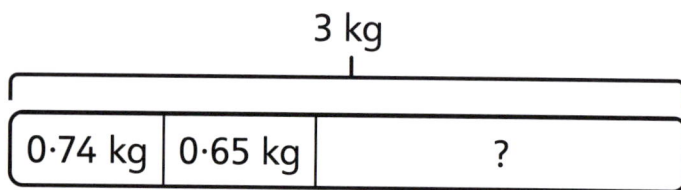

2 A tablespoon holds 18·6 g of flour. A teaspoon holds 15·9 g less flour than the tablespoon.

What is the total mass of flour on the two spoons?

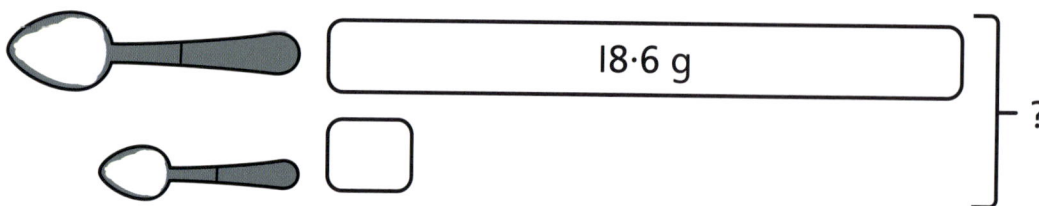

18·6 g

?

CHALLENGE

3 A street has four lamp posts in a line. Jen measures the distances between some of the lamp posts.

> The distance between the 1st and 2nd lamp posts is 5·85 m. Between the 2nd and 3rd it is 6·189 m. The distance between the 1st and 4th lamp posts is 3 times the distance between the 1st and 2nd.

Jen

What is the distance between the 3rd and 4th lamp posts?

> I think I need to multiply decimals.

> I do not think you have to. I think you can add the number three times instead.

→ Practice book 5C p93

Decimal sequences

Discover

These rose bushes grow 2·5 cm every month.

Mo

Olivia

1 **a)** The rose bush Mo and Olivia are planting is 15·4 cm tall in April. How tall will it be each coming month for the next 6 months?

b) The other rose bush is 87·2 cm. For how many months has the rose bush been over 60 cm tall?

128

Share

a) The rose bush starts at 15·4 cm and grows 2·5 cm each month. Add on 2·5 cm to its height from the previous month.

> I made a table to organise the results. I also showed the same sequence on a number line.

Month	April	May	June	July	Aug	Sept	Oct
Height (cm)	15·4	17·9	20·4	22·9	25·4	27·9	30·4

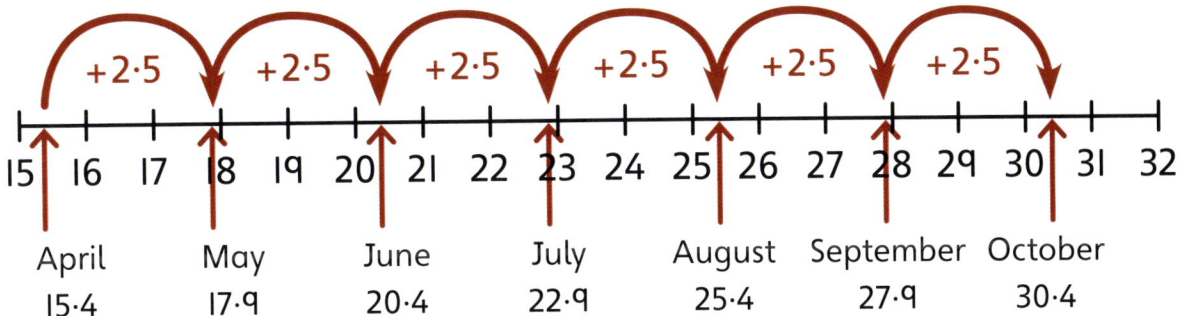

The rule is to add 2·5 each time.

> These numbers are in a sequence. A sequence is when related things happen in an order. This sequence goes up by the same amount each time.

b) Subtract 2·5 each time, until you get less than 60.

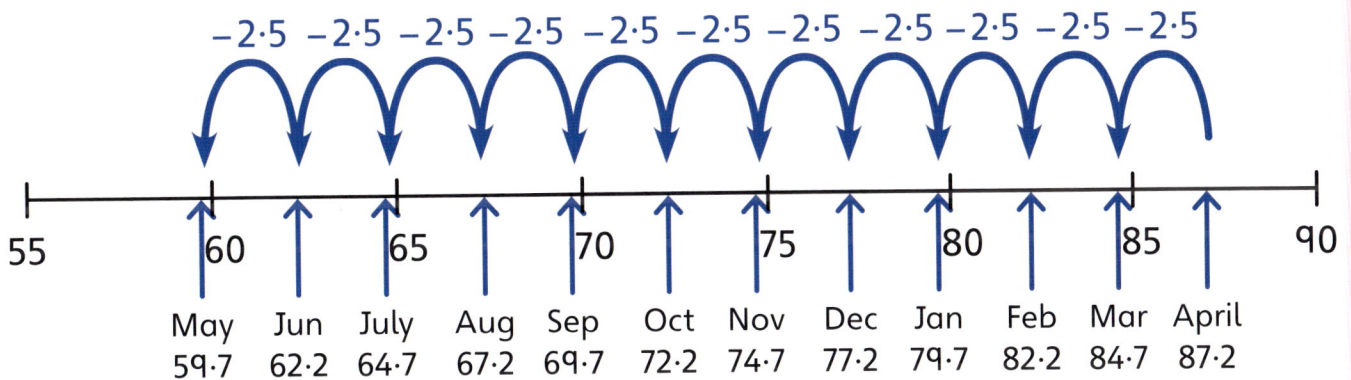

11 months ago, the rose bush was shorter than 60 cm. So, the rose bush has been over 60 cm tall for the last 10 months.

Think together

I wonder if I can find the rule by looking at how much each rose has grown by each month.

1) The changes in heights of these three roses each month make a sequence.

All the heights are in centimetres.

Find the rules and complete the missing numbers.

	April	May	June	July	Aug	Sept	Oct
White rose	15·1	15·2	15·3	☐	☐	☐	☐
Climbing rose	10·0	12·6	15·2	☐	☐	☐	☐
Wild rose	☐	12·43	12·431	12·432	☐	☐	☐

2) Work out the sequences and complete the missing values.

a)

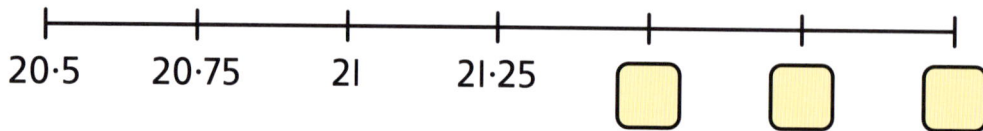

20·5   20·75   21   21·25   ☐   ☐   ☐

b)

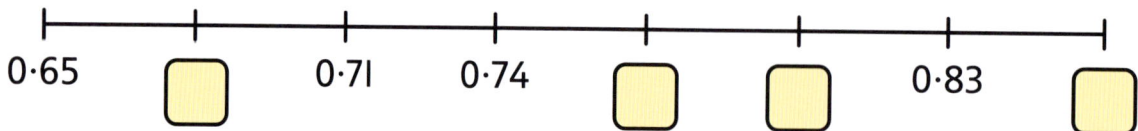

0·65   ☐   0·71   0·74   ☐   ☐   0·83   ☐

c)

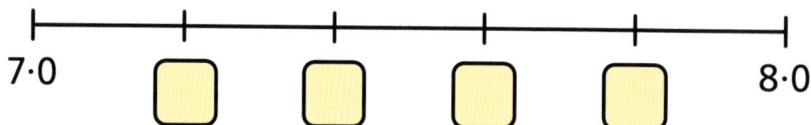

7·0   ☐   ☐   ☐   ☐   8·0

CHALLENGE

3 These two sets of decimal cards form sequences when arranged in ascending order.

Two of the cards in each set are covered up.
What could they be?

Describe to a partner the sequence that each set of decimals makes.

a)

| 3·7 | 3·5 | 3·9 | 4·0 |

I am going to put the cards in order and try to work out what they go up in.

I will look to see how the decimals on the covered cards might make the sequences work.

b)

| 35·6 | 38·7 | 32·5 | 41·8 | 29·4 |

What would be the first number above 50 in the second sequence?

→ Practice book 5C p96

Multiply by 10

Discover

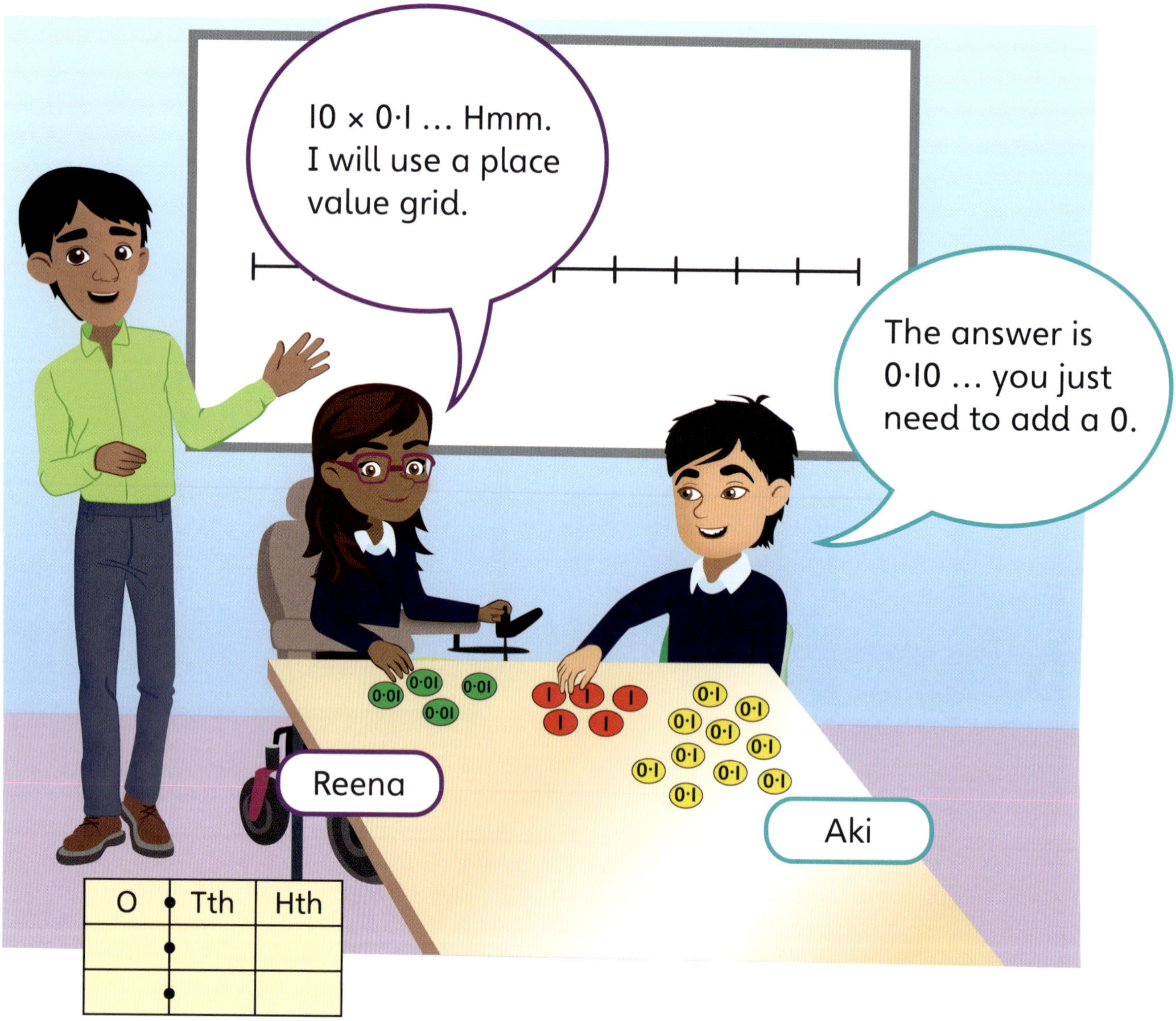

1 **a)** Discuss Aki's thinking. Why might he think this is a good idea?

b) Show 10 groups of 0·1 using place value equipment.

Use this to convince a partner of the correct calculation.

Share

a) Aki is thinking about a quick way to multiply whole numbers by 10.

$10 \times 3 = 30$ $10 \times 8 = 80$ $15 \times 10 = 150$

> This is a helpful, quick mental process but it doesn't work with decimals.

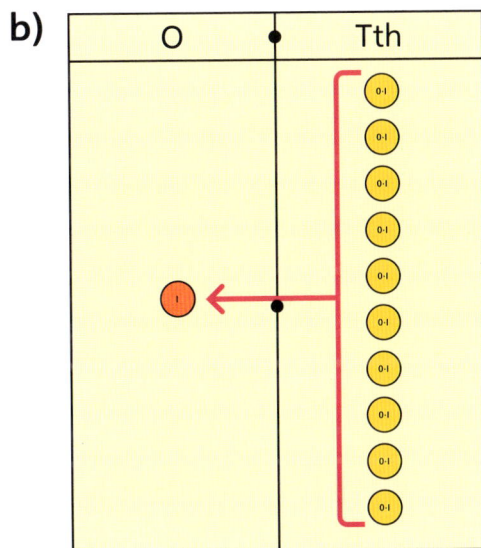

b)

> I is ten times the size of 0·I.

$10 \times 0·1 = 1$

Think together

1 **a)** Use the counters and a place value grid to work out these multiplications.

i) 0·14 × 10 = ☐

O	•	Tth	Hth

ii) 2·3 × 10 = ☐

T		O	•	Tth

b) Multiply each of these numbers by 10.

i)

T	O	•	Tth	Hth
	3	•	7	
		•		

iii)

T	O	•	Tth	Hth
	2	•	3	9
		•		

ii)

T	O	•	Tth	Hth
	4	•	5	
		•		

iv)

T	O	•	Tth	Hth	Thth
	0	•	1	9	6
		•			

2 Complete the multiplications.

a) $0.1 \times 10 = \boxed{}$

$1.2 \times 10 = \boxed{}$

$5.7 \times 10 = \boxed{}$

$19.1 \times 10 = \boxed{}$

b) $0.72 \times 10 = \boxed{}$

$1.25 \times 10 = \boxed{}$

$5.71 \times 10 = \boxed{}$

$19.16 \times 10 = \boxed{}$

c) $0.256 \times 10 = \boxed{}$

$1.256 \times 10 = \boxed{}$

$31.126 \times 10 = \boxed{}$

d) With a partner, look at the digits in each number that is being multiplied by 10.

What do you notice about the digits in the answers?
What is the same and what is different?

CHALLENGE

3 Find the missing numbers in these multiplications.

a) $10 \times 3.9 = \boxed{}$

b) $10 \times 11.6 = \boxed{}$

c) $\boxed{} \times 10 = 4.56$

d) $\boxed{} \times 10 = 12.62$

e) $\boxed{} \times 10 = 3.2$

f) $\boxed{} \times 10 = 15.86$

I can multiply numbers by 10 without using counters and a place value grid.

I notice that when I multiply by 10, the digits move 1 place to the left. I wonder if this always happens.

135

→ Practice book 5C p99

Multiply by 10, 100 and 1,000

Discover

I wonder where these potatoes came from.

10 bags go in each sack.

1 a) How many bags are on the lorry?

b) What is the mass of potatoes in one sack?

What is the mass of potatoes on one pallet?

What is the mass of potatoes on the lorry?

Share

a) There are 10 pallets on the lorry. There are 10 sacks on each pallet.

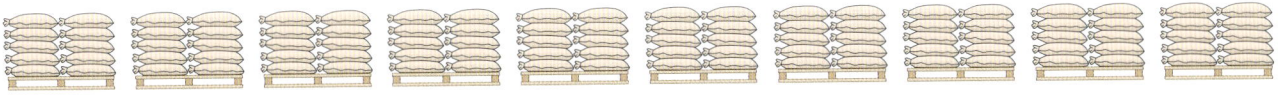

10 × 10 = 100 sacks

Each sack contains 10 bags.

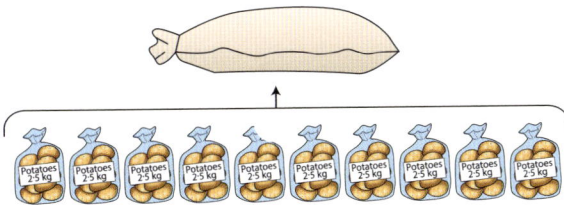

There are 10 × 10 × 10 bags on the lorry.

That is 1,000 bags.

b) The mass of one bag of potatoes is 2·5 kg.

The mass of potatoes in one sack is 25 kg.

The mass of potatoes on one pallet is 250 kg.

2·5 × 10 = 25
2·5 × 100 = 250
2·5 × 1,000 = 2,500

Th	H	T	O	• Tth
			2	• 5
		2	5	•
	2	5	0	•
2	5	0	0	•

When multiplying by 100, the digits move two places to the left. When multiplying by 1,000, the digits move three places to the left.

Multiplying by 1,000 is the same as multiplying by 10, then 10 and then 10 again.

So 2·5 × 1,000 is the same as 2·5 × 10 × 10 × 10 = 2,500 kg. The mass of all the potatoes on the lorry is 2,500 kg.

Think together

1 Draw a place value grid and complete the calculations.

Th	H	T	O	•	Tth
			3	•	7
				•	
				•	
				•	

$3·7 \times 10 = \boxed{}$

$3·7 \times 100 = \boxed{}$

$3·7 \times 1,000 = \boxed{}$

2 Use a place value grid to help you complete the multiplications.

Th	H	T	O	•	Tth	Hth	Thth
				•			
				•			
				•			

a) $1·72 \times 10 = \boxed{}$

$1·72 \times 100 = \boxed{}$

$1·72 \times 1,000 = \boxed{}$

b) $4·13 \times 1,000 = \boxed{}$

$0·413 \times 1,000 = \boxed{}$

$0·041 \times 1,000 = \boxed{}$

c) $39·3 \times 100 = \boxed{}$

$3·93 \times 100 = \boxed{}$

$0·393 \times 100 = \boxed{}$

CHALLENGE

3 **a)** This chart shows different multiples.

1,000	2,000	3,000	4,000	5,000	6,000	7,000	8,000	9,000
100	200	300	400	500	600	700	800	900
10	20	30	40	50	60	70	80	90
1	2	3	4	5	6	7	8	9
0·1	0·2	0·3	0·4	0·5	0·6	0·7	0·8	0·9
0·01	0·02	0·03	0·04	0·05	0·06	0·07	0·08	0·09

Use the chart to work out

$0.8 \times 10 = \boxed{}$

$0.4 \times 100 = \boxed{}$

$0.2 \times 1,000 = \boxed{}$

b) How could you use this chart to multiply 12·47 by 100?

1,000	2,000	3,000	4,000	5,000	6,000	7,000	8,000	9,000
100	200	300	400	500	600	700	800	900
10	20	30	40	50	60	70	80	90
1	2	3	4	5	6	7	8	9
0·1	0·2	0·3	0·4	0·5	0·6	0·7	0·8	0·9
0·01	0·02	0·03	0·04	0·05	0·06	0·07	0·08	0·09

→ **Practice book 5C p102**

Divide by 10

Discover

Lexi

1 **a)** What is the width of one hand span?

b) Show $0.9 \div 10$ on a place value grid.

Share

a)

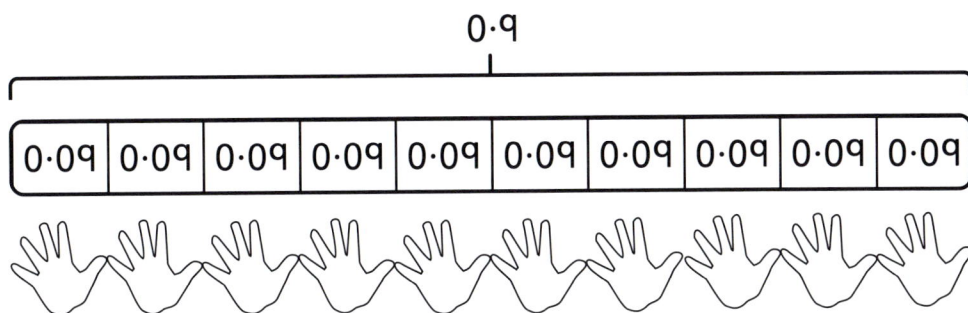

$0.09 \times 10 = 0.9$, so $0.9 \div 10 = 0.09$.

Each hand span is 0.09 m wide.

> I converted to cm first and then divided by 10. So $90 \div 10 = 9$. Each hand span is 9 cm wide. This is the same as 0.09 m.

b) The digits move one place to the left when you divide by 10.

O		Tth	Hth
0	•	9	
0	•	0	9

> The 0s are important because they ensure the other digits are in the correct columns.

Think together

1 Toshi makes a line of 10 footsteps.

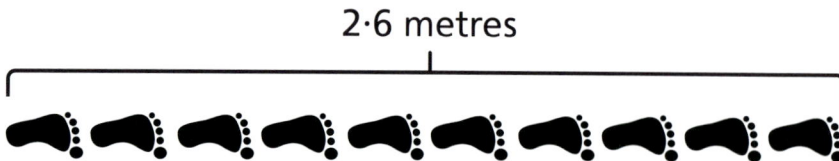

2·6 metres

How long is each of Toshi's footsteps in metres?

O	•	Tth	Hth
2	•	6	
	•		

2 Work out the missing numbers.

H	T	O	•	Tth	Hth	Thth
			•			
			•			

a) $0·92 \div 10 = \boxed{}$

b) $53·6 \div 10 = \boxed{}$

c) $95 \div 10 = \boxed{}$

d) $\boxed{} \div 10 = 5·86$

e) $89·02 \div 10 = \boxed{}$

f) $\boxed{} \div 10 = 1·002$

CHALLENGE

3 Use the pictures to answer the questions.

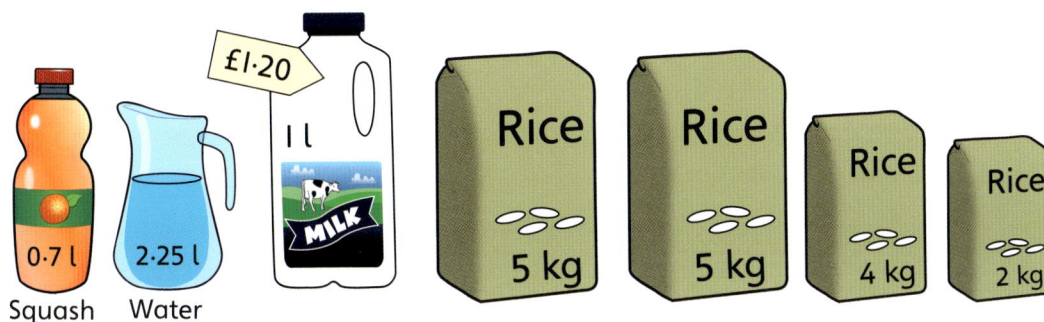

£1·20

1 l

MILK

0·7 l
Squash

2·25 l
Water

Rice 5 kg

Rice 5 kg

Rice 4 kg

Rice 2 kg

a) Danny mixes the water and squash.
He shares it equally between 10 glasses.

How much drink is in each glass?

b) How much does 100 ml of milk cost?
What about 200 ml?

c) The rice is shared between 20 saucepans.

How much rice is in each saucepan?

d) Make up your own decimal questions which involve dividing by 10.

I know there are 10 equal parts of 100 ml in 1 litre.

I think I can put half the rice in 10 pans and work it out from there.

143

→ Practice book 5C p105

Divide by 10, 100 and 1,000

Discover

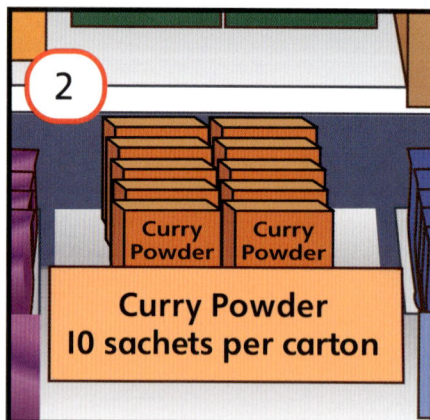

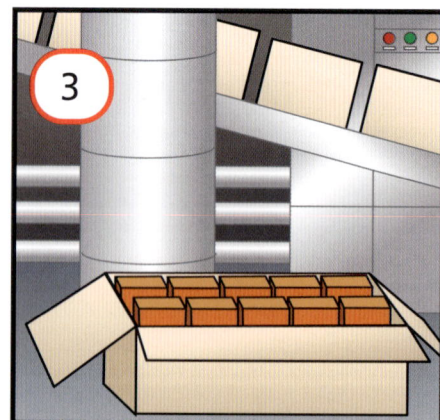

1 a) How many sachets of curry powder are in the large box?

b) The total mass of the curry powder in the large box is 8·5 kg.

How many kilograms of curry powder are in each sachet?

Share

a) There are 10 sachets in each carton. There are 10 cartons in each large box.

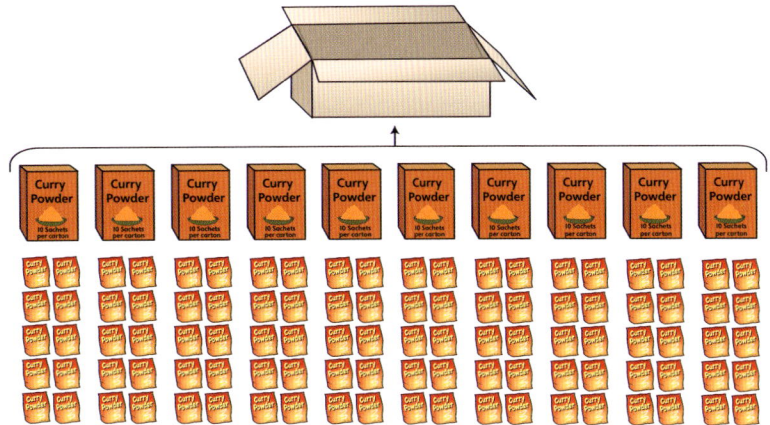

$10 \times 10 = 100$

There are 100 sachets of curry powder in the large box.

b) The total mass of the large box is 8·5 kg.

Method 1

> I divided by 10 to work out how much is in each carton.

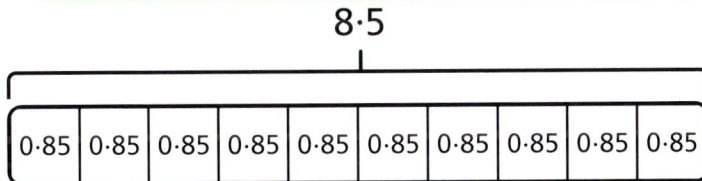

8·5

0·85	0·85	0·85	0·85	0·85	0·85	0·85	0·85	0·85	0·85

O	•	Tth	Hth	Thth
8	•	5		
0	•	8	5	

$8·5 \div 10 = 0·85$

> I divided by 10 again to work out how much curry powder is in each sachet.

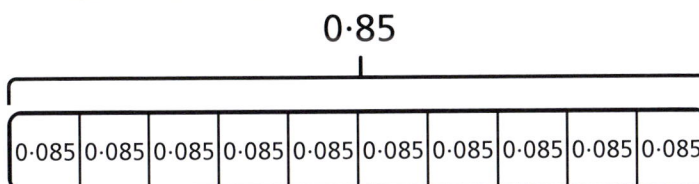

0·85

0·085	0·085	0·085	0·085	0·085	0·085	0·085	0·085	0·085	0·085

O	•	Tth	Hth	Thth
0	•	8	5	
0	•	0	8	5

$0·85 \div 10 = 0·085$

There is 0·085 kg of curry powder in each sachet.

Method 2

I divided by 100 instead as there are 100 sachets in the large box.

O	•	Tth	Hth	Thth
8	•	5		
0	•	0	8	5

When dividing by 100, the digits move 2 places to the right.

Dividing by 100 is the same as dividing by 10 and then 10 again.

There is 0·085 kg of curry powder in each sachet.

Think together

1 a) Divide each of these numbers or amounts by 100.

H	T	O	•	Tth	Hth	Thth
			•			
			•			

12·8 kg ÷ 100 = ☐ kg   128 ÷ 100 = ☐

2·52 m ÷ 100 = ☐ m   0·9 ÷ 100 = ☐

b) Divide each of these numbers or amounts by 1,000.

i) 12   ii) 6 m   iii) 718 km   iv) £70

2 All the milk in the bottle is used in a recipe for 100 scones.

How much milk is in each scone?

☐ ÷ ☐ = ☐

4 l
MILK

CHALLENGE

3 In a bakery there is a trolley that holds 10 trays. Each tray contains 10 loaves of bread. Each loaf of bread is cut into 10 equal slices.

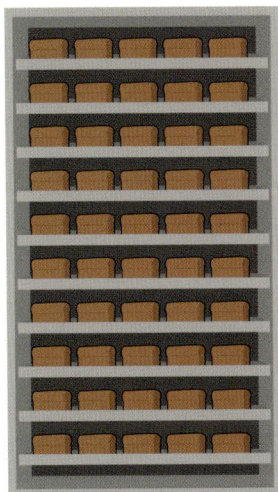

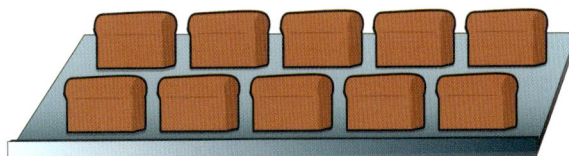

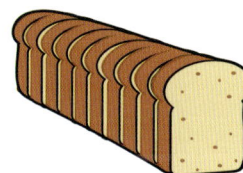

a) If the total mass of all the bread on the trolley is 46 kg, how much does a single slice weigh?

Explain your method.

b) What rule can you think of to show your method?

I will work out the number of slices and then divide the mass by this.

I will work out the mass of the loaves on a tray, then the mass of each loaf and then the mass of each slice.

→ Practice book 5C p108

End of unit check

1 What is the answer when these two numbers are added together?

| 2·53 | | 3·64 |

A 5·17   B 5·117   C 6·17   D 6·67

2 What is 0·35 subtracted from 15·6?

A 12·1   B 15·25   C 15·35   D 15·95

3 Which of the following is **not** equivalent to 5 – 3·45?

A 6 – 4·45   B 4·99 – 3·46   C 4·99 – 3·44   D 4·98 – 3·43

4 What is the answer to 0·2 × 100?

A 0·02   B 0·2   C 2   D 20

5 Which of these calculations is equal to 0·015?

A 15 ÷ 1,000   B 0·15 × 10   C 1·5 ÷ 10   D 15 × 100

6 Which statement is false?

A When you multiply by 10, the digits move one place to the left.

B When you multiply by 100, the digits move two places to the right.

C When you divide by 10, the digits move one place to the right.

D When you divide by 1,000, the digits move three places to the right.

7 A tube contains two tennis balls.

Each tennis balls weighs 0·16 kg.

The total mass of the tube and two balls is 0·5 kg.

What is the mass of the empty tube?

8 A, B and C are plotted on a number line.

A   B   C
├────┼────┼──────────────────────────────────┤
   15·48

The difference between A and B is 3·5.

The difference between A and C is 10 times the difference between A and B.

What are the values of B and C?

→ Practice book 5C p111

Unit 15
Negative numbers

In this unit we will …

- ⚡ Learn how to count back past 0
- ⚡ Learn how to read and write negative numbers
- ⚡ Learn how to place negative numbers on a number line
- ⚡ Learn how to read thermometers with sub-zero temperatures
- ⚡ Compare and order negative and positive numbers
- ⚡ Find the difference between two numbers, including negative numbers

We will use number lines to think about numbers. Can you count on and back on a number line?

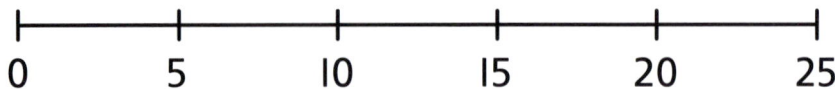

```
0    5    10   15   20   25
```

We will need some maths words.
Which of these do you know?

positive   negative   increase

decrease   temperature   interval

step   counting sequence

We will use thermometers to think about negative and positive numbers in real-life contexts.
Can you read these temperatures?

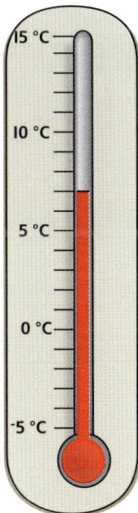

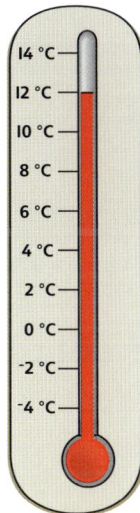

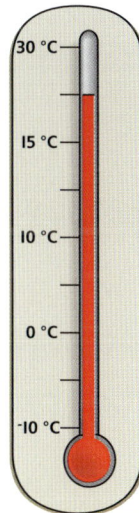

Understand negative numbers

Discover

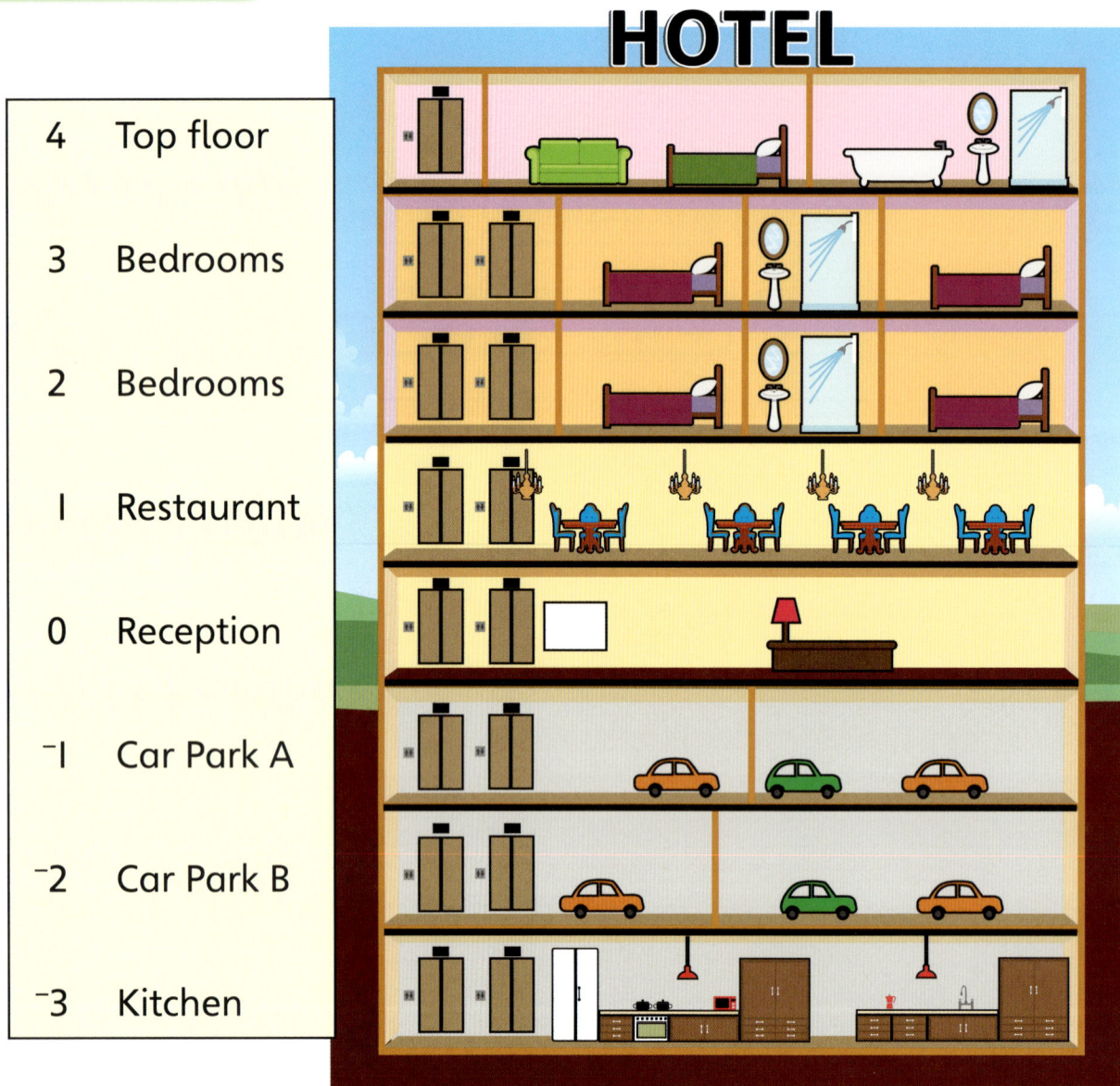

4	Top floor
3	Bedrooms
2	Bedrooms
1	Restaurant
0	Reception
⁻1	Car Park A
⁻2	Car Park B
⁻3	Kitchen

1 **a)** What is the same and what is different about the floor above Reception and the floor below Reception?

b) The waiter is in the Restaurant. He travels down 4 floors.

Where is the waiter now?

Share

a) The Restaurant is up one level from Reception on the ground floor. In the United Kingdom this is called the 'first floor'.

Reception is at ground level: floor 0.

Car Park A is one level below 0. This is floor '**negative** 1'.

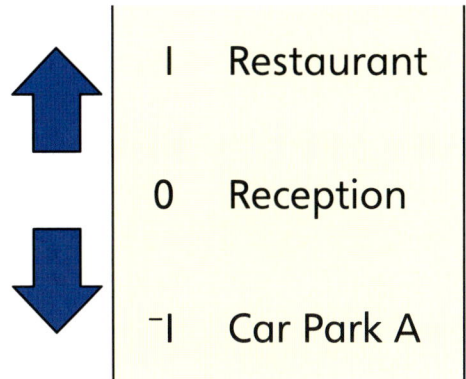

1	Restaurant
0	Reception
⁻1	Car Park A

b) The waiter starts in the Restaurant on floor 1. He travels down 4 floors.

> There are 4 floors so I counted back 4 jumps.

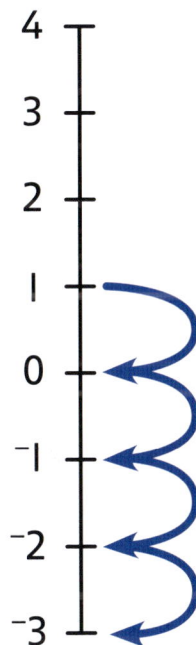

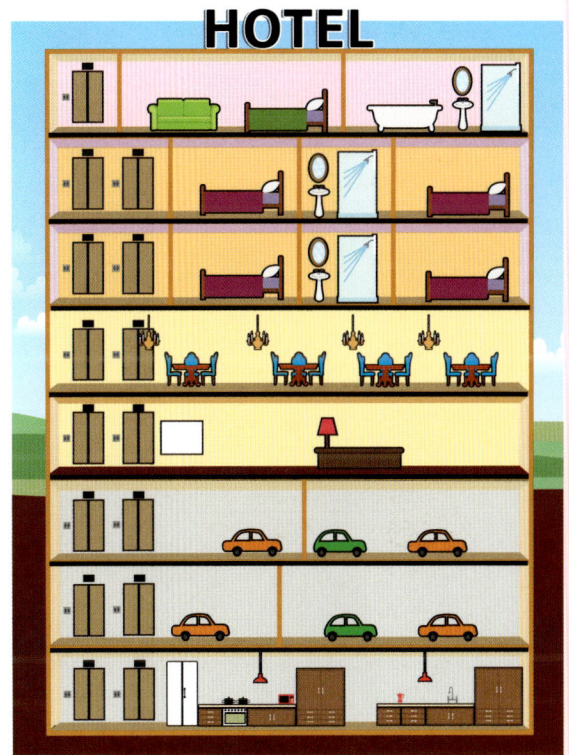

HOTEL

4
3
2
1
0
⁻1
⁻2
⁻3

The waiter is in the Kitchen on floor ⁻3.

153

Think together

1 What is the temperature shown on each thermometer?

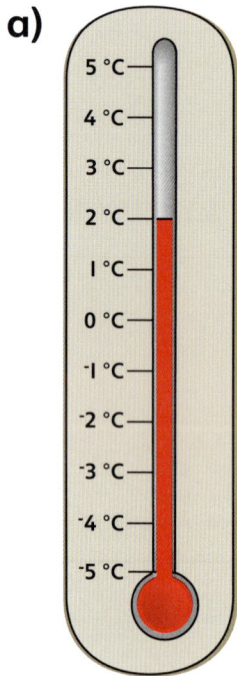

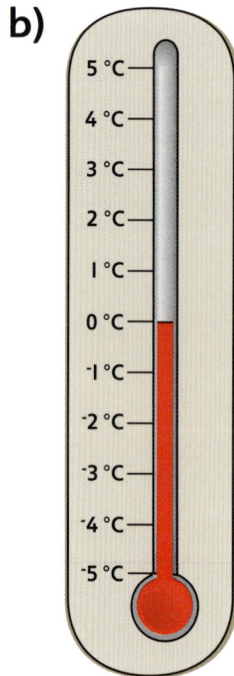

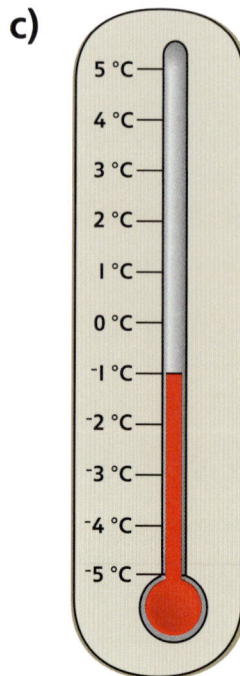

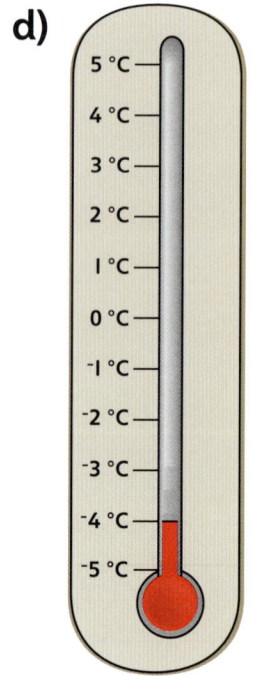

a)

b)

c)

d)

2 a) Start on 10. Count back to ⁻10.

... 3, 2, 1, ⁻1, ⁻2, ⁻3 ...
My teacher says I keep making a mistake.
I wonder what it is.

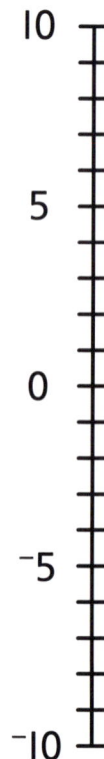

10

5

0

⁻5

⁻10

b) Start on ⁻10. Count on to 10.

3 Say the next two numbers in the sequences.
Use the number line to help you.

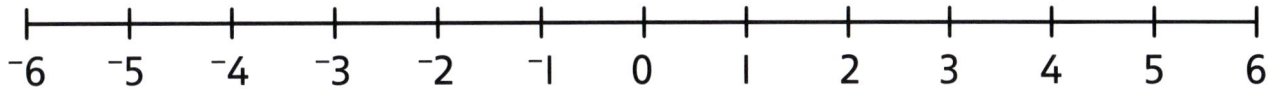

CHALLENGE

```
├──┼──┼──┼──┼──┼──┼──┼──┼──┼──┼──┼──┤
⁻6  ⁻5  ⁻4  ⁻3  ⁻2  ⁻1   0   1   2   3   4   5   6
```

a) 5, 4, 3, 2, 1, 0, ⁻1, ☐ , ☐

b) 2, 1, 0, ⁻1, ⁻2, ⁻3, ⁻4, ☐ , ☐

c) ⁻4, ⁻3, ⁻2, ☐ , ☐

4 What numbers are shown by the arrows?

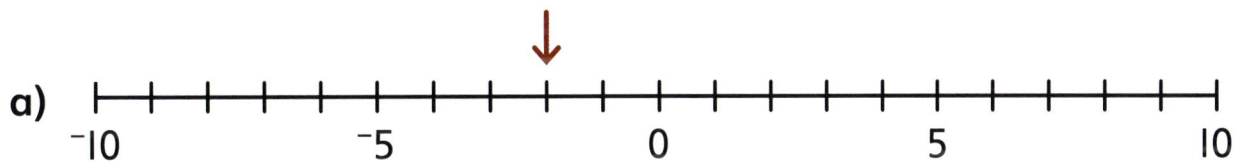

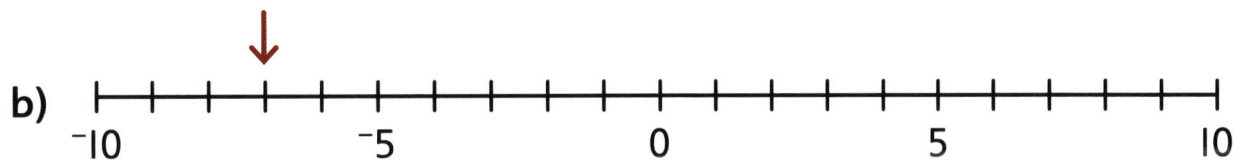

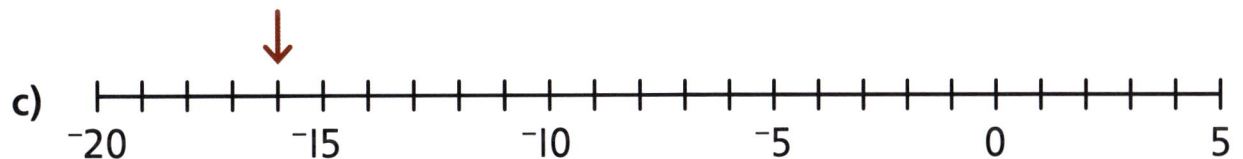

a)
```
          ↓
├┼┼┼┼┼┼┼┼┼┼┼┼┼┼┼┼┼┼┼┤
⁻10        ⁻5        0         5        10
```

b)
```
      ↓
├┼┼┼┼┼┼┼┼┼┼┼┼┼┼┼┼┼┼┼┤
⁻10        ⁻5        0         5        10
```

c)
```
     ↓
├┼┼┼┼┼┼┼┼┼┼┼┼┼┼┼┼┼┼┼┤
⁻20      ⁻15       ⁻10       ⁻5        0         5
```

155

→ Practice book 5C p114

Count through zero

Discover

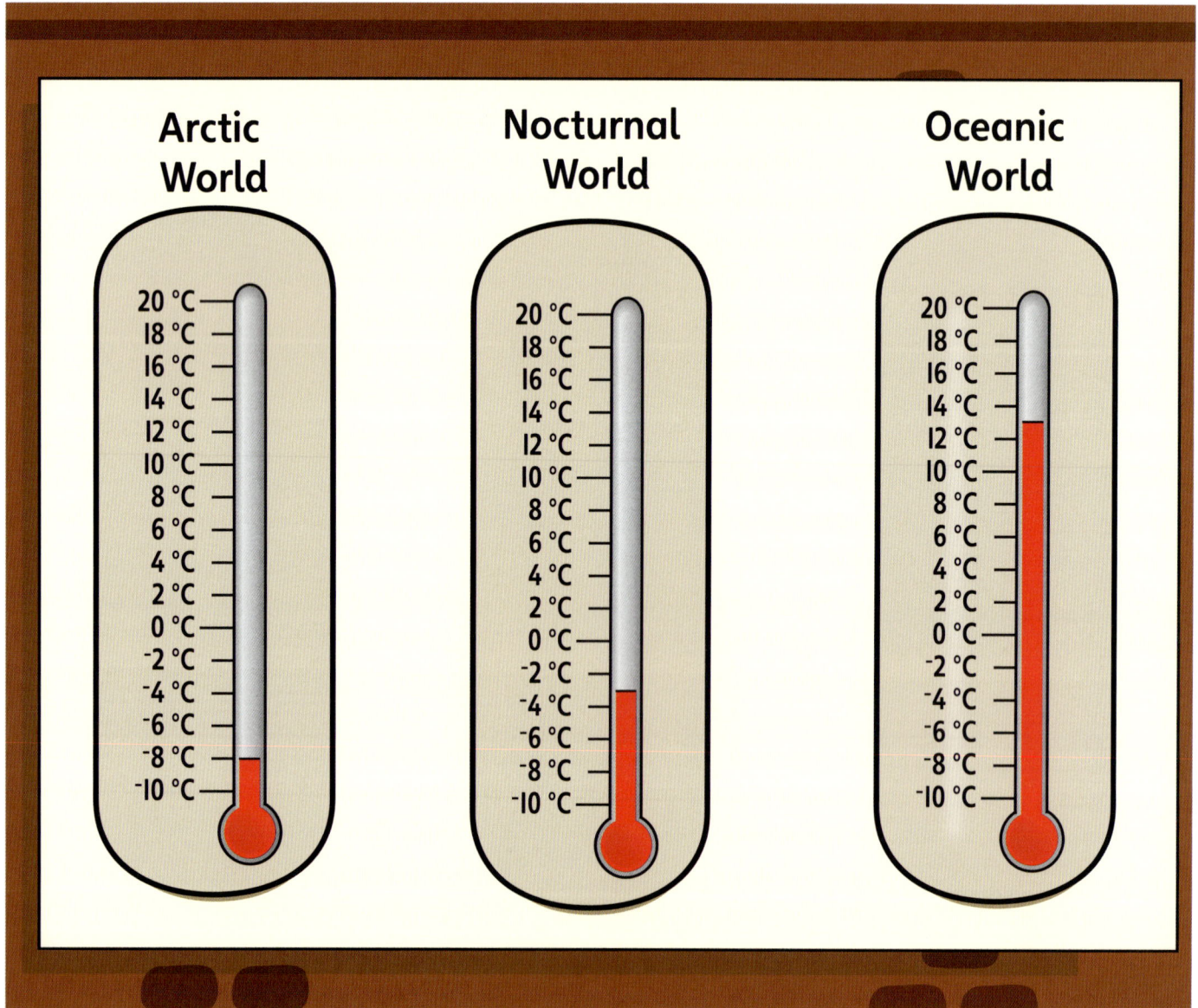

1 a) Examine the scales on the thermometers. What do you notice?

b) What is the temperature in each 'world'?

Share

a) The thermometers go up in jumps of 2 °C. For example, there are 8 intervals from 0 °C to 16 °C.

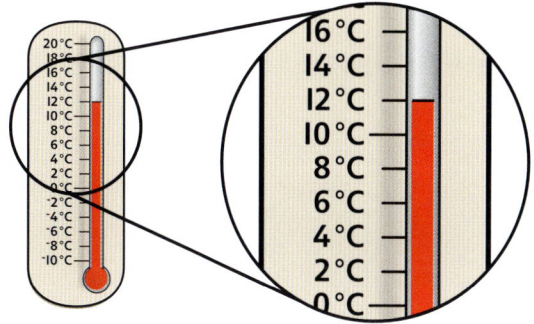

b)

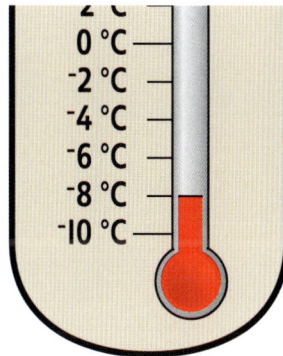

Arctic World is at exactly ⁻8 °C.

Temperature is measured in degrees Celsius. This is written as °C.

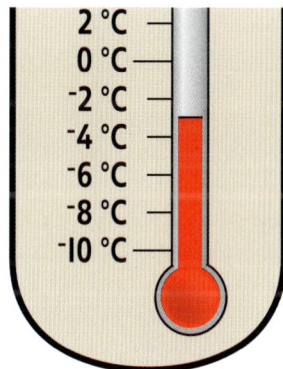

Nocturnal World is between ⁻2 °C and ⁻4 °C.

This is ⁻3 °C.

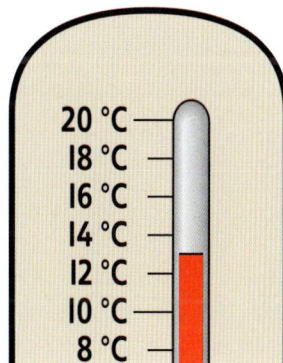

Oceanic World is above 0° C. It is between 12 °C and 14 °C.

This is 13 °C.

Think together

1 Talk about the scales on these thermometers. Read the temperatures accurately.

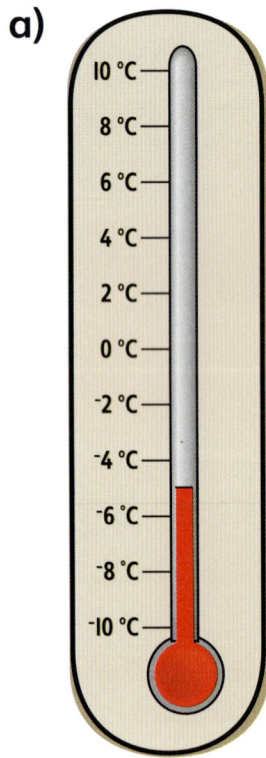

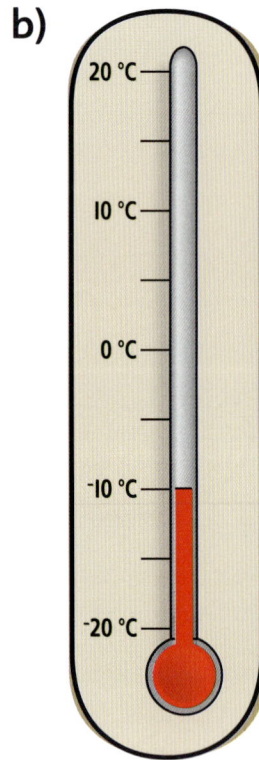

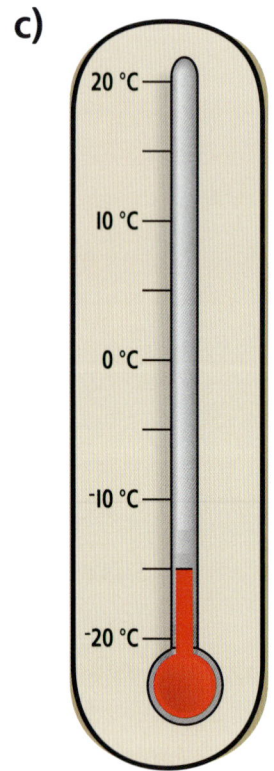

a)

| 10 °C |
| 8 °C |
| 6 °C |
| 4 °C |
| 2 °C |
| 0 °C |
| ⁻2 °C |
| ⁻4 °C |
| ⁻6 °C |
| ⁻8 °C |
| ⁻10 °C |

b)

| 20 °C |
| 10 °C |
| 0 °C |
| ⁻10 °C |
| ⁻20 °C |

c)

| 20 °C |
| 10 °C |
| 0 °C |
| ⁻10 °C |
| ⁻20 °C |

2 a) Count on from ⁻50 to 50 in 10s.
Count back from 50 to ⁻50 in 10s.

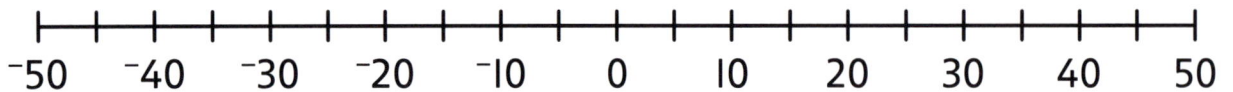

```
├─┼─┼─┼─┼─┼─┼─┼─┼─┼─┼─┼─┼─┼─┼─┼─┼─┼─┼─┼─┤
⁻50   ⁻40   ⁻30   ⁻20   ⁻10    0    10    20    30    40    50
```

b) Count on from ⁻50 to 50 in 5s.
Count back from 50 to ⁻50 in 5s.

3 Are these children correct?

CHALLENGE

I am counting back from 10 in 5s. One of the numbers I will say is ⁻20.

I am counting back from 5 in 2s. I will say ⁻20 too.

I am counting back from 8 in 4s. I will say ⁻20 too.

Lee

Zac

Emma

I am going to use a number line to help me work this out. I will start at the number and count back through 0.

→ Practice book 5C p117

Compare and order negative numbers

Discover

Hmm. That's strange, I think the fridge is cooler than the freezer.

Temperature
Fridge   4 °C
Freezer   -18 °C

Alex

1 a) Discuss Alex's thinking. Is she right? How would you compare and order these two numbers?

b) How far is each temperature from 0 °C?

Share

a) 18 is greater than 4, but a negative number is always less than a **positive** number.

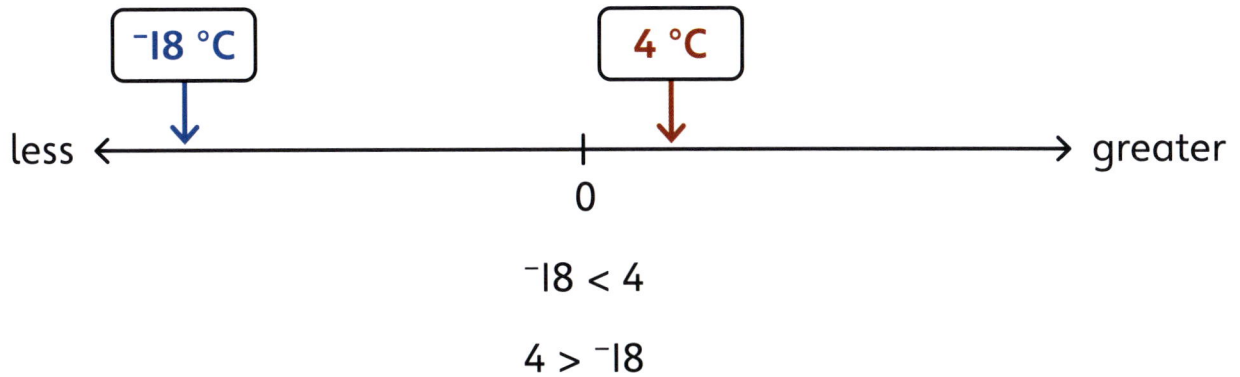

$$^-18 < 4$$

$$4 > ^-18$$

b)

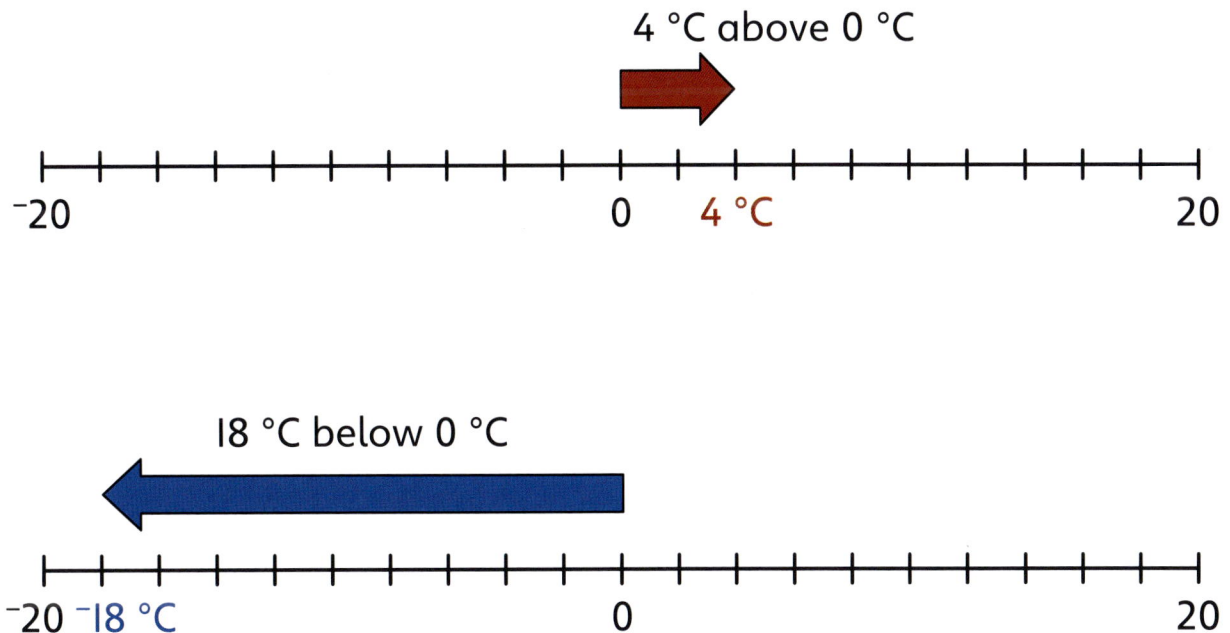

Think together

1 Complete the comparisons using <, > or =.

a) 0 ◯ ⁻10

b) ⁻5 ◯ ⁻10

c) 10 ◯ ⁻10

d) ⁻10 ◯ ⁻1

e) ⁻10 ◯ 1

f) ⁻9 ◯ ⁻10

⁻10 — — — — — — — — — 0 — — — — — — — — — 10

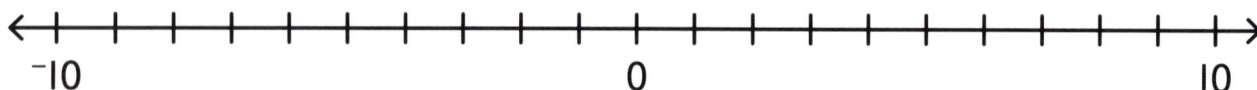

2 Order the set of numbers from smallest to greatest.

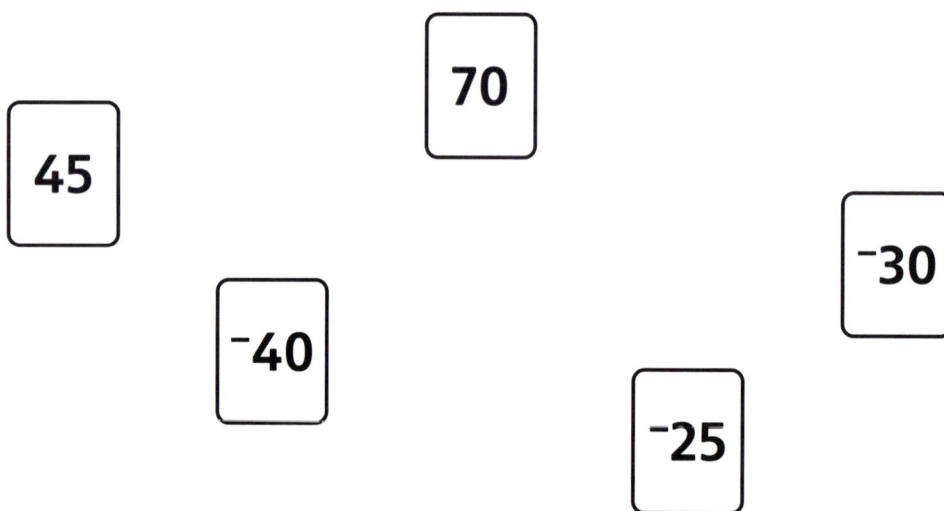

70

45

⁻30

⁻40

⁻25

smallest ☐ < ☐ < ☐ < ☐ < ☐ greatest

CHALLENGE

3 Estimate the numbers shown on the number lines.

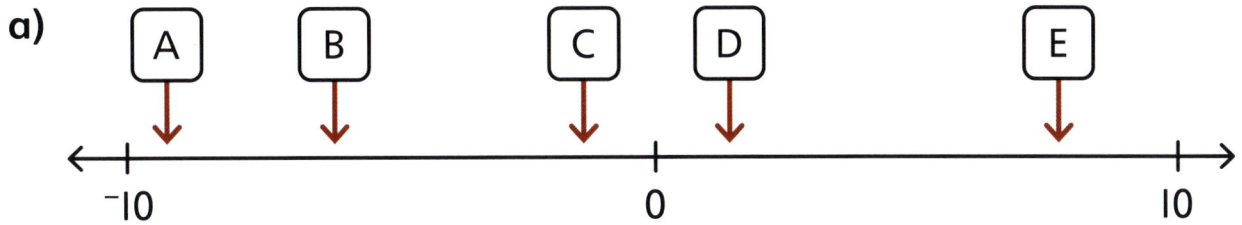

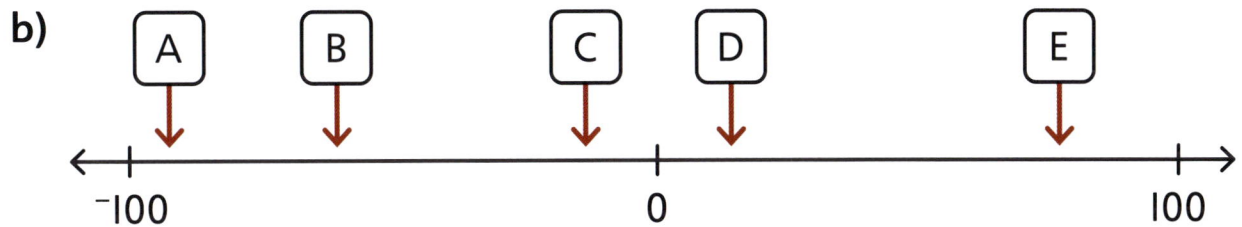

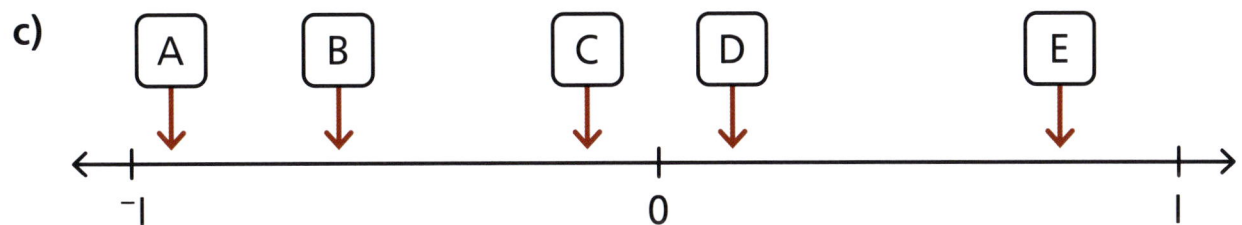

a)

A   B   C   D   E

←——|————————————————————|————————————————————|——→
  ⁻10   0   10

b)

A   B   C   D   E

←——|————————————————————|————————————————————|——→
  ⁻100   0   100

c)

A   B   C   D   E

←——|————————————————————|————————————————————|——→
  ⁻1   0   1

→ **Practice book 5C p120**

Find the difference

Discover

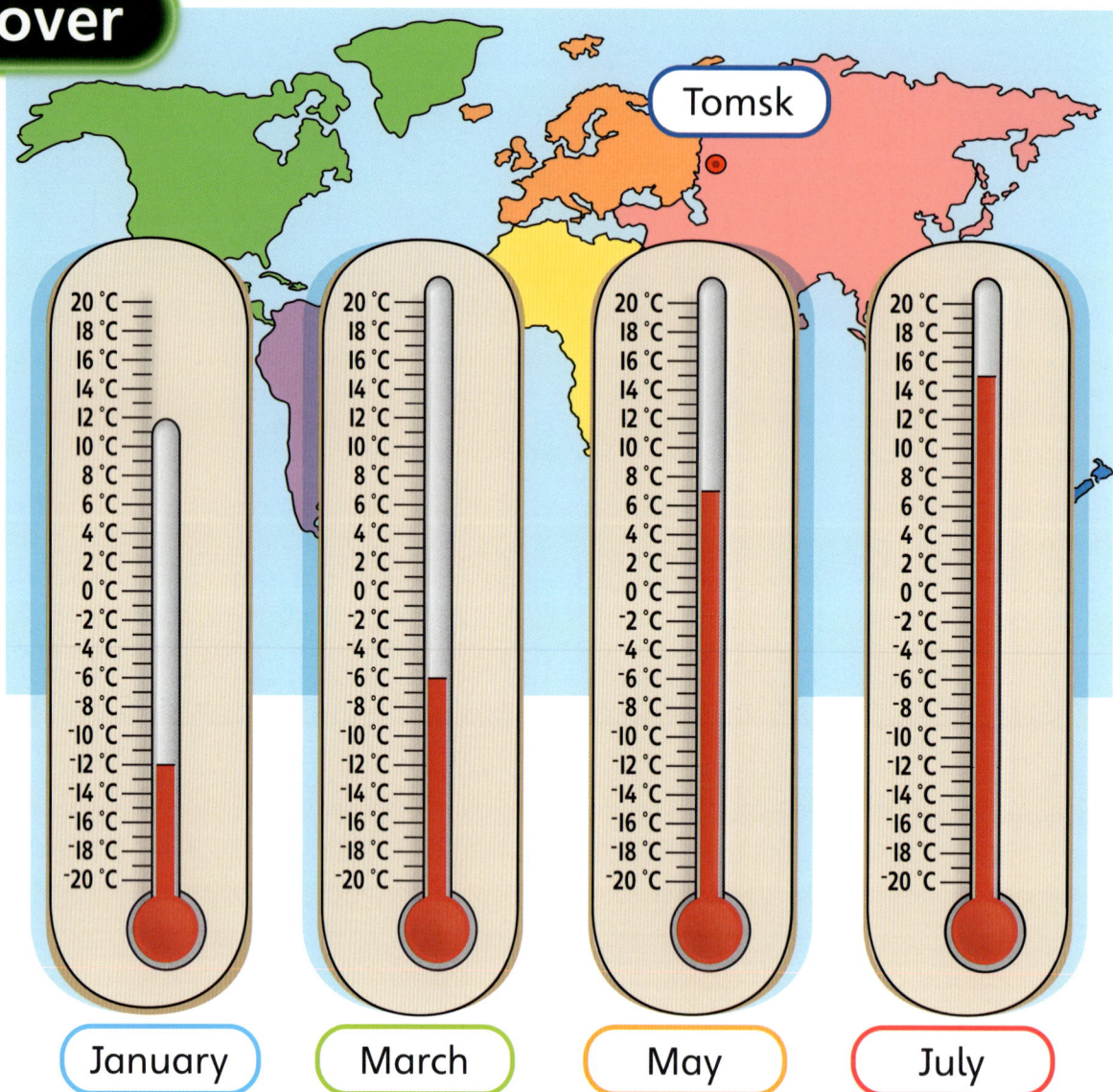

Tomsk

| 20 °C | 20 °C | 20 °C | 20 °C |
| January | March | May | July |

1 **a)** In Tomsk, how much warmer is May than March?

b) Which two months have the greatest difference in temperature?

What is the greatest difference?

Share

a) The temperature in March is ⁻6 °C.

The temperature in May is 7 °C.

> I used a number line and counted how many degrees warmer it was. First I counted to 0, then on to 7.

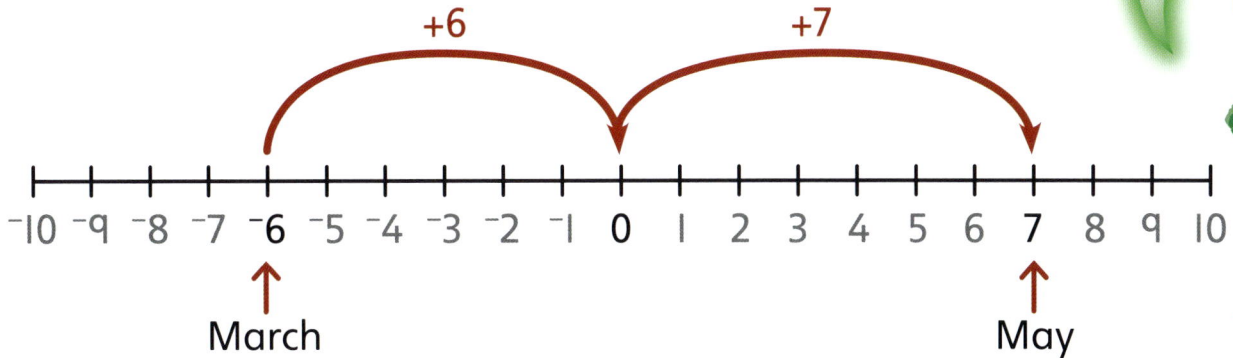

In Tomsk, May is 13 °C warmer than March.

b) The two months that have the greatest temperature difference are January and July.

> January has the coldest temperature and July has the warmest.

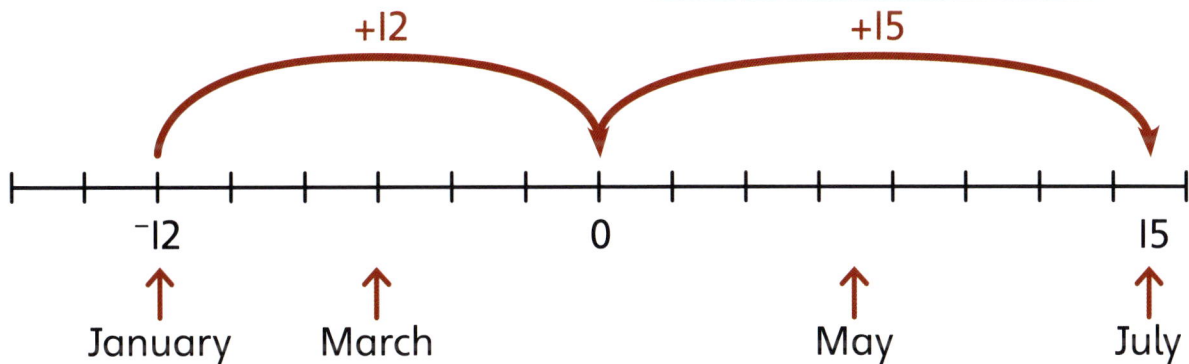

The difference in temperature between January and July is 27 °C.

> The difference between ⁻12 and 0 is 12 °C.
> The difference between 0 and 15 is 15 °C.
> I added 12 and 15 to get 27 °C.

165

Think together

1 The table shows the temperatures in New York and Cairo.

New York	Cairo
⁻12 °C	9 °C

How much warmer is the temperature in Cairo than in New York?

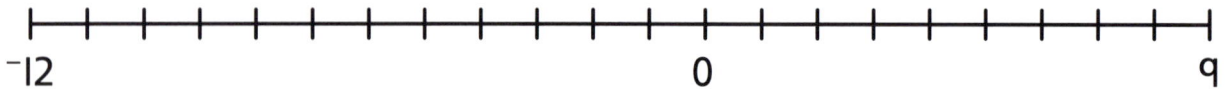

⁻12   0   9

2 A hotel has floors above and below ground.

Mrs Dean gets into the lift on floor 14.

She travels to the underground car park on floor ⁻5.

How many floors does she travel down?

> I wonder which floors are above ground and which are below ground.

CHALLENGE

3 The thermometers show the temperatures at different times of the day in a city.

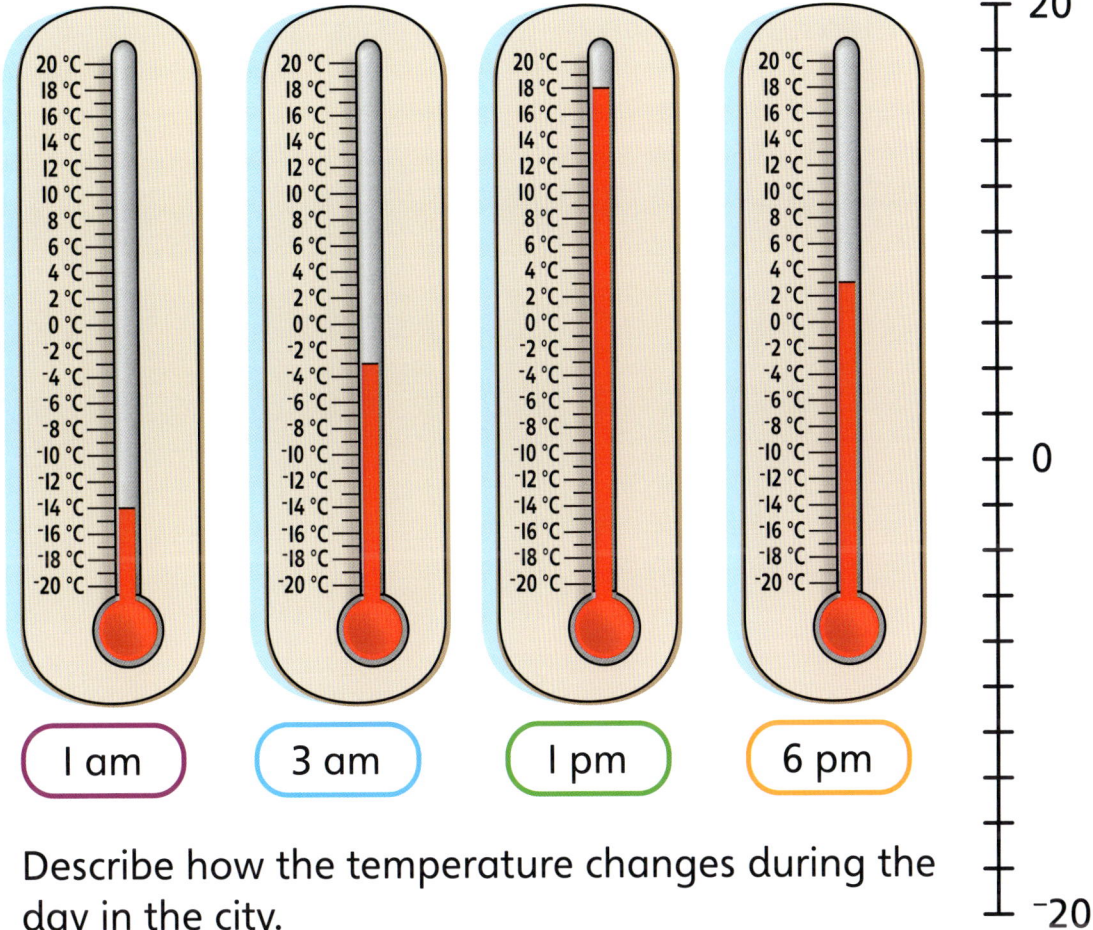

(I am)   (3 am)   (I pm)   (6 pm)

20

0

−20

Describe how the temperature changes during the day in the city.

I will talk about how much it **increases** and **decreases**. I will use the number line to help me.

I might turn it into a weather report and present it to a partner.

167

→ Practice book 5C p123

End of unit check

1 What is the temperature shown on the thermometer?

A 4 °C

B ⁻4 °C

C 6 °C

D ⁻6 °C

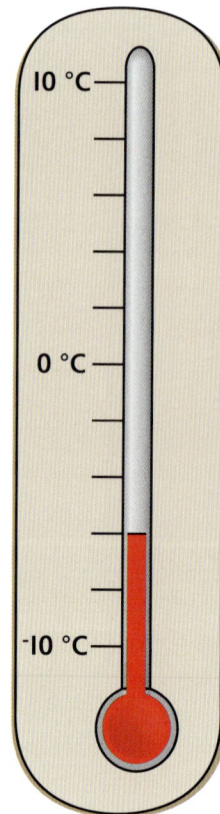

2 What number comes next?

20   15   10   5   0

A ⁻1

B ⁻5

C ⁻10

D 5

3 What is the missing number?

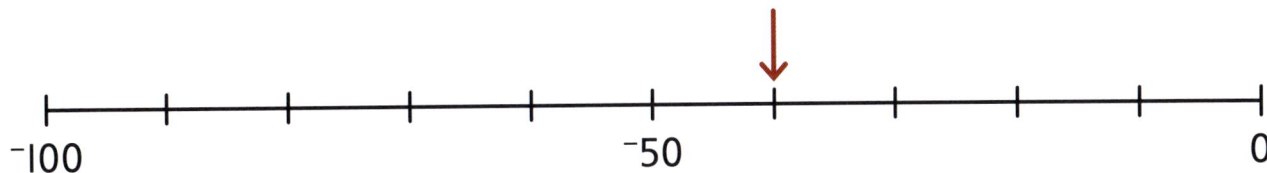

-100 -50 0

A -60 B -4 C -40 D -6

4 Which statement is incorrect?

A $-9 < -7$

B $-10 > -11$

C $-3 < 2$

D $2 < -7$

5 What is the difference between -8 and 5?

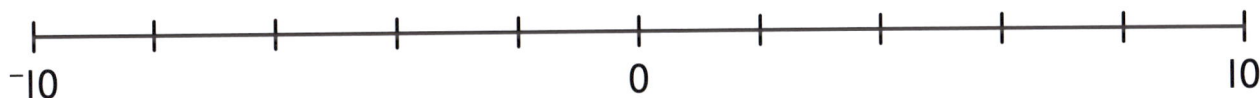

-10 0   10

A 3   B 12   C 13   D 15

6 Count on in steps of 5 from -21. Write down the numbers you will say.

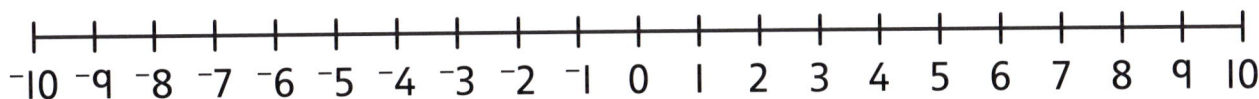

-10 -9 -8 -7 -6 -5 -4 -3 -2 -1 0 1 2 3 4 5 6 7 8 9 10

169

→ Practice book 5C p126

Unit 16
Measure – converting units

In this unit we will …

⚡ Convert between metric units of length, mass, volume and capacity

⚡ Recognise imperial units and understand how to convert them into metric units

⚡ Convert between units of time

⚡ Read timetables and understand the information they show

⚡ Solve problems based on measures

How many centimetres are approximately the same as 5 inches?

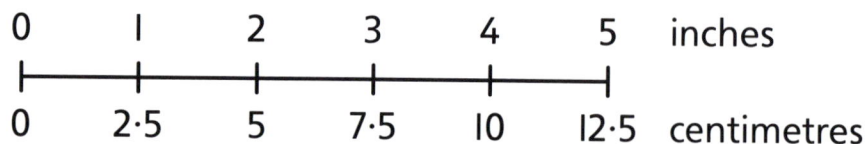

inches	0	1	2	3	4	5
centimetres	0	2·5	5	7·5	10	12·5

Here are some maths words we will be using. Are any of these words new?

convert   metric units   imperial units

kilo   kilogram   gram   milli

millimetre   centimetre   metre

kilometre   litre   millilitre

pound (lb)   ounce (oz)   inch (in)

foot (ft)   yard (yd)   pint   gallon

stone (st)   approximately   timetable

How many millilitres of orange juice are in this jug?

1 litre

0·5

0

Kilograms and kilometres

Discover

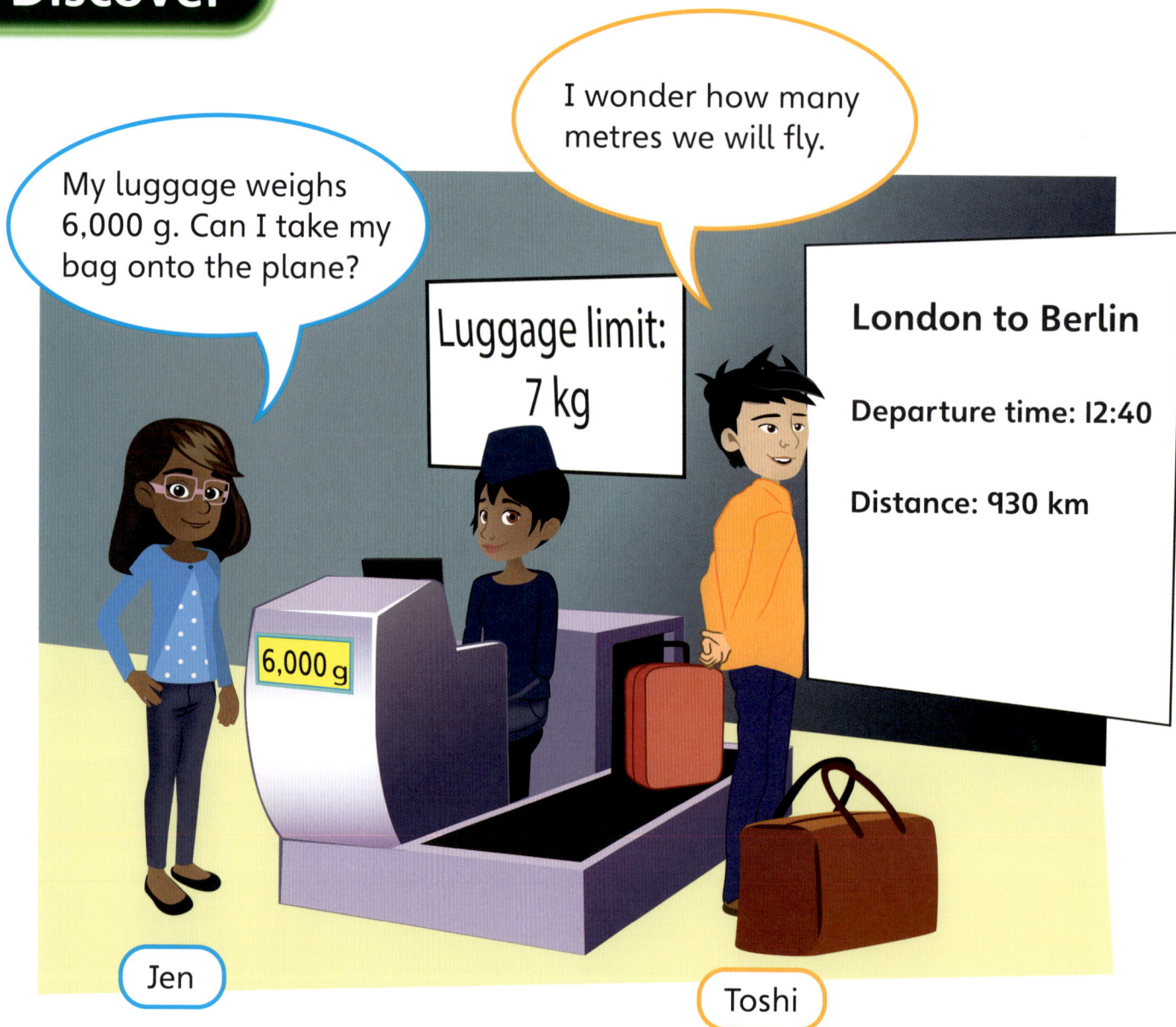

Speech bubble (Jen): My luggage weighs 6,000 g. Can I take my bag onto the plane?

Speech bubble (Toshi): I wonder how many metres we will fly.

Sign: Luggage limit: 7 kg

Scale display: 6,000 g

Sign: **London to Berlin**

Departure time: 12:40

Distance: 930 km

Jen

Toshi

1 **a)** How many metres is it from London to Berlin?

b) Can Jen take her bag on to the plane?

Share

a)

1 km
1,000 m

Kilometres (km) and kilograms (kg) both begin with '**kilo**'. The prefix 'kilo' comes from Greek. It means 'thousand'.

1 kilometre = 1,000 metres

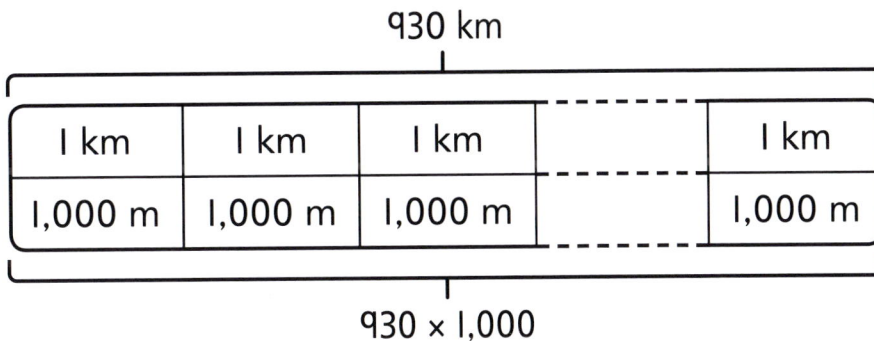

930 km

1 km	1 km	1 km		1 km
1,000 m	1,000 m	1,000 m		1,000 m

930 × 1,000

HTh	TTh	Th	H	T	O	
			9	3	0	km
9	3	0	0	0	0	m

To convert between kilometres and metres, I multiplied by 1,000. I did this by moving each digit three places to the left.

9 hundreds become 9 hundred thousands.

3 tens become 3 ten thousands.

930 × 1,000 = 930,000

It is 930,000 metres from London to Berlin.

b) 1 kilogram = 1,000 grams

Th	H	T	O	•	Tth	Hth	
6	0	0	0	•			g
			6	•			kg

6,000 ÷ 1,000 = 6

6 kg < 7 kg, so Jen can take her bag onto the plane.

To convert from a smaller unit (grams) into a larger unit (kilograms), I used division.

Think together

1 These scales measure mass in grams.

a) What will the scales show when the rucksack is placed on them?

b) What is the mass of each bag in kg?

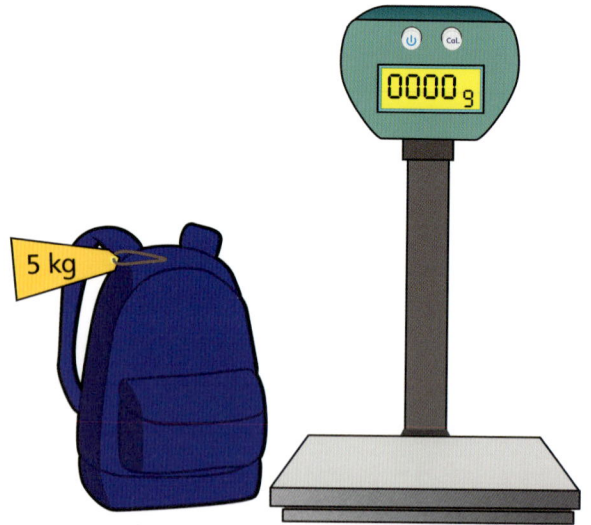

5 kg

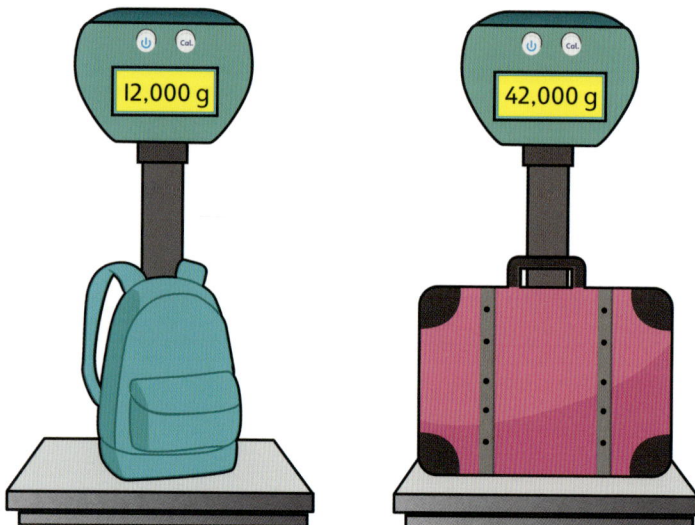

12,000 g

42,000 g

2 Complete these conversions.

a) 3 km = ☐ m

5 km = ☐ m

17 km = ☐ m

4·8 km = ☐ m

11·3 km = ☐ m

0·6 km = ☐ m

b) 6,000 m = ☐ km

19,000 m = ☐ km

260,000 m = ☐ km

7,600 m = ☐ km

750 m = ☐ km

26,500 m = ☐ km

CHALLENGE

3 Lee is working out how many grams are in 8·3 kg.

> I know how to multiply by 1,000 quickly! I am going to write three 0s on the end.

Lee

> It is not as easy as that! I think I need to move the digits.

What mistake has Lee made?

How can you work out the correct answer?

175

→ Practice book 5C p128

Millimetres and millilitres

Discover

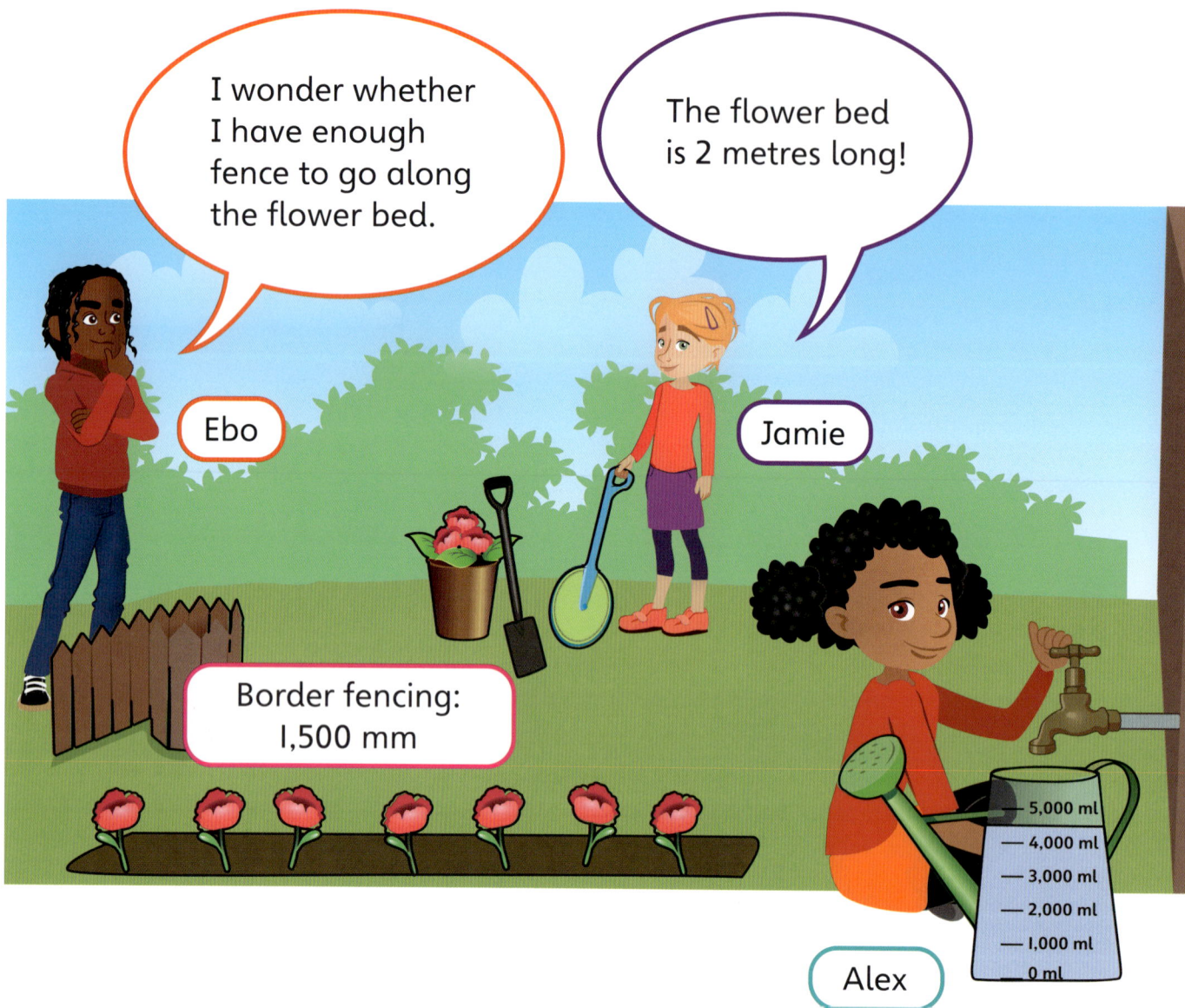

I wonder whether I have enough fence to go along the flower bed.

Ebo

The flower bed is 2 metres long!

Jamie

Border fencing: 1,500 mm

5,000 ml
4,000 ml
3,000 ml
2,000 ml
1,000 ml
0 ml

Alex

1 a) Has Ebo got enough fencing to go along the flower bed?

b) How many litres of water has Alex put in the watering can?

Share

a) 1 m = 100 cm and 1 cm = 10 millimetres (mm)

100 × 10 = 1,000 so there are 1,000 mm in 1 m.

Ebo has 1,500 mm of fencing.
The flower bed is 2 m long.

2 m = 2,000 mm

1,500 < 2,000, so Ebo does
not have enough fencing to
go along the flower bed.

> Millimetres and millilitres
> both begin with '**milli**'. The
> prefix 'milli' comes from
> Latin. We use it to mean 'one
> thousandth' of something.

Th	H	T	O	
			2	m
2	0	0	0	mm

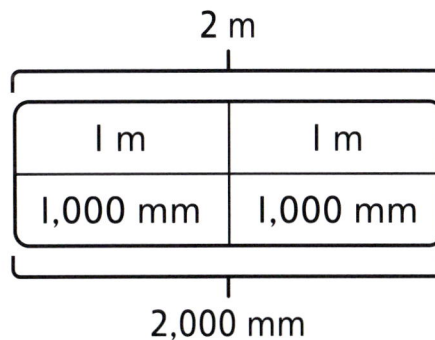

2 m

1 m	1 m
1,000 mm	1,000 mm

2,000 mm

b) Alex has put 4,500 ml of
water in the watering can.

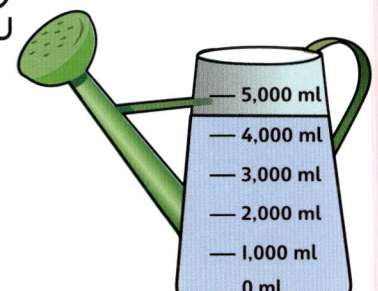

> 1,000 ml = 1 l, so I divided by
> 1,000 to convert from millilitres
> to litres.

4,500 ml

1,000 ml	1,000 ml	1,000 ml	1,000 ml	500 ml
1 l	1 l	1 l	1 l	0·5 l

4·5 l

4,500 ÷ 1,000 = 4·5

Alex has put 4·5 l of water in the watering can.

5,000 ml
4,000 ml
3,000 ml
2,000 ml
1,000 ml
0 ml

177

Think together

1 How many millilitres of plant food are in the bottle?

> To convert from a larger unit to a smaller unit you multiply. To convert from a smaller unit to a larger unit you divide.

PLANT FOOD

0·7 litres

2 Complete these conversions.

a) 4 l = ☐ ml

9 m = ☐ mm

14 l = ☐ ml

b) 4,000 mm = ☐ m

19,000 mm = ☐ m

185,000 mm = ☐ m

c) 8·2 l = ☐ ml

24·5 m = ☐ mm

0·6 l = ☐ ml

d) 6,900 mm = ☐ m

750 ml = ☐ litres

26,500 ml = ☐ l

3 **a)** Complete the table.

CHALLENGE

Length	Capacity
1 mm = $\dfrac{1}{\boxed{}}$ of a metre	1 ml = $\dfrac{1}{\boxed{}}$ of a litre
1 cm = $\dfrac{1}{\boxed{}}$ of a metre	
1 m = 1,000 _____	1 l = 1,000 _____
1 m = 100 _____	
1 _____ is 0·001 _____	1 _____ is 0·001 _____

Explain your answers.

b) What is the same about the two columns? What is different?

For the last line, I will look at the place value of the digit 1 to help me.

I can think of more than one possible answer for length in that last part!

→ **Practice book 5C p131**

Convert units of length

Discover

I know that each Ip coin is about I cm long.

Charity chain of coins
Let's raise I km of Ip coins for charity!

I wonder how much money we will raise!

I think we would raise more money if we placed them on their sides. Each coin is about I mm thick.

Jamilla   Olivia   Zac

I **a)** How many Ip coins do the children need to lay flat to make a line I km long?

How much money will they have raised for charity?

b) How much more money would the children raise if they use Zac's idea and placed the coins on their sides?

Share

a)

I **milli**metre = $\frac{1}{1,000}$ m   I **centi**metre = $\frac{1}{100}$ m

I **kilo**metre = 1,000 m

> The base **metric unit** of length is the metre.

I m
100 cm
1,000 mm

One Ip coin is I cm long.

100 Ip coins will be I m.

So each metre is £1.

I km is 1,000 m, so the children will have raised £1,000.

> I know there are 100p in £1 and that 100 Ip coins laid flat measure 100 cm, which is I m. So I multiplied £1 by 1,000 m to get £1,000.

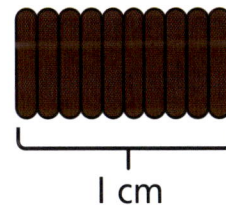

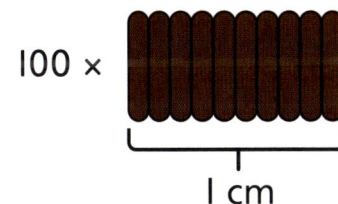

b) I cm = 10 mm. Each coin is I mm thick.

So, there are 10 coins for every I cm.

I m = 100 cm

So, in I m there are 10 × 100 = 1,000 coins.

1,000p = £10   I km = 1,000 m

So, in I km there must be coins worth £10 × 1,000 = £10,000.

£10,000 − £1,000 = £9,000

The children would raise £9,000 more if they placed the coins on their sides.

I cm

100 ×

I cm

= 1,000p = £10

Think together

1 Here are some barrels.

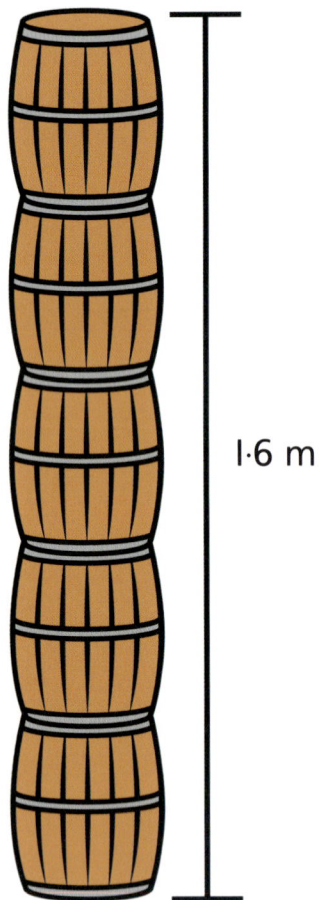

1·6 m

Remember. There are 100 centimetres in a metre.

a) Convert 1·6 m to cm.

1·6 m = ☐ cm

b) How tall is each barrel?

2 **a)** Max walks $\frac{1}{2}$ km to Bella's house.

Put these steps in the correct order to show how to work out how far he walks in centimetres.

> **A** Change metres into centimetres by multiplying by 100.

> **B** Convert $\frac{1}{2}$ to a decimal.

> **C** Change kilometres into metres by multiplying by 1,000.

b) Now work out the answer.

3

When we convert between millilitres and litres or between grams and kilograms I only need to know how to multiply and divide by 1,000.

Reena

But when we convert between metric units of length, there seems to be more to remember!

Luis

CHALLENGE

mm   cm   m   km

Although there are more conversions, the numbers involved are very similar!

Explain what you need to do to convert between each pair of units and why.

→ **Practice book 5C p134**

Imperial units of length

Discover

The bird that swallowed my wedding ring was about 3 feet tall.

POLICE LINE UP

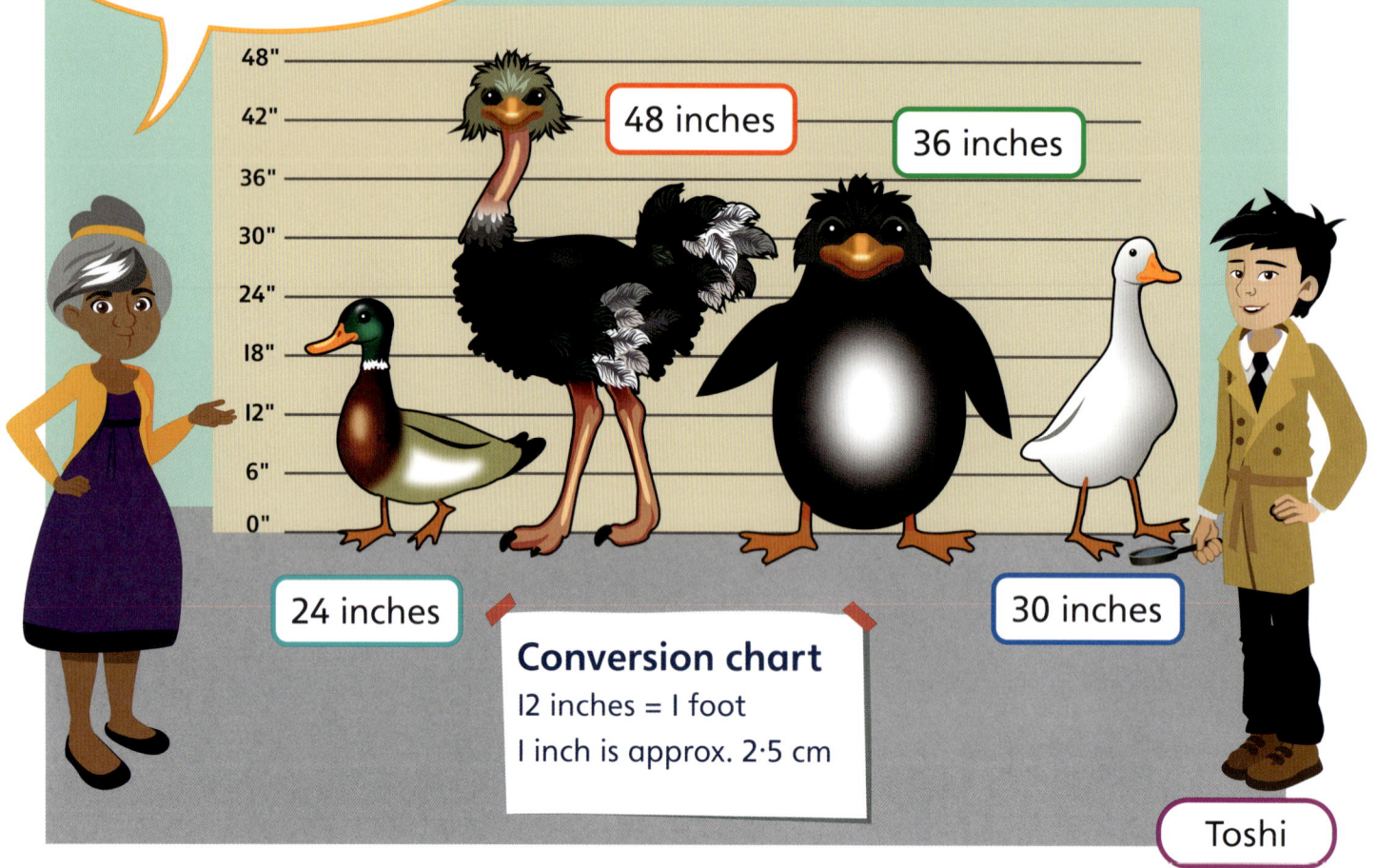

48"
42"
36"
30"
24"
18"
12"
6"
0"

48 inches

36 inches

24 inches

30 inches

Conversion chart

12 inches = 1 foot

1 inch is approx. 2·5 cm

Toshi

1 **a)** Which bird swallowed the ring?

b) How tall is the ostrich in metric units?

Share

Inches and feet are imperial units of length. Imperial units were used in the UK until the metric system was introduced in 1965. The metric system made things easier as it deals with 10s, 100s and 1,000s. Imperial units are still sometimes used.

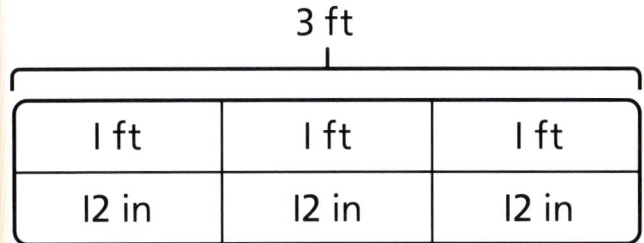

3 ft		
1 ft	1 ft	1 ft
12 in	12 in	12 in

12 inches 3 ft
12 inches
12 inches

a) 12 inches (in) = 1 foot (ft)

12 × 3 = 36

3 feet = 36 in

The penguin swallowed the ring.

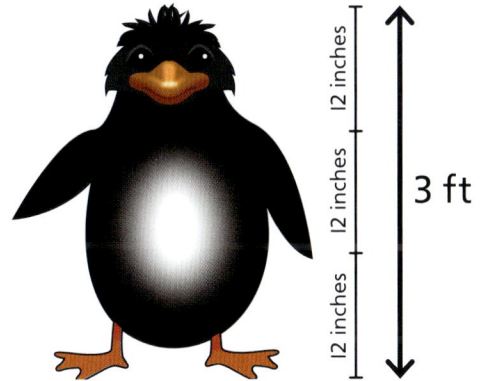

b) 1 inch is approximately 2·5 cm. The ostrich is 48 in tall.

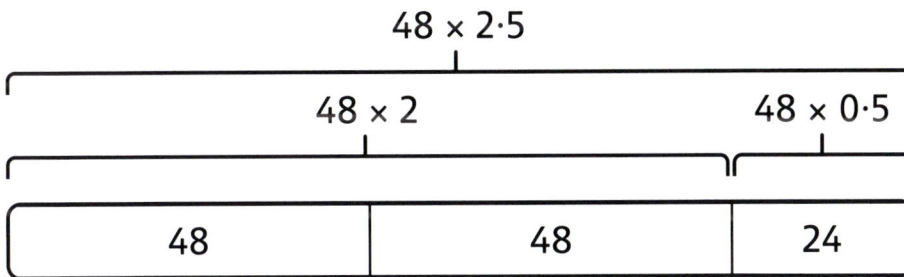

48 × 2·5

48 × 2		48 × 0·5

48	48	24

I knew that 48 × 0·5 means 48 lots of $\frac{1}{2}$. This is the same as finding half of 48!

48 × 2 = 96

48 × 0·5 = 24

96 + 24 = 120 cm

120 ÷ 100 = 1·2 m

The ostrich is 120 cm tall, which is the same as 1·2 m.

120 cm or 1·2 m

185

Think together

1 This emu is 5 ft and 3 in tall. How tall is it in inches?

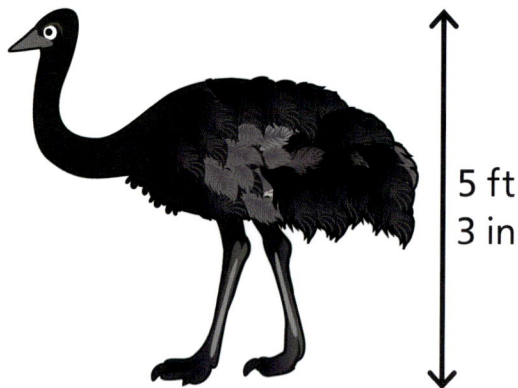

> 1 foot (ft) = 12 inches (in)

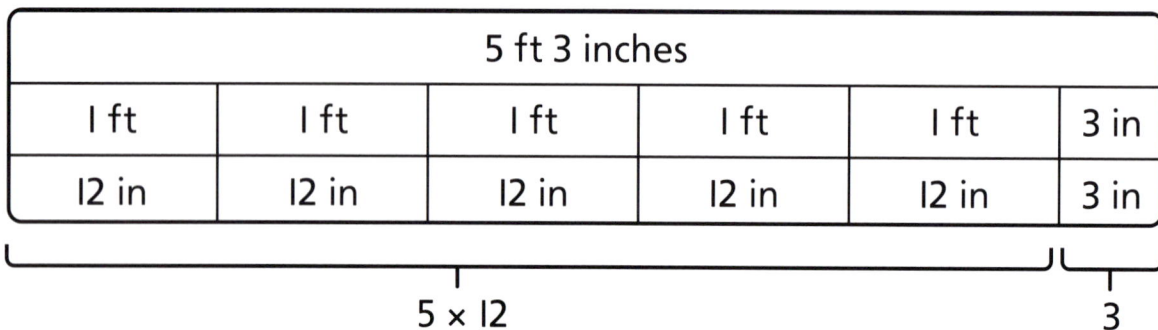

5 ft
3 in

5 ft 3 inches					
1 ft	1 ft	1 ft	1 ft	1 ft	3 in
12 in	12 in	12 in	12 in	12 in	3 in

5 × 12

3

$5 \times 12 = \boxed{}$ $\boxed{} + 3 = \boxed{}$

2 A duck's pond is 15 yds wide. How wide is it in inches?

> 1 **yard** (yd) = 3 feet (ft)

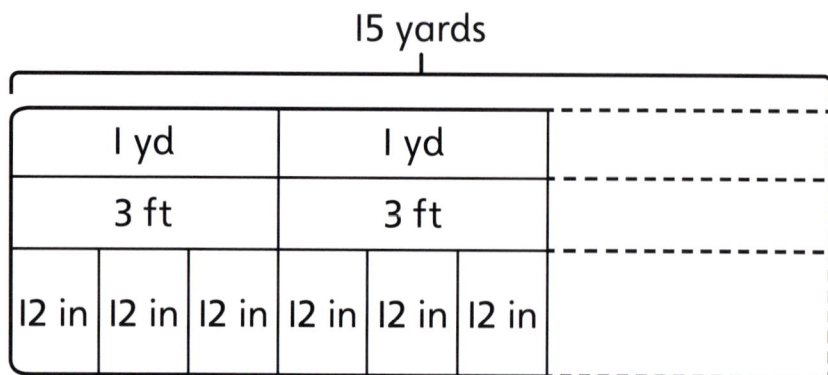

15 yards

1 yd		1 yd			
3 ft		3 ft			
12 in	12 in	12 in	12 in	12 in	12 in

I am going to multiply twice to find the answer: once to convert into feet and once to convert into inches.

CHALLENGE

3 Convert each of these imperial units into metric units.

Choose a range of metric units to convert to. For example, you could convert 1 inch into millimetres, 1 foot into centimetres and 1 yard into metres.

| 1 inch | 1 foot | 1 yard |

Explain how you can work out the answer.

Use these conversion facts to help.

1 inch is about the same as 2·5 cm.

10 mm = 1 cm

12 inches = 1 foot

100 cm = 1 m

3 feet = 1 yard

1,000 m = 1 km

I wonder if I will need to convert all the measurements into inches first.

I am going to use the fact that 1 inch is about the same as $2\frac{1}{2}$ cm to help me.

187

→ Practice book 5C p137

Imperial units of mass

Discover

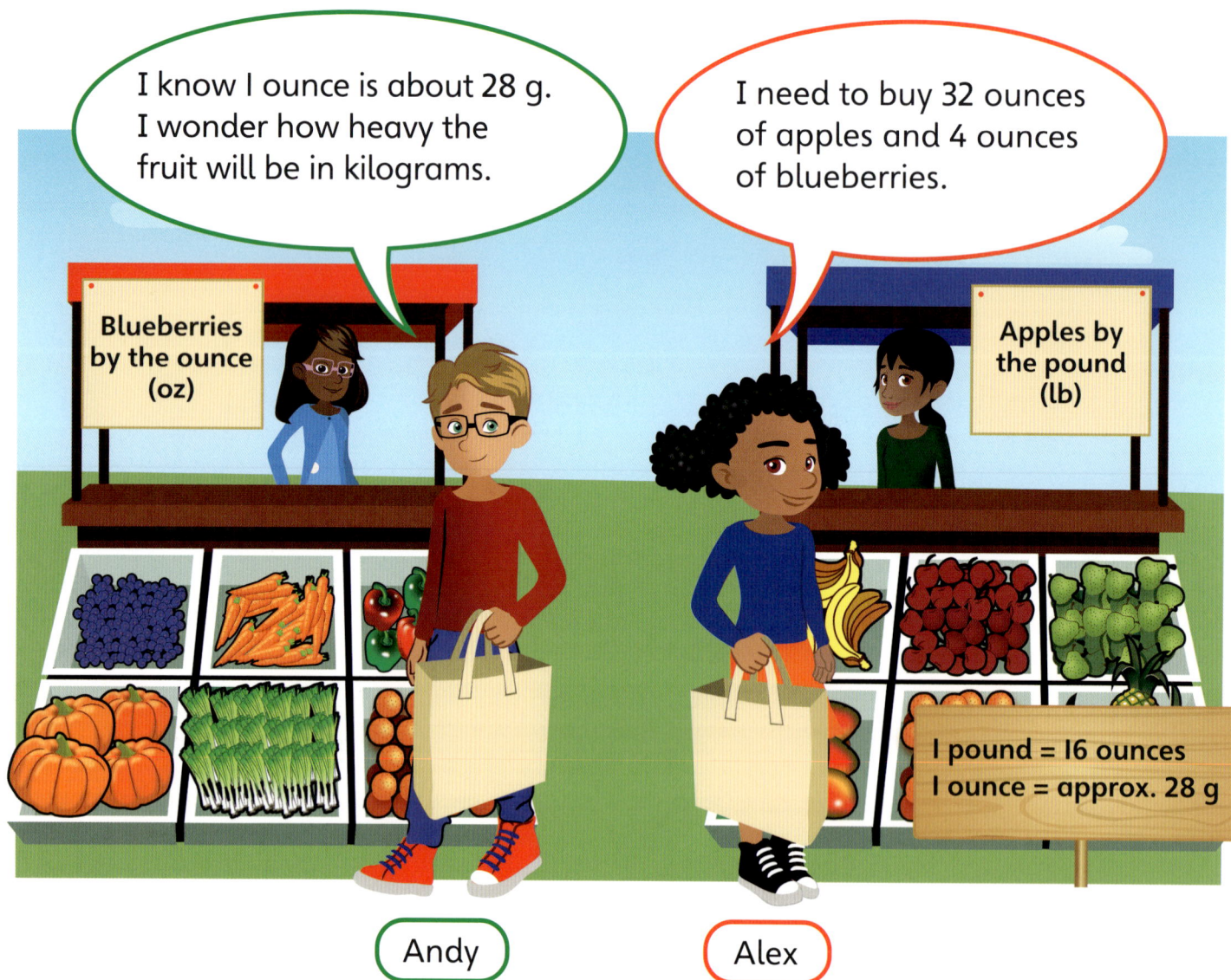

I know 1 ounce is about 28 g. I wonder how heavy the fruit will be in kilograms.

I need to buy 32 ounces of apples and 4 ounces of blueberries.

Blueberries by the ounce (oz)

Apples by the pound (lb)

1 pound = 16 ounces
1 ounce = approx. 28 g

Andy

Alex

1 a) How many **pounds** of each type of fruit should Alex ask for?

b) What will the total mass of Alex's fruit be in kilograms?

Share

a)

Pounds and **ounces** are imperial measures of mass. I pound (lb) equals 16 ounces (oz).

32 oz	
16 oz	16 oz
1 lb	1 lb

$32 \div 16 = 2$

$32 \text{ oz} = 2 \text{ lb}$

Alex should ask for 2 lbs of apples.

I calculated how many lots of 4 oz are in 16 oz to help with the second amount.

16 oz			
4 oz	4 oz	4 oz	4 oz

$1 \div 4 =$

1 lb			
$\frac{1}{4}$ lb	$\frac{1}{4}$ lb	$\frac{1}{4}$ lb	$\frac{1}{4}$ lb

$4 \text{ oz} = \frac{1}{4} \text{ lb}$

Alex should ask for $\frac{1}{4}$ of a pound of blueberries.

b) $32 + 4 = 36$

Alex's fruit will weigh 36 oz altogether.

I know that 1 oz is about 28 g. First I used long multiplication to convert into grams.

36×28

×	20	8
30	600	240
6	120	48

$600 + 240 + 120 + 48 = 1,008$

	Th	H	T	O
		6	0	0
		2	4	0
		1	2	0
+			4	8
	1	0	0	8
		1		

$36 \times 28 = 1,008$ $1,008 \div 1,000 = 1 \cdot 008$

Alex's fruit will weigh about 1,008 g, which is equal to $1 \cdot 008$ kg.

189

Think together

1 How many grams of raspberries are there in this container?

15 oz														
1 oz	1 oz	1 oz	1 oz	1 oz	1 oz	1 oz	1 oz	1 oz	1 oz	1 oz	1 oz	1 oz	1 oz	1 oz
28 g	28 g	28 g												

$28 \times 15 = \boxed{}$

2 a) There are 16 ounces in 1 pound.

1 lb															
1 oz	1 oz	1 oz	1 oz	1 oz	1 oz	1 oz	1 oz	1 oz	1 oz	1 oz	1 oz	1 oz	1 oz	1 oz	1 oz

Work out the number of ounces in these amounts.

4 lb $= \boxed{} \times \boxed{} = \boxed{}$ oz

10 lb $= \boxed{} \times \boxed{} = \boxed{}$ oz

$\frac{1}{2}$ lb $= \boxed{} \div \boxed{} = \boxed{}$ oz

b) Describe how you would find out what $\frac{3}{4}$ lb weighs in ounces.

CHALLENGE

3 **a)** Amelia is weighing a gift.

What will the second set of scales show if Amelia weighs the gift using them?

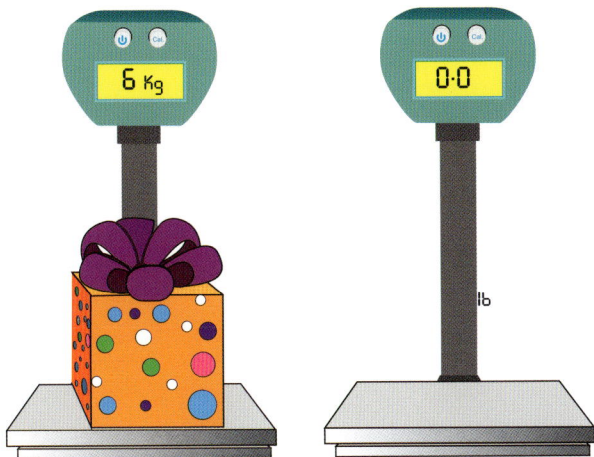

6 Kg

0·0

lb

I lb is approximately 450 g.

I kg is approximately 2·2 lb.

I think I need to multiply 450 by 6 to find the answer.

I do not think that is right. I think you need to multiply 2·2 by 6 instead!

b) How many pounds does the dog weigh?

Estimate the number of kilograms that the dog weighs.

3·5 st

I **stone** (st) = 14 lb

→ **Practice book 5C p140**

Imperial units of capacity

Discover

I gallon = 8 pints
I pint = approx. 570 ml

Jamilla

500 ml 500 ml 500 ml 500 ml 500 ml 500 ml 500 ml 500 ml

MILK 4 pints 4 pints 4 pints 4 pints 4 pints MILK MILK MILK

Water $\frac{3}{4}$ of a gallon   Water $\frac{3}{4}$ of a gallon   Water $\frac{3}{4}$ of a gallon   MILK MILK MILK MILK MILK MILK

I have one big bottle of water, which contains $\frac{3}{4}$ of a gallon.

I know that I pint is about the same as 570 ml. That is just over half a litre.

I wonder how many litres are the same as 4 pints.

Zac

Mo

1 **a)** How many litres are approximately equal to 4 **pints** of milk?

b) How many litres of water does Mo have?

Share

a)

Pints and **gallons** are imperial units of capacity.

4 pints

1 pint	1 pint	1 pint	1 pint
570 ml	570 ml	570 ml	570 ml

		5	7	0
×				4
	2	2	8	0
			2	

I used short multiplication to find the total in millilitres. Then I converted my answer into litres using division.

Th	H	T	O	•	Tth	Hth	
2	2	8	0	•			ml
			2	•	2	8	l

$2{,}280 \div 1{,}000 = 2{\cdot}28$

2·28 l are approximately equal to 4 pints of milk.

b) 1 gallon = 8 pints. So $\frac{3}{4}$ of a gallon = 6 pints.

1 pint = 570 ml

		5	7	0
×				6
	3	4	2	0
		4		

1 gallon
8 pints

$8 \div 4 = 2$

2 pints	2 pints	2 pints	2 pints

$\frac{1}{4}$ of a gallon

$2 \times 3 = 6$

2 pints	2 pints	2 pints	2 pints

$\frac{3}{4}$ of a gallon

Mo has 3,420 ml of water.

$3{,}420 \div 1{,}000 = 3{\cdot}42$ Mo has 3·42 l of water.

Think together

1 **a)** This water container holds 5 pints of water.

Approximately how many litres is this the same as?

5 pints

1 pint	1 pint	1 pint	1 pint	1 pint
570 ml	570 ml	570 ml	570 ml	570 ml

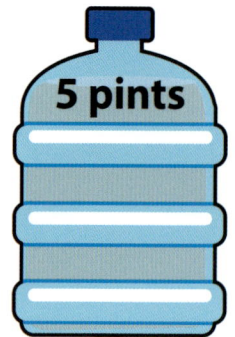

$5 \times \boxed{} = \boxed{}$

$\boxed{} \div 1{,}000 = \boxed{}$

b) What is the difference between the capacity of the container and 1 gallon? Write your answer in litres.

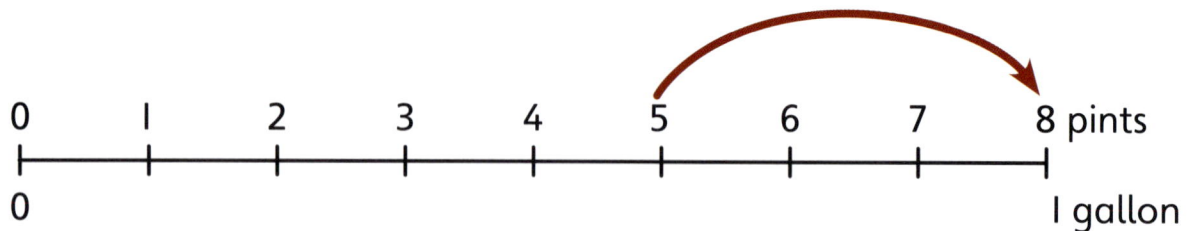

```
0    1    2    3    4    5    6    7    8 pints
├────┼────┼────┼────┼────┼────┼────┼────┤
0                                    1 gallon
```

1 gallon = 8 pints

2 Is half a pint of milk more or less than a 330 ml can of lemonade?

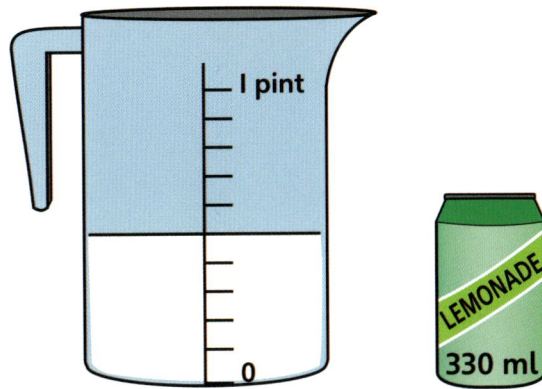

I pint

LEMONADE 330 ml

3 Can you fill up the bucket using the water in the container?

Will there be any left?

CHALLENGE

I gallon

4·3 litres

I gallon = 8 pints

I pint = approximately 570 ml

I gallon is 570 ml, so there is not enough water in the container to fill the bucket.

That is not right! You need to use the number of pints in a gallon to help.

195

Convert units of time

Discover

I am taking my phone back to the shop. The charger has broken already and I have only had it 39 days!

Buy one like mine! My battery has 5 bars and each bar takes an hour to charge.

Toshi

Amal

Warning: Low Battery

On charge for 285 minutes

1 a) How many weeks has Toshi had his phone for?

b) How many bars of Amal's battery should be charged fully?

How long until the next bar is charged?

Share

a)

There are 7 days in I week. 39 is not a multiple of 7, so I predicted that there would be a remainder.

39 days					
7 days	7 days	7 days	7 days	7 days	

35 days or 5 weeks   remainder

$39 \div 7 = 5$ remainder 4

35 days or 5 weeks

So 39 days equals 5 weeks and 4 days.

Toshi has had his phone for 5 weeks and 4 days.   remainder

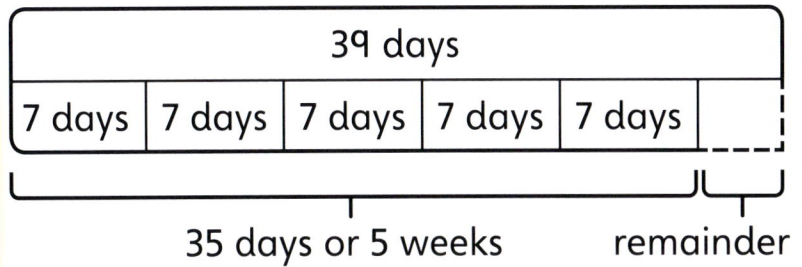

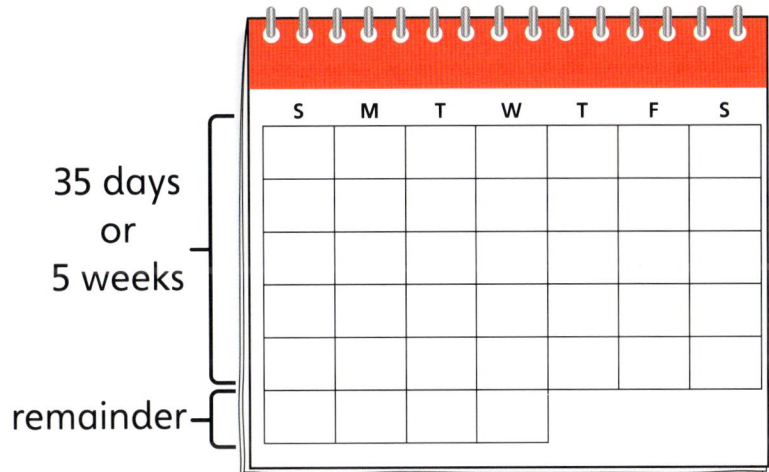

	S	M	T	W	T	F	S

b) 60 minutes equals I hour.

285 minutes is between 240 minutes (4 hours) and 300 minutes (5 hours).

285 minutes				
60 min	60 min	60 min	60 min	

240 minutes or 4 hours   remainder

Amal's phone should have 4 bars fully charged.

Four hours equals 240 minutes.

$285 - 240 = 45$

Amal's phone has been charging for 4 hours and 45 minutes.

$60 - 45 = 15$

There are 15 minutes left until the next bar is charged.

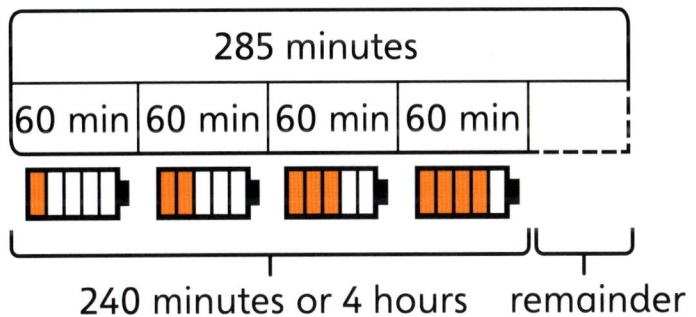

Think together

1 Amal's phone is downloading updates. How many minutes has his phone been downloading updates for?

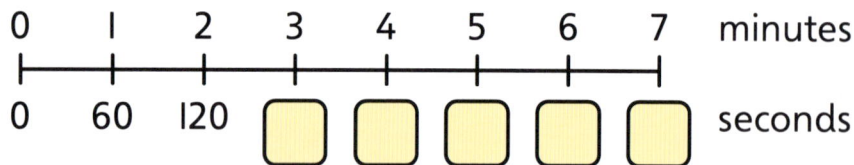

Downloading updates ...

378 seconds

```
0    1    2    3    4    5    6    7    minutes
├────┼────┼────┼────┼────┼────┼────┤
0    60  120  ☐    ☐    ☐    ☐    ☐    seconds
```

I am going to count up in 60s until I get close to 378 and then work out the difference.

I wonder if there is another way to work it out.

2 How many days is it until the sale ends?

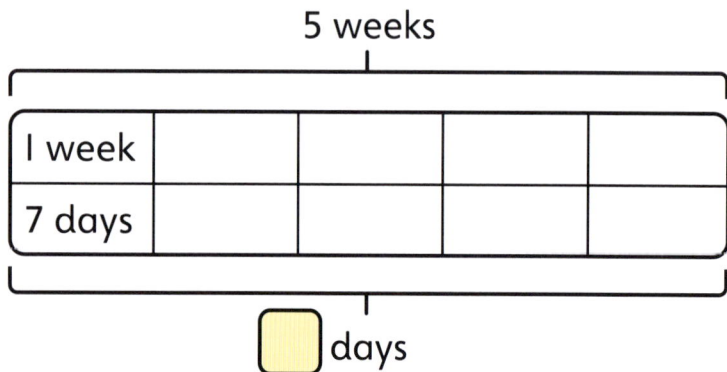

5 weeks

1 week				
7 days				

☐ days

Day 22 of our
5 week phone sale!
Be quick!!
Ends soon!

3 Jen's watch shows this time:

MON
13:00

CHALLENGE

In 24 hours, we will be on a ferry, sailing to Ireland!

In 30 hours, we will have arrived.

Jen

In 72 hours, we will be visiting my auntie.

Our ferry home is on Sunday at 11 pm.

In 93 hours, we will be going to a theme park!

a) What will Jen's watch look like at each of these times?

b) How many hours is it from the time on the watch until Jen returns home on the ferry?

I know that there are 24 hours in a day. I can use the remainder to work out each time.

199

→ **Practice book 5C p146**

Timetables – calculating

Discover

I go to Breakfast Club, so the school bus picks me up from Clemence Way at twenty-five minutes to 8.

Anderton Primary School Buses

Stop	Bus A	Bus B	Bus C
Nicolson Street	07:15	07:30	07:45
Clemence Way	07:35	07:50	08:05
Hart Lane Shops	07:42	07:57	08:12
Mason Avenue	07:46	08:01	08:16
Marigold Crescent	07:56	08:11	08:26
Anderton Primary School	08:05	08:20	

Emma

Max

1 **a)** What time does Emma arrive at school?

b) All the buses take the same time to get to school.
What time does Bus C arrive?

Share

a) Each column of the timetable shows a different bus. Each row shows a different place.

Stop	Bus A
Nicolson Street	07:15
Clemence Way	**07:35**
Hart Lane Shops	07:42
Mason Avenue	07:46
Marigold Crescent	07:56
Anderton Primary School	**08:05**

→ Twenty-five minutes to 8
= 7:35 am
= 07:35

> Timetables are usually written in 24-hour digital time, so you will have to convert first.

Emma catches Bus A. Emma arrives at school at 08:05 (five minutes past 8).

b)

> I used the information from the other buses to work out the hidden time.

Stop	Bus A	Bus B
Nicolson Street	07:15	07:30
Anderton Primary School	08:05	08:20

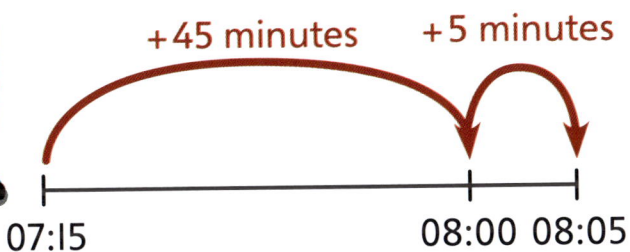

Bus A

+45 minutes   +5 minutes

07:15   08:00 08:05

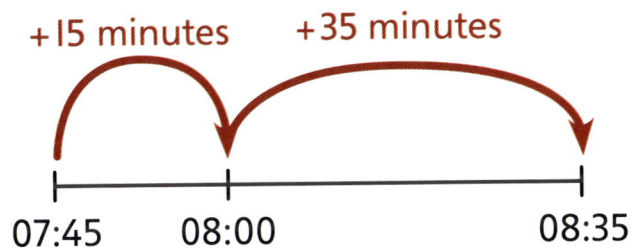

Bus C

+15 minutes   +35 minutes

07:45   08:00   08:35

Each bus takes 50 minutes to get from Nicholson Street to school.

Bus C arrives at school at 08:35.

Think together

1 Look at this train timetable.

Littleborough	14:13	14:43	15:13	15:43
Birchfield	14:37	15:07	–	16:07
Ashtown Parkway	15:09	15:39	–	16:39
Ashtown Central	15:20	15:50	16:00	16:50

a) Lexi gets on the 15:07 train at Birchfield.

What time does she arrive in Ashtown Central?

b) Andy gets on the 14:13 train at Littleborough.

14:13   14:37

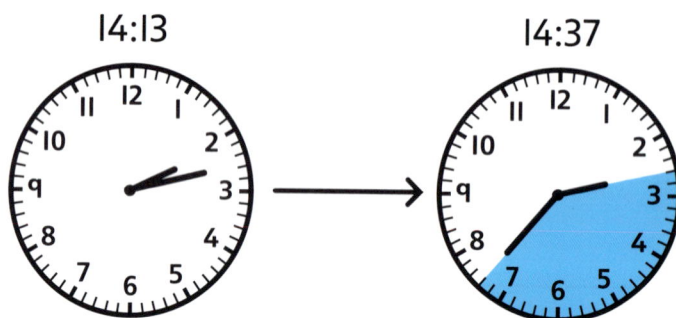

Littleborough	14:13
Birchfield	14:37
Ashtown Parkway	15:09
Ashtown Central	15:20

How long does it take to get to Birchfield?

2 How long does it take to get from Birchfield to Ashtown Parkway?

Littleborough	14:13
Birchfield	14:37
Ashtown Parkway	15:09
Ashtown Central	15:20

The journey crosses the o'clock boundary, so I am going to count in two jumps.

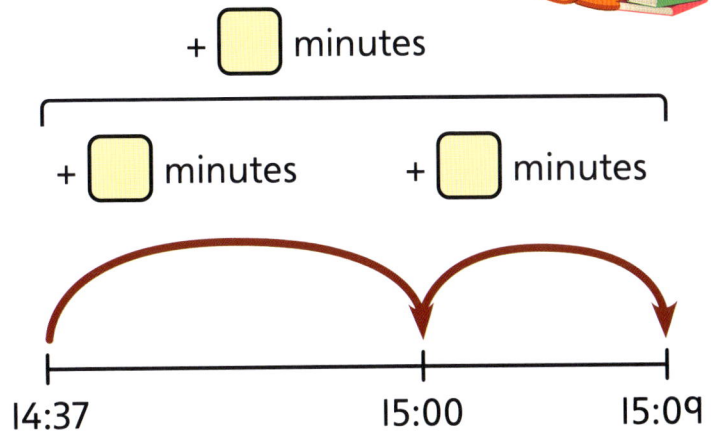

+ ☐ minutes

+ ☐ minutes   + ☐ minutes

14:37   15:00   15:09

3 The 15:13 train from Littleborough to Ashtown Central is an express train. It does not stop anywhere else.

CHALLENGE

Littleborough	15:13
Birchfield	–
Ashtown Parkway	–
Ashtown Central	16:00

Aki

I want to get from Littleborough to Ashtown Central as quickly as possible!

How much quicker is it for Aki to catch the express train than one of the other trains?

I am going to work out how long each journey is before finding the difference.

I think there is a quicker way. I can compare the departure and arrival times of two of the journeys.

203

→ Practice book 5C p149

Problem solving – units of measure ❶

Discover

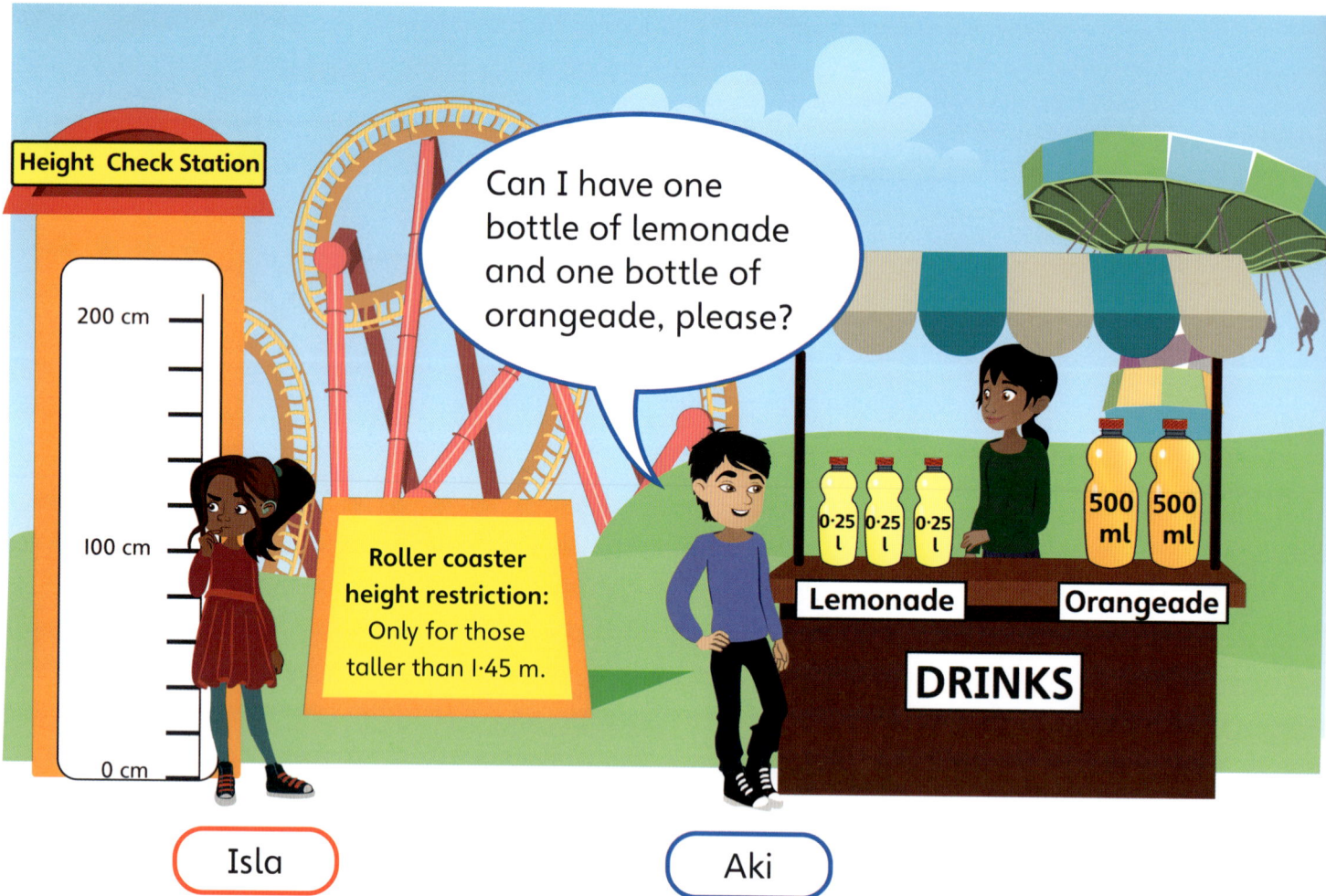

Height Check Station

200 cm

100 cm

0 cm

Can I have one bottle of lemonade and one bottle of orangeade, please?

Roller coaster height restriction: Only for those taller than 1·45 m.

0·25 l 0·25 l 0·25 l

Lemonade

500 ml 500 ml

Orangeade

DRINKS

Isla

Aki

❶ a) Is Isla tall enough to go on the roller coaster?

b) How many millilitres of fizzy pop is Aki buying altogether?

Share

a) Isla needs to convert 140 cm into metres.

140 cm ⟵ ? m

Smaller unit ⟵ larger unit, so you need to divide.

Divide by 100 as there are 100 cm in 1 m.

H	T	O	•	Tth	Hth
1	4	0	•		
		1	•	4	0

$140 \div 100 = 1 \cdot 40$ 140 cm = 1·40 m = 1·4 m

> The number line helps you convert between cm (along the top) and m (along the bottom).

```
0  10  20  30  40  50  60  70  80  90  100  110  120  130  140  150  160  170  180  190  200 cm
|---|---|---|---|---|---|---|---|---|---|----|----|----|----|----|----|----|----|----|----|
0  0·1 0·2 0·3 0·4 0·5 0·6 0·7 0·8 0·9  1   1·1  1·2  1·3  1·4  1·5  1·6  1·7  1·8  1·9   2  m
```

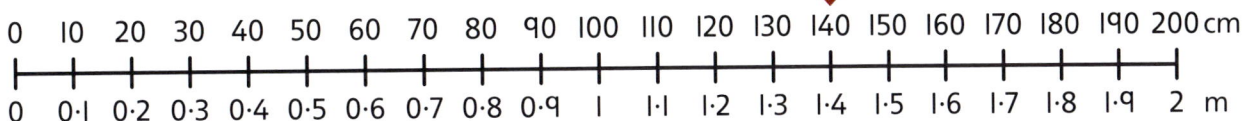

1·40 m < 1·45 m so Isla is not tall enough to go on the roller coaster.

b) Aki buys one 0·25 l bottle and one 500 ml bottle.

Larger unit ⟵ smaller unit, so you need to multiply.

> The question asks for the answer to be given in millilitres. One of the amounts is in litres, so I converted it first.

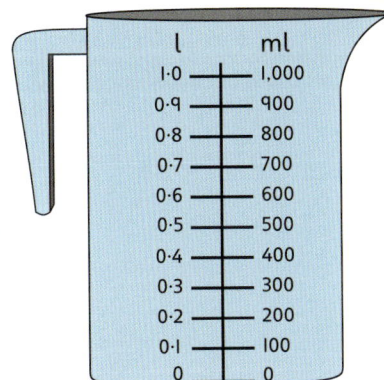

Multiply by 1,000 as there are 1,000 ml in 1 l.

$0 \cdot 25 \times 1{,}000 = 250$, so 0·25 l = 250 ml.

250 ml + 500 ml = 750 ml

Aki is buying 750 ml of fizzy pop altogether.

l	ml
1·0	1,000
0·9	900
0·8	800
0·7	700
0·6	600
0·5	500
0·4	400
0·3	300
0·2	200
0·1	100
0	0

205

Think together

Guess the total mass of the cakes!

Answers in grams please!

1 What should Ambika's total guess be in grams?

The larger cake looks like it might weigh about 0·9 kg.

Ambika

The smaller cake looks like it might weigh about 0·3 kg.

0·9 kg = ☐ g   0·3 kg = ☐ g

0·9 kg + 0·3 kg = ☐ g + ☐ g = ☐ g

2 How long is the roller coaster now?

Give your answer in metres.

The roller coaster is now ☐ metres long.

Please note: Due to a broken track, our 600 m roller coaster is now 300 cm shorter!

CHALLENGE

3 Here are the masses of five parcels.

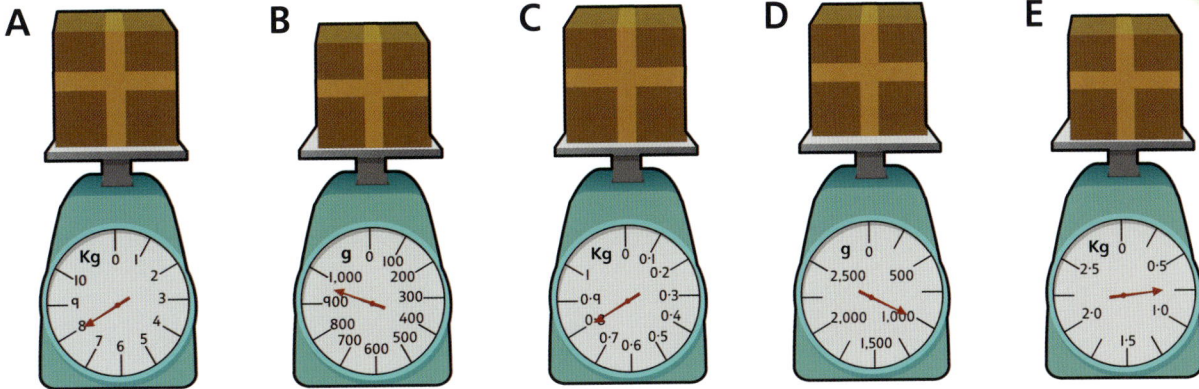

A   B   C   D   E

a) Put the masses in order from heaviest to lightest.

I think you can just look at the position of the dial. The further around it is, the heavier it will be.

I don't think that's right. You need to convert the masses of the parcels into the same unit.

b) If you converted the masses to a different unit, would you get the same order?

Explain your answer.

207

→ Practice book 5C p152

Problem solving – units of measure ❷

Discover

Oh dear! My scales only measure in grams!

Reena

I am going to make enough apple crumble for 5 people.

Lee

APPLE CRUMBLE
(Serves 4 people)

Ingredients
4 cooking apples
2 oz oats
4 oz brown sugar
5 oz plain flour
4 oz butter

I oz is approximately 28 g.

I **a)** How can Reena measure the ingredients listed on the recipe using her scales?

b) What quantities should Lee use to make enough apple crumble for 5 people?

Share

a) Reena needs to convert from ounces (oz) to grams (g).

$$5 \text{ oz} = 4 \text{ oz} + 1 \text{ oz} = 112 \text{ g} + 28 \text{ g} = 140 \text{ g}$$

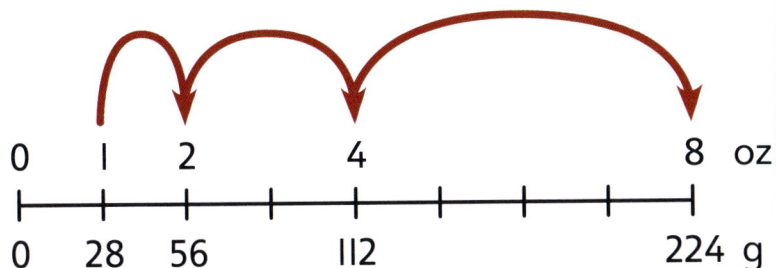

| 0 | 1 | 2 | | 4 | | | | 8 | oz |

| 0 | 28 | 56 | | 112 | | | | 224 | g |

> I could have multiplied each weight by 28, but I saw a way to use doubling facts to help me multiply more quickly!

Reena can use the scales to measure these amounts:

2 oz = 56 g oats   4 oz = 112 g brown sugar
4 oz = 112 g butter   5 oz = 140 g plain flour

b) The recipe is for 4 people. Lee can divide each ingredient by 4 and multiply by 5.

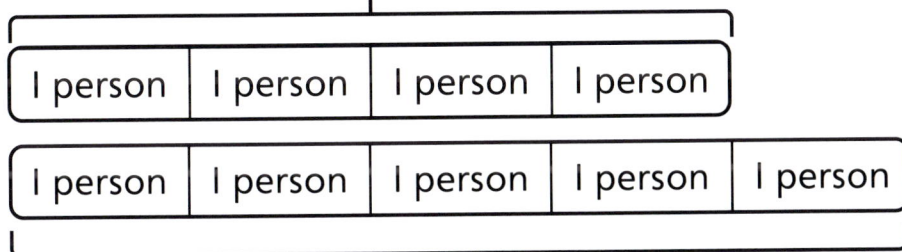

4 people

| 1 person | 1 person | 1 person | 1 person |

| 1 person | 1 person | 1 person | 1 person | 1 person |

5 people

> I divided by 4 to find the quantities for one person. I used this to alter the recipe for 5 people!

Ingredient	÷ 4 (one person)	× 5 (five people)
4 cooking apples	4 ÷ 4 = 1	1 × 5 = 5 cooking apples
56 g oats	56 ÷ 4 = 14 g	14 × 5 = 70 g oats
112 g brown sugar	112 ÷ 4 = 28 g	28 × 5 = 140 g brown sugar
112 g butter	112 ÷ 4 = 28 g	28 × 5 = 140 g butter
140 g plain flour	140 ÷ 4 = 35 g	35 × 5 = 175 g plain flour

Think together

1 Jamie wants to fill a 2 litre jug with milk.

a) How many cartons of milk does she need to pour into the jug?

I pint is approximately 570 ml.

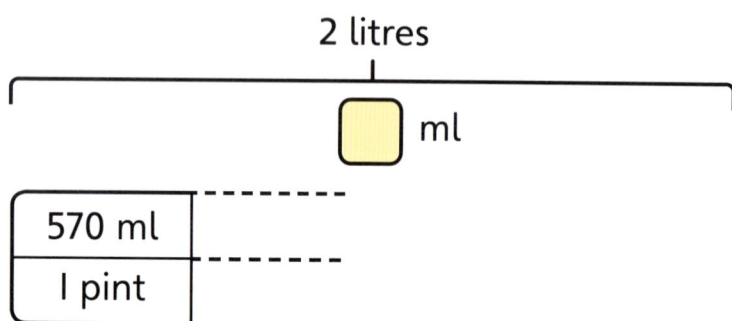

2 litres

☐ ml

570 ml
I pint

b) How much milk will Jamie have left over?

2 Danny is making a fruit pie.

He wants to serve it at 17:10.

Read the instructions. What is the latest time he should start preparing it?

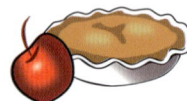

Fruit pie

Preparation time: 25 minutes

Cooking time: 55 minutes

Serve hot!

CHALLENGE

3 These bags of sugar are all the same price.

A
Sugar
1·4 kg

B
Sugar
10 oz

C
Sugar
1,250 g

D
Sugar
2 lb

I ounce (oz) is approximately 28 g.

I pound (lb) is approximately 0·45 kg.

Which one is the best value?

Explain how to find the answer.

It would be easier if all the bags were in the same unit of measurement.

I know how to convert all these units into grams. I will then be able to compare them!

→ **Practice book 5C p155**

End of unit check

1 There are 9·2 l of water in a fish tank. How many millilitres is this?

A 9·2000 ml B 920 ml C 9,200 ml D 0·0092 ml

2 Which of these statements is not correct?

A To convert from grams into kilograms, divide by 1,000.

B To convert from kilograms into grams, multiply by 1,000.

C To convert from kilograms into grams, divide by 1,000.

D There are 2,000 g in 2 kg.

3 A marathon runner takes 3 hours and 48 minutes to complete the race.

How many minutes is this?

A 3·48 minutes C 348 minutes

B 180 minutes D 228 minutes

4 Bella has three bags of rice weighing 1·2 kg, 200 g and 5 kg. What mass of rice does she have in total?

A 6·4 kg B 1,405 g C 206·2 kg D 820 g

5 This is part of a bus timetable.

Bus Station	08:47	08:57	09:07	09:17	09:27
Kingsway	08:52	09:02	09:12	09:22	09:32
Mount Pleasant	09:04	09:14	09:24	09:34	09:44
High Street	09:11	09:21	09:31	09:41	09:51
Oakfield Avenue	09:15	09:25	09:35	09:45	09:55
Leisure Centre	09:25	09:35	09:45	09:55	10:05

Ambika wants to catch a bus from Kingsway to the Leisure Centre. She needs to be at the Leisure Centre at five minutes to 10.

What time should she catch the bus?

A 9:17 am   **B** 9:22 am   **C** 9:32 am   **D** 9:22 pm

6 This piece of string is being measured in inches. What is its length in centimetres?

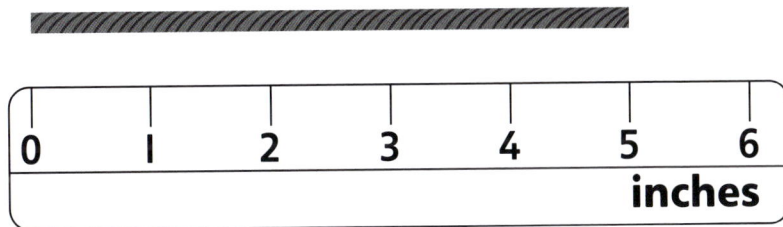

A 2 cm   **B** 5 cm   **C** 2·5 cm   **D** 12·5 cm

7 These durations show the length of time a bus takes between stops.

300 seconds $\frac{1}{4}$ of an hour $4\frac{1}{2}$ minutes   5 minutes 10 seconds

Put the lengths of time in order, from shortest to longest.

→ **Practice book 5C p158**

Unit 17
Measure – volume

In this unit we will …

- ⚡ Learn what the volume of a shape is
- ⚡ Find volumes of shapes by counting the number of cm³ cubes
- ⚡ Draw shapes with different volumes
- ⚡ Compare the volume of different shapes
- ⚡ Estimate the volume of different shapes

How many cm³ cubes are used to make this cube?

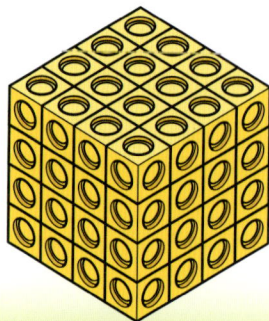

We will need some maths words. Which of these are new?

volume   cube   cuboid   3D shape

solid   capacity   cm³ cube

estimate   least   greatest

Which shape do you think has the greatest volume? Why?

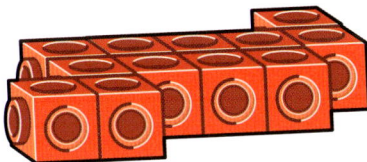

Cubic centimetres

Discover

> I think our cubes have the same volume.

> Our shapes look different, though.

Reena

Zac

1 Reena and Zac are making shapes using **cm³ cubes**.

a) Is Zac correct?

What do you think is meant by volume?

b) Build three other 3D shapes using cubes that have the same volume as Zac and Reena's shapes.

Share

a)

Volume means the amount of space that an object fills. We can use cm³ cubes as a way to measure volume.

I counted the number of cm³ cubes in each shape.

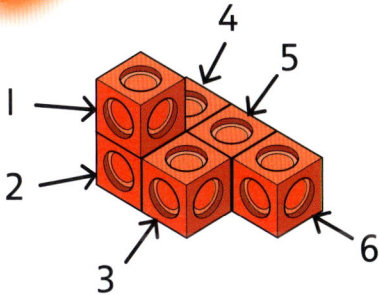

Reena's shape uses 6 cm³ cubes.

We can write the volume of this shape as 6 cm³.

I noticed that one of the cubes in Zac's shape is hidden.

Zac's shape also uses 6 cm³ cubes.

It has the same volume as Reena's shape.

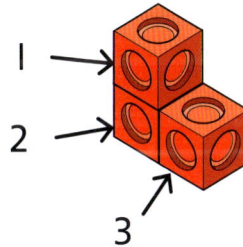

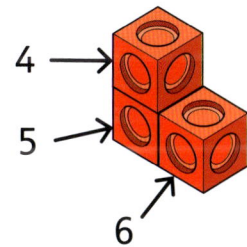

b) Each of these shapes has a volume of 6 cm³, the same volume as Reena's and Zac's shapes.

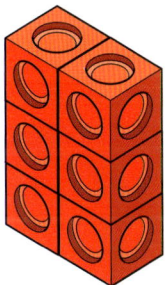

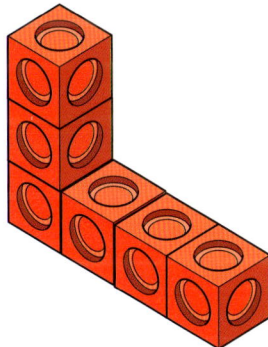

Think together

1 What is the volume of each shape?

a)

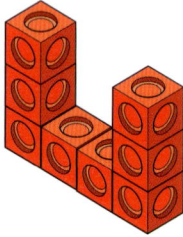

Volume = ☐ cm³

b)

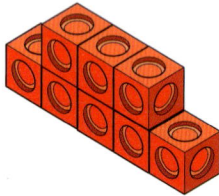

Volume = ☐ cm³

c)

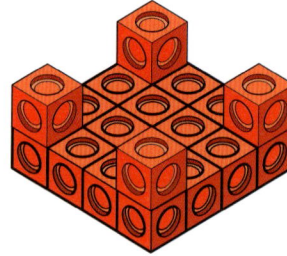

Volume = ☐ cm³

d)

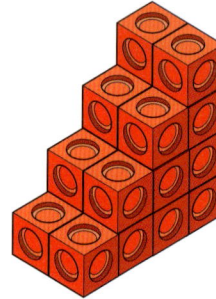

Volume = ☐ cm³

2 Using 12 cubes, build three different 3D shapes.

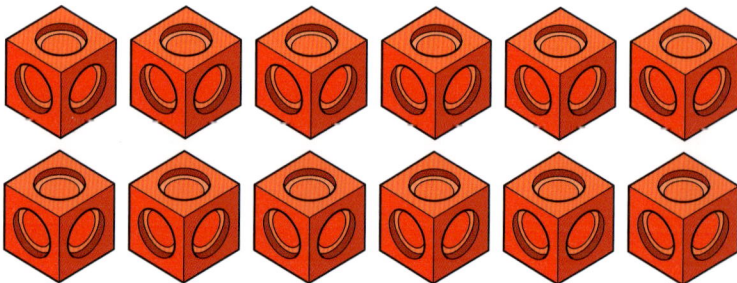

I am going to try to make a cuboid.

3

CHALLENGE

Reena: Drawing 3D shapes is challenging.

Zac: We can use isometric paper. It makes it a bit easier.

a) On isometric paper, draw more cubes like this one.

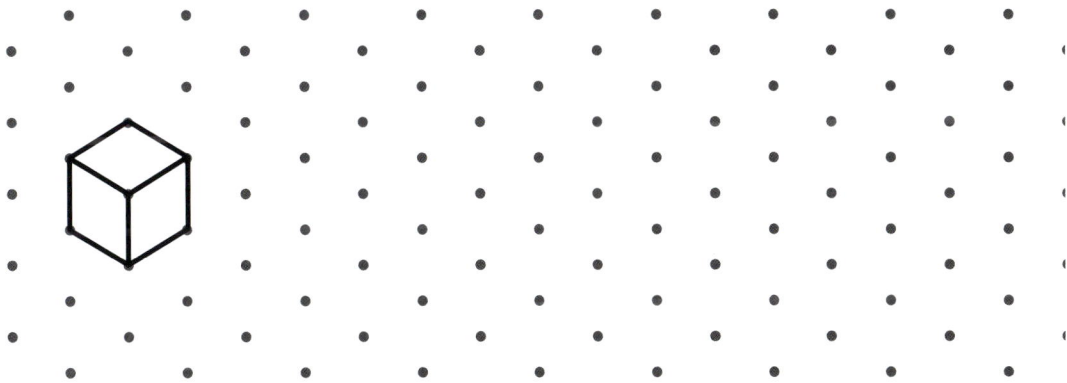

b) Draw the following 3D shapes on isometric paper.

What is the volume of each of your shapes?

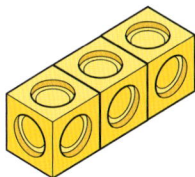

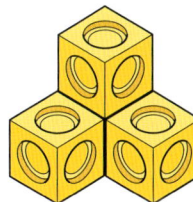

These look difficult to draw. I may need to make a few attempts. I am sure I can do it though.

I think one of these shapes has a hidden cube.

219

Compare volumes

Discover

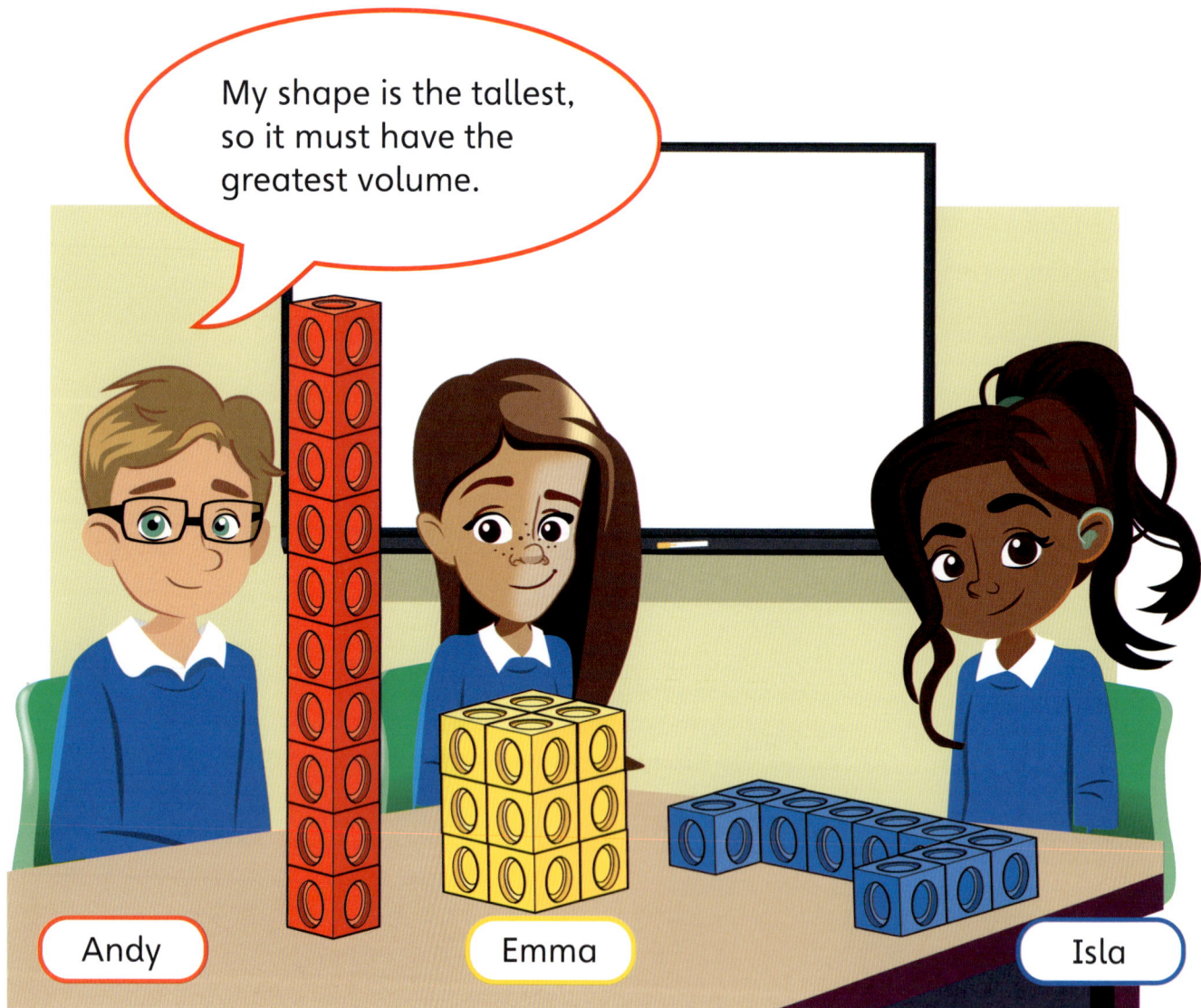

My shape is the tallest, so it must have the greatest volume.

Andy

Emma

Isla

1 **a)** Who has built the 3D shape with the greatest volume?

b) Isla adds more cubes to her shape so that it has the same volume as Emma's shape.

What could Isla's shape look like now?

Share

a) Andy and Emma have made cuboids. Isla's shape is not a cuboid.

Andy's shape

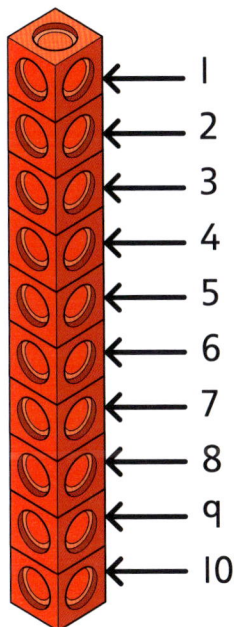

Isla's shape

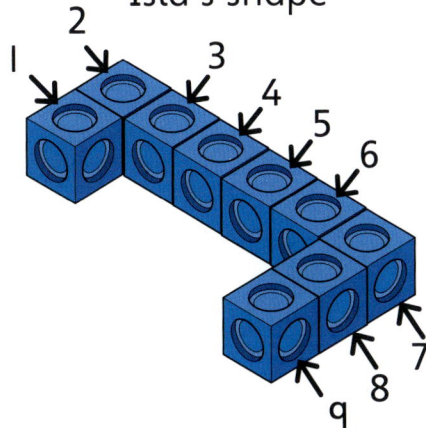

I counted the cubes in each shape.

Emma's shape

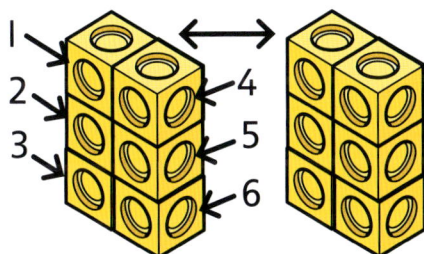

I split Emma's shape into 2 layers. There are 6 cubes in each layer.

$6 \times 2 = 12$.

Andy's shape has a volume of 10 cm^3.
Isla's shape has a volume of 9 cm^3.
Emma's shape has a volume of 12 cm^3.

$9 < 10 < 12$

Emma has built the shape with the greatest volume.

b) Isla's shape has 9 cubes. Emma's shape has 12. Isla needs to add 3 more cubes for her shape to have the same volume as Emma's. It might look like one of these two shapes.

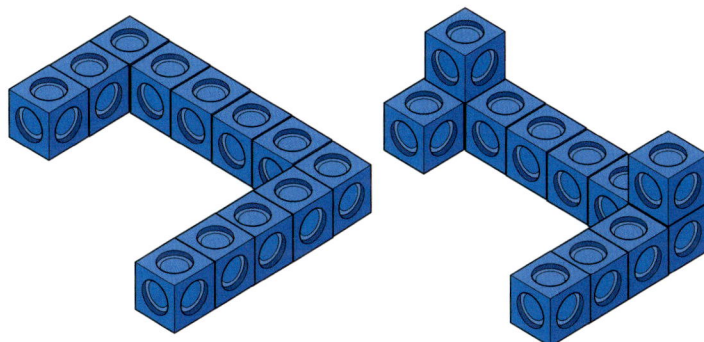

Think together

1 Isla and Emma make another two shapes.

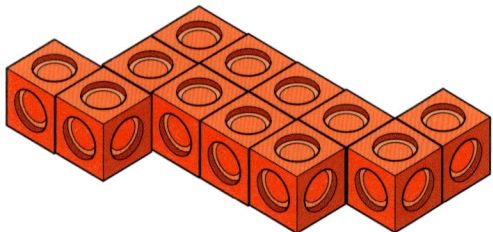

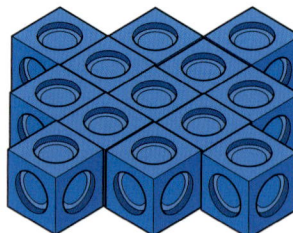

Emma's shape

Isla's shape

Whose shape has the smaller volume?

2 Order these shapes from least to greatest volume.

A

B

C

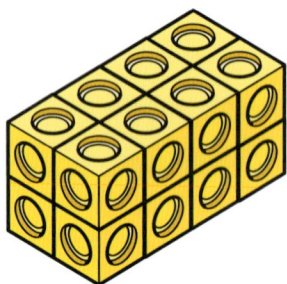

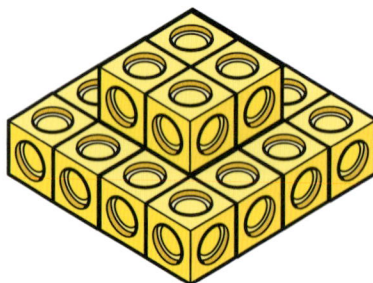

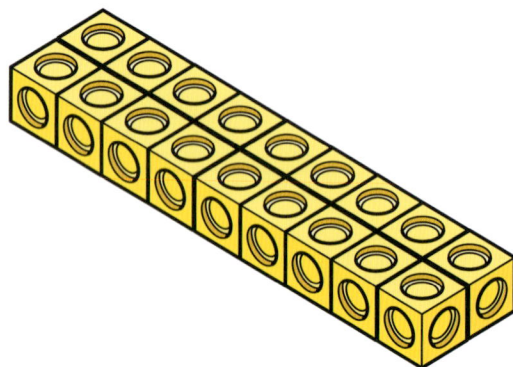

I will count all the cubes. I wonder if there is a different method I could also use.

222

3 **a)** Andy and Emma have made some more 3D shapes.

CHALLENGE

I think my shape has a larger volume as I have used more cubes.

Are you sure? I think our shapes have the same volume.

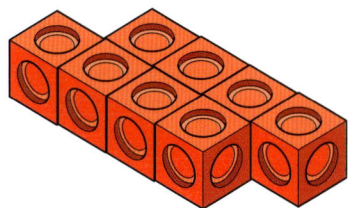

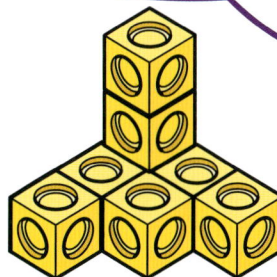

Andy

Emma

Who is correct? Explain your answer.

b) Isla makes the following shape, using bigger cubes.

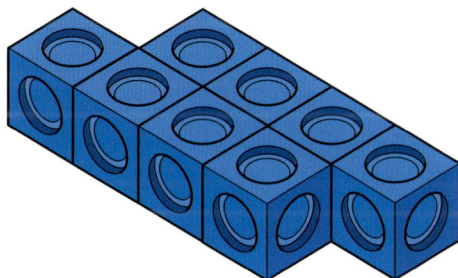

Does Isla's shape have the same volume as Andy's?

They must have the same volume as they have the same number of cubes.

They have the same number of cubes, but Isla's cubes do not look the same size as Andy's.

223

→ Practice book 5C p170

Estimate volume

Discover

Estimate the volume of each shape with cubes.

This is my estimate for the volume of one of the shapes.

Jamilla

Miss Hall

1 **a)** Which 3D shape did Jamilla estimate the volume of?

What is the estimate of the volume of the shape?

b) Why is it only an estimate?

Share

a) Jamilla estimated the volume of the triangular prism by making a shape out of cm^3 cubes that could fit inside it.

> I worked out the volume of each layer and added them together.

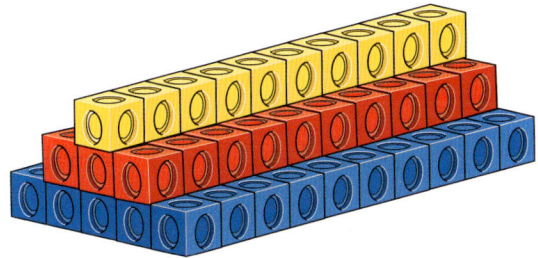

$10 \times 1 = 10$ cubes

$10 \times 3 = 30$ cubes

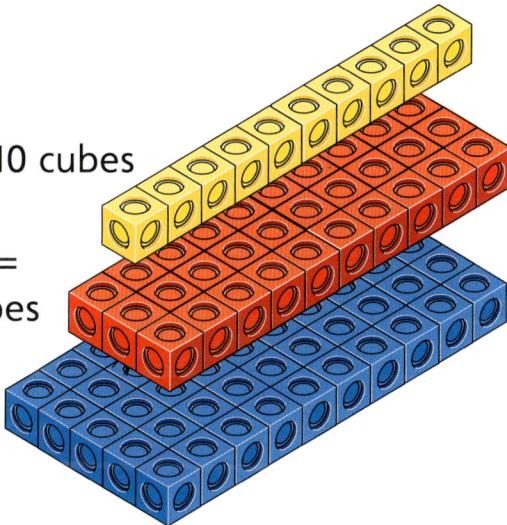

$10 \times 5 = 50$ cubes

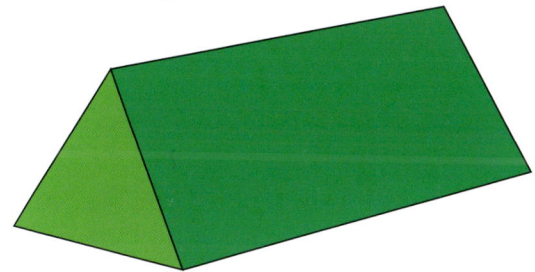

$50 + 30 + 10 = 90$ cubes

> I tried another way. I worked out the volume in each 'slice' and multiplied.

$10 \times 9 = 90$ cubes

Each cube has a volume of $1\ cm^3$. An estimate of the volume of the triangular prism is therefore $90\ cm^3$.

b) The volume is an estimate because it is not exact, as there would still be spaces left in the triangular prism if it were filled with the cubes.

> The volume of the 3D shape is likely to be a bit more than $90\ cm^3$.

Think together

1 Use the models to estimate the volume of each of the 3D shapes.

a)

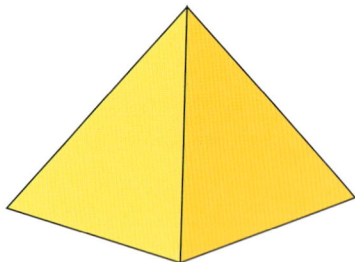 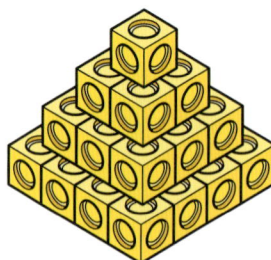

b)

 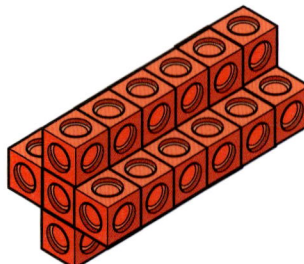

c)

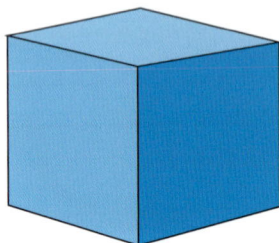 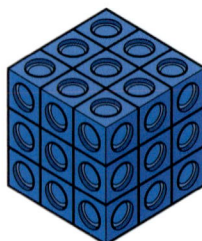

Which do you think is your most accurate estimate?
Explain your answer.

2 Pick an object in your classroom.

How can you use cubes to estimate the volume of the object?

3 **a)** Discuss how to compare the volume of each ball.

CHALLENGE

I will make a model of each shape with cubes.

b)

Reena

The football is about three times as tall as the tennis ball, so I think the volume will be three times greater, too.

Do you agree with Reena?

I will imagine each ball is inside a cube.

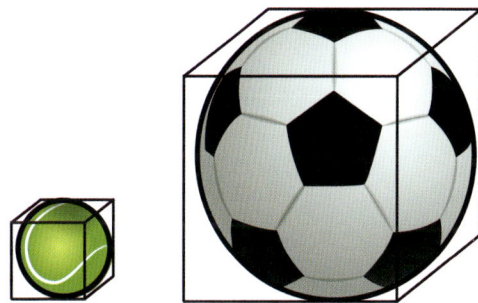

227

End of unit check

1 What is the volume of this shape?

 A 8 cm^3

 B 7 cm^3

 C 9 cm^3

 D 17 cm^3

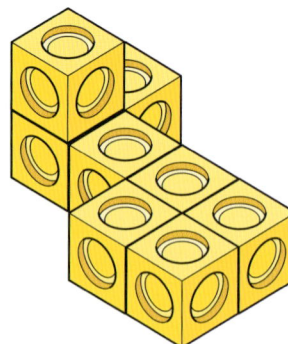

2 Which shape does not have the same volume as the other shapes?

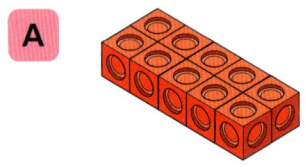

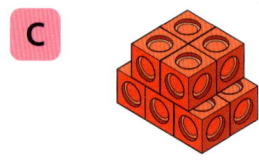

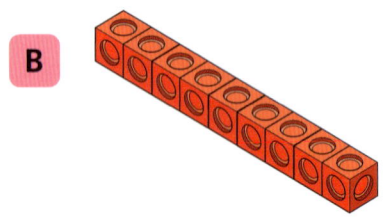

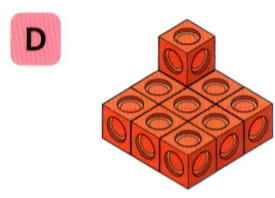

 A

 C

 B

 D

3 Which shape has the greatest volume?

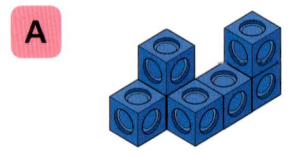

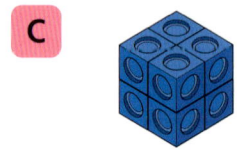

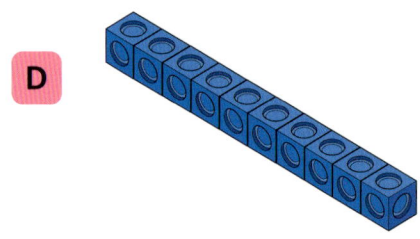

 A

 C

 B

 D

4 Use cm³ cubes to build this shape.

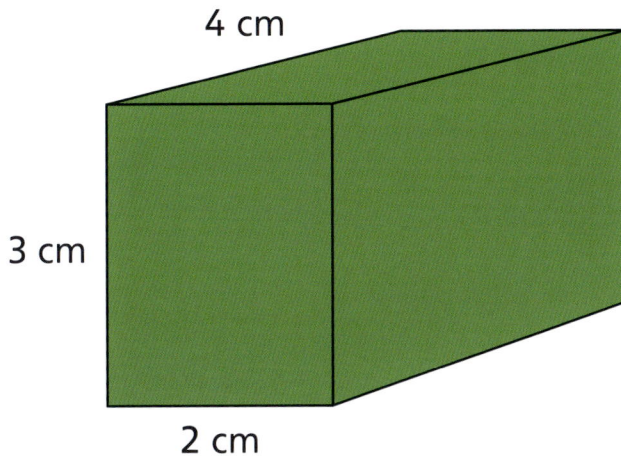

4 cm

3 cm

2 cm

What is the volume of the shape?

5 Explain how can you estimate the volume of a triangular prism.

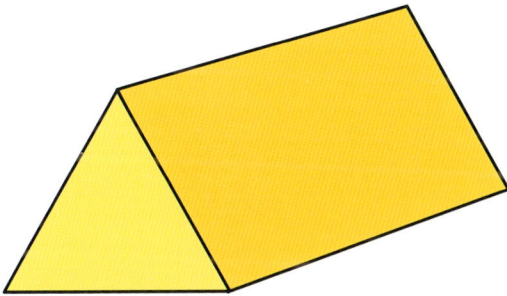

6 Estimate how many spheres of this size will fit in the box.
Explain your workings.

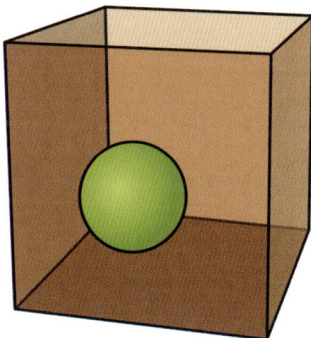

→ Practice book 5C p176

I enjoy listening to my partners to learn from them.

It is great to share ideas!

What have we learnt?

Can you do all these things?

⚡ Calculate and measure angles

⚡ Problem solve with coordinates

⚡ Add and subtract decimals

⚡ Understand negative numbers

⚡ Convert units of measure

Some of it was difficult, but we did not give up!

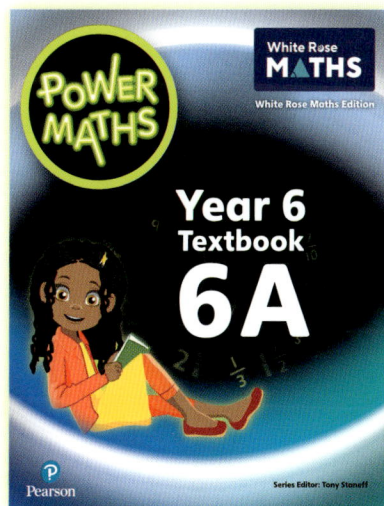

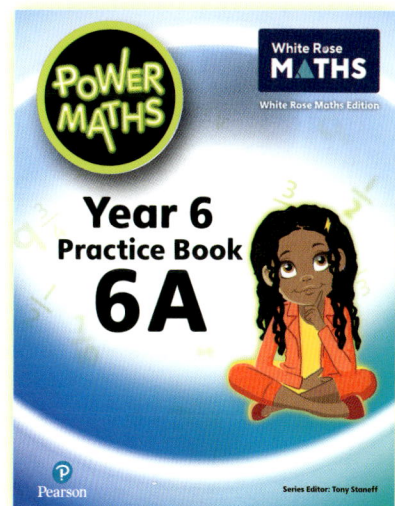

Now you are ready for the next books!

Published by Pearson Education Limited, 80 Strand, London, WC2R 0RL.

www.pearsonschools.co.uk

Text © Pearson Education Limited 2018, 2023
Edited by Pearson and Florence Production Ltd
First edition edited by Pearson, Little Grey Cells Publishing Services and Haremi Ltd
Designed and typeset by Pearson Ltd and PDQ Digital Media Solutions Ltd
First edition designed and typeset by Kamae Design
Original illustrations © Pearson Education Limited 2018, 2023
Illustrated by Laura Arias, John Batten, Fran and David Brylewski, Diego Diaz, Nigel Dobbyn and Nadene Naude at Beehive Illustration; Emily Skinner at Graham-Cameron Illustration; and Kamae Design
Cover design by Pearson Education Ltd
Front and back cover illustrations by Diego Diaz and Nadene Naude at Beehive Illustration

Series editor: Tony Staneff
Lead author: Josh Lury
Consultants (first edition): Professor Liu Jian and Professor Zhang Dan

The rights of Tony Staneff and Josh Lury to be identified as authors of this work have been asserted by them in accordance with the Copyright, Designs and Patents Act 1988.

This publication is protected by copyright, and permission should be obtained from the publisher prior to any prohibited reproduction, storage in a retrieval system, or transmission in any form or by any means, electronic, mechanical, photocopying, recording, or otherwise. For information regarding permissions, request forms and the appropriate contacts, please visit https://www.pearson.com/us/contact-us/permissions.html Pearson Education Limited Rights and Permissions Department.

First published 2018
This edition first published 2023

27 26 25 24 23
10 9 8 7 6 5 4 3 2

British Library Cataloguing in Publication Data
A catalogue record for this book is available from the British Library

ISBN 978 1 292 41959 6

Printed in the UK by Bell & Bain Ltd, Glasgow

For Power Maths resources go to
www.activelearnprimary.co.uk

Note from the publisher
Pearson has robust editorial processes, including answer and fact checks, to ensure the accuracy of the content in this publication, and every effort is made to ensure this publication is free of errors. We are, however, only human, and occasionally errors do occur. Pearson is not liable for any misunderstandings that arise as a result of errors in this publication, but it is our priority to ensure that the content is accurate. If you spot an error, please do contact us at resourcescorrections@pearson.com so we can make sure it is corrected.